MELVILLE'S SOURCES

MELVILLE'S
SOURCES

MARY K. BERCAW

Northwestern University Press
Evanston, Illinois

For my teacher, Harrison Hayford

Northwestern University Press
Evanston, Illinois 60201

Printed in the United States of America

Library of Congress Cataloging in Publication Data

Bercaw, Mary K.
  Melville's sources.

  Revision of the author's thesis (Ph.D.)—
Northwestern University.
  Bibliography: p.
  Includes index.
  1. Melville, Herman, 1819–1891—Sources—Bibliography. 2. Melville,
Herman, 1819–1891—Bibliography. I. Title.
Z8562.58.B47 1987 [PS2387] 016.813'3 87–5670 ISBN 0–8101–0734–1

CONTENTS

PREFACE

This book, based on my dissertation, grew out of the desire to solve a pervasive problem in literary study: the repetition of scholarship. Too often scholars will discover the source of a passage in a literary work, find out as much at they can about that source, write up their findings, and send them off to a journal— only to learn that the source had been discovered twenty years earlier and the find reported in a now-defunct journal. This is especially true of studies of Herman Melville, who drew in his works from many sources and who has been extensively studied.

Another problem this book will try to solve is that of misplaced credit. Sometimes a scholar has been cited for years as the discoverer of a major Melville source, when that source was actually pointed out by another scholar years before or even by reviewers in Melville's own day.

I wish to express my gratitude here to the staff of The Newberry Library, especially the guards who so often and so patiently opened the door to the Melville Collection when my keycard wouldn't work; to Hershel Parker, Gerald Graff, Carl Smith, and Paul Breslin for their promptness in reading the successive drafts of the introductory essay and for their many valuable suggestions; to my parents and to Mrs. Patricia Case, my high school Marine Biology teacher, who helped me go to college in the first place and encouraged me all the way through the Ph.D. and then through the book; to Susan Jerome, Susan Stucke Funk, and especially to Jennifer Johnson for their assistance with proofreading; to Alma MacDougall for copy-editing; to John Phelan, who patiently cross-referenced the checklists with me; to Guy Hermann, who spent countless hours working with the book on the computer; and especially to Bob Madison and to my teacher Harrison Hayford, without whom (and this is beyond doubt) this book would never have been written.

I

INTRODUCTION

*M*ELVILLE'S SOURCES is a checklist, keyed to Melville's works, of all the sources scholars have suggested that Melville used. It is different in scope from, but complementary to, *Melville's Reading: A Check-List of Books Owned and Borrowed* by Merton M. Sealts, Jr.[1] Sealts's checklist claims only "to set forth the established objective evidence concerning the books Herman Melville owned and borrowed" (p. v); it does not assert that he used them as sources. Sealts lists all volumes known to survive from Melville's library, those he acquired by verifiable purchase or gift, those recorded as his borrowings from friends and institutional libraries, and those available to Melville through members of his family.

Because Sealts restricts his checklist to specific works which were physically available to Melville, the list, as he recognizes, has limitations of two kinds. First, though it is titled "Melville's Reading," it does not undertake to establish whether Melville actually read any work listed or, if so, where or how he may have used it as a source. For example, nine romances by Amelia Edith Barr, such as *The Bow of Orange Ribbon* and *Friend Olivia*, are included (Sealts #39–47) because the New York Society Library has a record that Melville borrowed them in 1890 and 1891—almost certainly for his wife and unmarried daughter, as Sealts points out (p. 25). Second, by the same criterion, Sealts's checklist excludes all sources which can be inferred only by internal evidence in Melville's writings (including allusions, citations, quotations, or references to authors). For example, William Ellis's

1

Polynesian Researches, Melville's pervasive source for *Omoo* and incidental source for *Typee* and *Mardi*, is not listed by Sealts because there is no evidence about any copy Melville owned or borrowed. The internal evidence, however, is abundant: Charles Roberts Anderson (133) proved that Melville drew on Ellis's work, and Harrison Hayford (480) identified the edition used as a source for specific passages in *Omoo*. This is but one example of *lacunae* in Sealts's checklist; there are many others. While many works shown to be major sources are listed by Sealts because Melville owned copies of them—e.g., the Bible, the *Works* of Sir Thomas Browne, and the *Dramatic Works* of Shakespeare—ultimately, though, many other demonstrated sources fail to appear.

In contrast to Sealts's checklist of works owned and borrowed, this checklist of works used relies not only on evidence of possession but also on such internal evidence as direct references and parallel passages. For each source listed, I cite the work or works in which Melville is thought to have used it and each reviewer, critic, or scholar who has made the attribution. I have listed dozens of works not included in Sealts's checklist and have omitted others that are, because no one has shown or suggested Melville used them. The categories of the two books may overlap in many cases: Sealts recorded, for example, that Melville acquired Charles Darwin's *Journal of Researches* on 10 April 1847. Though I do not list a work as a source solely because Melville owned it, I include Darwin's *Journal* because it has been proposed as a source for *Moby-Dick*, "The Encantadas," and *Clarel*—and I list the scholars who proposed it. Like *Melville's Reading*, this checklist may include works Melville did not in fact read or use, since my criterion for inclusion is suggested rather than proven use. In sum, both Sealts's *Melville's Reading* and my *Melville's Sources* are needed for a thorough study of Melville's reading.

One important category of possible sources, Melville's own allusions to writers or works, is not, as such, included in either this checklist or Sealts's. Even so a fair percentage of the writers and works involved are listed by both—including all the major authors such as Shakespeare, Carlyle, Milton, and Spenser—on Sealts's checklist because Melville owned works by them and on mine because some scholar has discussed Melville's use of them. Nevertheless, allusions of themselves are not covered. A third checklist of at least Melville's literary allusions is needed.[2]

The following introduction is divided into four parts: (1) a brief history of Melville source study; (2) a general discussion of Melville's acquisition and use of his sources; (3) an explanation of how I assembled the lists that follow; and (4) a note on possibilities for future research.

A HISTORY OF MELVILLE SOURCE STUDY

During Melville's lifetime few questions were raised about his printed sources. Most of his reviewers assumed that in his early works he was writing, as he claimed, from his own experiences and observations, and not many suspected he was often adapting material from other writers. Many reviewers sensed, however, that Melville's reading indirectly affected his writing. In the London *Examiner* one reviewer of *Mardi* observed that Melville's writing was "much in the manner of Sir Thomas Browne, and with a dash of old Burton and Sterne." He even suggested certain chapters as "examples of thoughtful writing, and *very extensive reading*."[3] A later reviewer, this time for the London *Morning Advertiser*, also noted the influence of Browne, writing of *The Whale* that it had "a quaintness reminding us of Sir Thomas Brown" (48, n.p.).

Reviewers pointed out resemblances to Defoe in *Typee*, *Omoo*, and *Redburn*, but most of these were only in tone and subject matter. The review in the *National Era* was typical: "Although entirely original, in many respects these volumes [*Typee* and *Omoo*] remind one of Robinson Crusoe. The author, like De Foe, has the faculty of telling a peculiarly captivating story in the simplest style" (13, p. 2). In *Redburn*, according to the *Literary World*, "Mr. Melville proves himself . . . the De Foe of the Ocean" (39, p. 395). A few reviewers did suggest direct borrowing: the *National Intelligencer* reported of *Typee* that the "points of resemblance between the inimitable novel of De Foe [*Robinson Crusoe*] and the production of Mr. Melville are neither few nor difficult to be traced" (53, n.p.)—though the reviewer did not point out specific parallels.

It was in *Mardi* (1849) that reviewers first saw Melville's reading, above all his reading of Rabelais, as seriously influencing his writing, though sometimes for the worse: "In a word, 'Mardi' greatly resembles Rabelais emasculated of every thing but prosiness and puerility" (26, n.p.). The French critic Philarete Chasles wrote that *Mardi* was "a symbolic Odyssey of the strangest nature, very clumsily imitated from Rabelais" (31, p. 102). Some reviewers were only slightly kinder: the Morning *Chronicle* thought *Mardi* was "a wonderful and unreadable compound of Ossian and Rabelais"—and of Thomas Moore, James Harrington, Swift, Cook, Macaulay, and Disraeli (32, n.p.). The bad effect of Melville's reading of Rabelais was still being deplored seven years later when the reviewer in the Newark *Daily Advertiser* wrote of *The Piazza Tales*, "One reads them with delight and with rejoicing that the author has laid his rhapsod[iz]ing aside, which savored too much of Swift, Rabelais and other such works, as suggest that they were the fruits of reading rather than of his imagination" (67, n.p.).

Melville clearly did read Rabelais, Swift, and Browne and was influenced by them. Contemporary reviewers, however, did little more than note and lament this fact, though a few delighted in the echoes. Because their purpose was not academic literary investigation they did not cite parallel passages or try to specify just *how* Rabelais influenced *Mardi*. All this changed with Melville's "rediscovery," which is usually dated from 1921, the year Raymond Weaver published *Herman Melville: Mariner and Mystic* (84), the first full-length biography.[4] Studies of Melville published in the 1920s were mostly biographical, and since such early biographers as Weaver, John Freeman, and Lewis Mumford took most of Melville's first-person narratives as reliable autobiography, they did not feel the need to attempt source study. What few conjectures they made about Melville's reading were inferred mostly from the books mentioned in Melville's journals and from books Melville owned, which were then in the possession of his granddaughter, Eleanor Melville Metcalf. For example, after mentioning Melville's buying a folio edition of the works of Sir Thomas Browne in London in 1849, Freeman noted only that "Browne and the Elizabethan dramatists appear constantly as an influence in some of his writings" (95, p. 48). Mumford, discussing Melville's trip home from London in 1850, commented, "what happens most importantly now, comes by way of books" and included Browne in a list of authors Melville presumably read (100, p. 131). Neither biographer attempted to detail the "influence" in question or to explain "what happens most importantly now."

What can be called "the great source studies," which first established Melville's extensive use of sources and identified specific source-books, began in June 1928 with the publication of Harold H. Scudder's discovery that Melville had based "Benito Cereno" on chapter 18 of Amasa Delano's *A Narrative of Voyages and Travels, in the Northern and Southern Hemispheres* (Boston, 1817). Though many scholars have since disputed Scudder's statement that Melville "merely rewrote this Chapter including a portion of one of the legal documents there appended, suppressing a few items, and making some small additions" (98, p. 502), they all acknowledge the importance of Scudder's discovery (see especially Rosalie Feltenstein's 1947 article [172] and Marjorie Dew's 1966 dissertation [415] for fuller analysis of Melville's use of this source). Scudder was the first to reprint Delano's chapter 18 with its documents and correspondence, and all subsequent articles on "Benito Cereno" which deal with that source depend on Scudder's discovery, refining and revising what he originally wrote.

In 1932 a second seminal source study, on "The Encantadas," was published by Russell Thomas (109). He identified the sources both of many prose passages and of all the poetical epigraphs to the sketches, most of which came from poems by Spenser. As Thomas admitted, he could not explain discrepancies between Melville's epigraphs and the original poems because he could not identify the edition of Spenser Melville had used (see 692). Nevertheless, Thomas pointed out various changes that were obviously deliberate, like the fact that Melville changed a few of Spenser's words to make his epigraphs fit his descriptions of the Galapagos Islands. Thomas also used parallel passages, placing Melville's words directly opposite those of his source, to show Melville's indebtedness to voyage narratives by David Porter and James Colnett. Finally, Thomas studied nineteenth-century maps of the Galapagos Islands and concluded that Melville used those of both Porter and Colnett.

Thomas's study was followed in 1940 by Victor Wolfgang von Hagen's edition of "The Encantadas." Von Hagen was a naturalist who had led a six-month expedition to the Galapagos and knew the islands intimately enough to supplement and correct Thomas's account. For example, von Hagen pointed out that Melville's "Barrington Isle" in Sketch Sixth was actually a description of James Island, and he showed that Melville's misnaming had been caused by a confusion in his source, Colnett (134, p. 105).

A third major source study, cited almost as often as Scudder's and Thomas's, is Willard Thorp's "Redburn's Prosy Old Guidebook," published in 1938 (132). Thorp compared a plate of the title page of an actual guidebook, *The Picture of Liverpool* (1808), to Melville's description in *Redburn*, and he included parallel passages to prove that the work was indeed the guidebook Redburn "inherited" from his father. Thorp's article leaves no doubt that this is the book on which Melville based many passages of *Redburn*, but neither Thorp nor a subsequent scholar has established whether Melville's own father Allan had a copy of *The Picture of Liverpool* in hand in 1811 or 1818 when he went to Liverpool or whether Melville himself took either that copy or any other one to Liverpool in 1839. (William H. Gilman discussed this problem, in 212, pp. 188–90, but could come to no conclusion.)

Scudder, Thomas, and Thorp all used evidence within Melville's books in order to identify his sources, but there was still important evidence outside them which had not been studied. Luther Stearns Mansfield in his 1936 dissertation, "Herman Melville: Author and New Yorker" (123), was the first to investigate Melville's use of his friend Evert A. Duyckinck's library. Mansfield's work was to earlier scholars what Sealts's checklist, *Melville's Reading* (1948–1950, 1966), would become to later ones: the standard reference to books Melville is known to have owned or borrowed. Mansfield's work has often been cited in source studies, because it showed when Melville borrowed specific books from Duyckinck and therefore when, presumably, he could have first drawn on them in his own works.

The source study which proved most influential in redirecting the course of Melville scholarship was Charles Roberts Anderson's *Melville in the South Seas*, completed as a Columbia University dissertation in 1935 and published in 1939. Anderson studied travel books along with naval and shipping records in order to give an account of Melville's experiences in the South Seas which was "more detailed and more authentic than [what] previous biographers have been able to draw from supposedly autobiographical passages in his writings" (133, p. 6). Anderson showed conclusively that the narratives in Melville's books were not literally true. No earlier biographer had looked at such obvious source materials as the log and official records of the frigate *United States*, the original of Melville's *Neversink* in *White-Jacket*. Studying these, Anderson found, for example, that Melville had not fallen from a yard on his voyage home. Had Anderson stopped with these records, his findings would have been noteworthy, but he also found most of the printed sources for the non-autobiographical material in Melville's South Sea books. In a 1935 article based on his dissertation Anderson first identified Nathaniel Ames's *A Mariner's Sketches* (Providence, 1830) as the "indisputable literary source" of White Jacket's fall from the yard (121, p. 131). Much study has since been devoted to Melville's use of Ames, but, like the work based on Scudder's discovery of Delano, the later scholarship is a refinement of an earlier seminal discovery.

Anderson read through many earlier South Sea travel books in order to identify sources for *Typee*, *Omoo*, parts of *Mardi*, *White-Jacket*, parts of *Moby-Dick*, and parts of *The Piazza Tales*. Although some scholars since 1939 have criticized Anderson for not making a more thorough critical analysis of the materials he quoted *en bloc* from such writers as William Ellis and Charles S. Stewart, his work permanently altered Melville scholarship. No longer could anyone safely identify Melville with his narrators or take their statements as reliable "autobiographical" facts.

Working on Melville's South Sea years at the same time as Anderson was Robert S. Forsythe of The Newberry Library in Chicago. Like Anderson, Forsythe sought out records of Melville's years in the Pacific, and he anticipated Anderson with "Herman Melville in Honolulu" (1935), "Herman Melville in the Marquesas" (1936), "Herman Melville in Tahiti" (1937), and "More upon Herman Melville in Tahiti" (1938). In these articles Forsythe questioned the literal truth of Melville's ostensibly factual statements in his early books—for example, those relating to the length of his stay in the Typee valley and the chronology in

Omoo—and he used both internal and external evidence to date Melville's stays in the Marquesas and Tahiti. Like Anderson's, Forsythe's findings were crucial in establishing that Melville's early books were something other than strict autobiography. But in his review of Anderson's *Melville in the South Seas* Forsythe sadly relinquished his own long-planned volume because Anderson had reported so much of what he himself had also discovered.[5]

The earliest source studies, then, were concerned mainly with correcting the impression that Melville's works were straight autobiography by demonstrating that Melville rewrote materials wholesale from other writers. The truth of events as implausible as Redburn's London trip had been maintained by Mumford on impressionistic grounds: "Mr. Weaver has cast doubts on this adventure in London: he regards it as one of the few wide inventions Melville made in Redburn: but to me its very vagueness and mysteriousness smells of reality" (100, p. 35). If the literary effectiveness of such a passage could be taken as proof of its autobiographical truth, who could doubt that Melville had himself spent four months as a captive of the Typees or had fallen from a yard?

In 1937 David Jaffe, one of Anderson's graduate students at Duke University, published "Some Sources of Melville's *Mardi*," in which he showed by means of parallel passages that Melville had drawn extensively from the works of F. D. Bennett, Charles Wilkes, William Ellis, and Daniel Tyerman and George Bennet. Jaffe found sources for "almost all the Polynesian background of *Mardi*" (127, p. 57). His article, often cited as an early, important source study, was typical of the kind generated by the positivistically oriented scholarly atmosphere of the 1930s. Like Scudder, Anderson, and W. Sprague Holden in his M.A. thesis, "Some Sources for Herman Melville's *Israel Potter*" (1932), Jaffe juxtaposed large sections of newly discovered source material with the passages Melville had derived from them, with, however, minimal literary analysis.

The major investigator to follow Anderson and Forsythe in tracing Melville's South Sea years was Wilson Heflin, who during the 1940s filled some of the *lacunae* in their work. Heflin made two important discoveries: in February 1947 he found in the National Archives an abstract log of the 1841-45 voyage of the

Acushnet, Melville's first whaler, and in 1949 he identified Melville's third whaler as the *Charles and Henry*. Before the discovery of this abstract log little had been known about Melville's first whaling voyage, and nothing about his third whaler, not even its name.

Heflin incorporated his findings into his 1952 dissertation, "Herman Melville's Whaling Years." Although most of Heflin's research was biographical rather than source-study, he established Melville's reliance on one source, William Scoresby's *Journal of a Voyage to the Northern Whale-Fishery*, in "The Needle" chapter in *Moby-Dick* (177). He also discussed Melville's reading of Owen Chase while writing *Moby-Dick* (214), as well as his study of navigation in Jeremiah Day's *The Mathematical Principles of Navigation and Surveying* (627).

Anderson's book and the growing critical interest in Melville had stimulated more comprehensive source studies, especially of *Moby-Dick*. Three scholars were working on the whaling sources of *Moby-Dick* during the 1940s: Wilbur S. Scott, Sumner W. D. Scott, and Howard P. Vincent. Wilbur Scott's Princeton University dissertation, "Melville's Originality: A Study of Some of the Sources of *Moby-Dick*," was finished in 1943 (147) and Sumner Scott's University of Chicago dissertation, "The Whale in *Moby Dick*," in 1950 (201), but only Vincent published his discoveries. Insofar as his *The Trying-Out of Moby-Dick* (1949 [182]) was a study of Melville's sources of information about whales, it lacked the thoroughness and accuracy of Sumner Scott's dissertation with its careful documentation, including a canvassing of all possible sources and the identification of the exact editions consulted by Melville. Though Wilbur Scott's discussion of the whaling sources as well as other sources was not as thorough as Sumner Scott's, neither did it have the careless errors of Vincent's.

Yet *The Trying-Out of Moby-Dick* had an interpretive dimension and stylistic verve which the two Scott dissertations lacked. Vincent combined source study with a running interpretation, a combination of scholarship and criticism which became a model for subsequent writing on Melville. An example of Vincent's method is his description of the way Melville transformed a passage from Thomas Beale into the scene about men caught out in whaleboats during a squall (chapter 48 of *Moby-Dick*):

The writing is splendid in its graphic realism, but it achieves true magnificence in Melville's perception of the scene as a symbol of man's terrifying loneliness amidst the hostile forces of the universe, of man's pathetic care for the flickering light of hope even as universal darkness engulfs him, of man's attempt to make a heaven in hell's despite. (182, p. 202)

Here can be seen Vincent's enthusiastic appreciation for Melville as an artist and his interpretive commentary which above all made his book important.

In the 1940s and 1950s a series of dissertations and books derived from them appeared by scholars who had studied under Stanley T. Williams at Yale University. Dorothee Metlitsky Finkelstein summed up Williams's importance in the preface to her *Melville's Orienda* (1961):

The list of those whose work on Melville took its first shape as a dissertation directed by Mr. Williams spans two decades: James Baird, Walter Bezanson, Merrell Davis, Charles Feidelson, Edward Fiess, Elizabeth Foster, William Gilman, Ethel-Mae Haave, Harrison Hayford, Tyrus Hillway, Henry Pommer, Merton Sealts, and Nathalia Wright. As the last one to have been guided to Melville by Mr. Williams, I feel a particular responsibility to pay tribute to his unique importance in Melville scholarship. (333, p. ix)

Much of the work of these scholars included important source-study, such as Sealts's dissertation, "Herman Melville's Reading in Ancient Philosophy" (143). In trying to determine what editions of specific works Melville used, Sealts found that Melville tended to read translated, modern editions that were inexpensive and thus easily available to him rather than early or foreign-language editions.

Nathalia Wright's *Melville's Use of the Bible* (1949), appropriately dedicated to Williams, studied one of the three major literary influences on Melville (the other two being Shakespeare and Milton). As she noted, "Melville echoed the Bible in novels, stories, and poems persistently from *Typee* in 1846 to *Billy Budd* in 1891—in every piece, in fact, of his collected work except five sketches and a few poems" (183, p. 8). Wright's book was divided thematically to trace the influence of the Bible on style, imagery, characters and types, and themes and plots of Melville's works. Though her analysis was not highly detailed, it is still the indispensable work on Melville's biblical borrowings.

Two other essential works by Stanley T. Williams's students were William H. Gilman's *Melville's Early Life and Redburn* (1951) and Merrell R. Davis's *Melville's Mardi: A Chartless Voyage* (1952). Gilman studied the letters and papers of Melville's family to rewrite and make more accurate the account of his youth. Like Anderson, he did archival research, identifying the ship on which Melville had sailed to Liverpool as the *St. Lawrence* and distinguishing facts about its voyage from his fictional account in *Redburn*. Gilman studied literary sources, too: for example, he noted that many of Redburn's experiences when he first boards the *Highlander* are "suspiciously like those in Captain Marryat's *Peter Simple*, published fifteen years before" (212, p. 184)—and he went on to show specific parallels. Davis's work (226) was similar to Gilman's in combining biography and literary source-study. He was above all concerned with the growth of *Mardi*, using both Melville's own statements and the evidence in the book itself to distinguish stages in its composition and to trace changes in Melville's plan for it.

The work of Gilman and Davis marked a shift in the direction of source-study in the 1950s. Scudder, Thorp, Anderson, and others having established that Melville worked from source-books as well as his own experiences in writing his narratives, scholars like Gilman, Davis, and Harrison Hayford began to use source study to investigate how Melville's works were conceived and written.

Leon Howard was central among those doing such compositional study. At Northwestern University Howard had directed Davis's earliest Melville studies (including his discovery of the use of books of flower symbolism in *Mardi*, 142) and was Hayford's senior colleague. Howard, Hayford, Davis, and Gilman collaborated closely in Jay Leyda's researches for the documentary *Melville Log* (1951). Howard's *Herman Melville: A Biography* (1951) included not only much discussion of Melville's reading but also an "account of the actual motives affecting Melville's composition and of the methods by which he put his books together" (213, p. viii). Howard's biography treated the composition of each of the books as an event in Melville's life. For example, Howard pointed out that Melville, in the first part of *The Confidence-Man*, frequently alluded to the Bible and seemed to be ironically parodying the Sermon on the Mount and the Epistles of St. Paul. But during the winter of 1856, when Melville's reading evidently "began to have a more humanizing effect upon his mind" (213, p. 231), he made many more allusions to Shakespeare while writing the second half of *The Confidence-Man*. Howard always gave priority to Melville's reading as source and inspiration, though he did not offer a full critical analysis of Melville's works or any detailed source-study.

During this time subsequent work on Melville's sources was made much easier by the series of Hendricks House editions of Melville's works, most of them heavily annotated. This projected complete edition was begun by Packard and Company (later Hendricks House) in 1947 with the publication of the *Collected Poems of Herman Melville*. Although Howard P. Vincent, the general editor, recruited qualified scholars to edit the volumes, the edition was plagued with problems. Most of the projected volumes were prepared during the later 1940s but to date only the following have been published:

> *Collected Poems*, Howard P. Vincent, ed. (1947)
> *The Piazza Tales*, Egbert S. Oliver, ed. (1948)
> *Pierre*, Henry A. Murray, ed. (1949)
> *Moby-Dick*, Luther S. Mansfield and Howard P. Vincent, eds. (1952)
> *The Confidence-Man*, Elizabeth S. Foster, ed. (1954)
> *Clarel*, Walter E. Bezanson, ed. (1960)
> *Omoo*, Harrison Hayford and Walter Blair, eds. (1969)

Charles R. Anderson and Gordon Roper edited the *Typee* volume, Nathalia Wright *Mardi*, Willard Thorp *Redburn*, and Merton M. Sealts, Jr., the short prose, all with new source discoveries, but these volumes remain unpublished.

Most of the published volumes provided extensive notes, not only identifying sources but speculating on how Melville used them. Vincent's edition of the *Collected Poems* involved little source study because he was primarily interested in "presenting an accurate text of all the poems which Herman Melville left to posterity" (166, p. v), and the source he discussed most extensively, *The Rebellion Record* (the major source for *Battle-Pieces*), had been discovered by Willard Thorp in 1938 (129, p. lxxxviii). The notes to Oliver's edition of *The Piazza Tales* were comparatively brief and involved few newly suggested sources. Murray's lengthy introduction focused on the psychological and bio-graphical dimensions of *Pierre*, but his explanatory notes also included much literary source-study. He suggested new sources, especially works by Sir Walter Scott and Horace Wal-pole, and emphasized "the immense influence of Byron" (181, p. 437) and of Thomas Moore's *Letters and Journals of Lord Byron; with Notices of His Life*.

For their edition of *Moby-Dick*, Mansfield and Vincent noted and discussed previously identified sources, some of which Vin-cent had recently examined in *The Trying-Out of Moby-Dick*. But their edition emphasized the influence on Melville of such liter-ary figures as Carlyle and Goethe, as *The Trying-Out*, which was concerned only with whaling sources, had not, and they also discussed at length his use of such works of "slight literary mer-it" as Robert Southey's *The Doctor* and Thomas Hope's *Anastasi-us* (229, p. 570). Indeed, Mansfield and Vincent so emphasized such minor sources that the really major ones—the Bible, Shakespeare, and Milton, for instance—seemed lost in the 260 pages of notes. In their annotation actual sources were too often obscured among the many analogues introduced with such vague directives as "See" and "Compare."

Both Foster's edition of *The Confidence-Man* and Bezanson's edition of *Clarel* made heavy use of their own Yale University dissertations, written at a time when very little work had been done on either book, so that the extensive source-work in their notes was almost all new. Hayford and Blair, on the other hand, reported in the preface to their edition of *Omoo* that Anderson's search for source-books was so exhaustive that they could find no additional ones. Hayford, who undertook the source-work, therefore set himself to study more closely the process by which Melville used his different source-books in the composition of *Omoo* (see below, pp. 23–24) and how he transformed the "mere factual lumber" of his sources into fiction. The published Hen-dricks House editions succeeded so well in reporting Melville's basic sources that for these works later source-hunters have found few additional ones.

Even more than the Hendricks House editions, Merton M. Sealts, Jr.'s *Melville's Reading: A Check-List of Books Owned and Borrowed* (1948–1950, 1966) shaped the course of later Melville source-study. As noted above, Sealts's checklist included only works which external evidence—such as surviving books, publishers' records, library call-slips, purchases or borrowings recorded in journals—suggested Melville owned or consulted and made no effort to identify which ones he may have drawn on in his works. It did not include books which had been proven or suggested to be sources solely on evidence within Melville's works. Unfortunately, since 1948 when Sealts's checklist began to appear, scholars have often overlooked this limitation and have given undue importance to books listed on it. Such scholars go first to Sealts, note the listed books relevant to their author or subject—Melville's knowledge of Egypt, for example—and then go only to those books, as if Melville could have had no access to others not listed. Had Anderson limited himself to such a list as Sealts's, he would not have found many of the major source-books turned up by his broad reading (e.g., those by F. D. Bennett, William Ellis, and Charles Stewart), for no external record survives of the copies of them which Melville used. Too often, moreover, scholars have assumed that they do not have to prove that Melville read a particular book as long as it is included in Sealts; they cite the Sealts number as "proof" and build from there. As Sealts himself warned, there are two possible misuses of his checklist: concluding that Melville in fact read all the books listed there, or that he did *not* read the books *not* so listed.

By the time Sealts's checklist was published in book form (1966), the results of Melville source-study had already begun to thin out, and now, in the 1980s, even less is being found than in the 1940s and 1950s. Though further identification of obscure sources is possible, much of the more recent source-study engages in reinterpretation of Melville's use of long-known and much-studied sources, or in speculative, repetitive, and even implausible suggestions about other sources. Even so, good source studies have recently been written in which scholars have determined the exact editions used by Melville and carefully sorted out his use of those sources in his works. The emphasis on criticism and interpretation has also injected new insights into source-study. Nonetheless, much that is done now is unoriginal or implausible.

In review, during the first years of attention to Melville—before there really was such a thing as source-study—contem-

porary reviewers only dimly sensed that Melville had read widely and that this reading had affected his writing. Then, in the
1920s, Melville was "rediscovered," but scholars at that period,
who were concerned mostly with biography, took Melville's
first-person narratives as literally true and therefore did not look
for sources. With Scudder's discovery of Delano's *Narrative* as
the major source for "Benito Cereno" in 1928 the early major
source studies began, the ones which established Melville's extensive dependence on literary sources. Next came more so-
phisticated literary study; e.g., using sources to study Melville's
method of composition. In the last two decades there has been
a decline in the quality of source-study, mostly because all the
major sources seem to have been discovered. Yet there is still
good work being done; e.g., Walter Bezanson's fine work on
Israel Potter for the Northwestern-Newberry edition. *Who* has
discovered Melville's sources has now been discussed; the next
question is *how* Melville acquired and used them.

MELVILLE'S ACQUISITION AND USE OF HIS SOURCES

In 1927, the year before the earliest of the major Melville source
studies appeared, John Livingston Lowes published *The Road to
Xanadu*, a study of Coleridge's writing of "The Rime of the Ancient Mariner" and "Kubla Khan." Lowes sought what he called
"the incongruous, chaotic, and variegated jumble out of which
emerged the two unique poems"[6] —and he studied how con-
stituents of that "jumble" had united to form unforgettable
passages of Coleridge's poems. Though Lowes's psychology of
composition is now considered naive, his book was important
as a model to source scholars. The questions he raised about
Coleridge's process of composition could aptly be applied to
Melville's: Did Melville write with books before him or did he
draw on memory? Did he go from a book to that book's sources
via its footnotes? Did he habitually read the whole book? Did he
integrate materials from different sources so that they coalesced
in one passage, or were his borrowings kept separate? Did Melville remember passages from works he had read earlier and return to them for verification? Or did he systematically search for
new inspiration? Do sources he used in early works reappear in
later ones?

The answers are not simple, of course, but some general patterns emerge. Melville usually wrote the informational parts of his narratives with one or more source-books before him. We know this from material he included *verbatim*: words, misspellings, dates, and figures that would not have been likely to stick in his memory. But Melville also drew on his memory, usually in his more inspired or dramatic passages. The likeness between Ahab and King Lear has often been noted: *King Lear* was certainly an inspiration for *Moby-Dick*, but Melville did not need to have his Hilliard and Gray edition of Shakespeare open before him. In late 1850 and early 1851, he was so steeped in Shakespeare that he was able to capture both the texture of Shakespeare's language and the grandeur of Shakespeare's conception of character without directly appropriating words or passages from *King Lear*, as he did, for example, from Scoresby and Beale. The complexity of Melville's borrowing, however, was shown by Leon Howard, who demonstrated that Coleridge's lecture on *Hamlet* (from his *Literary Remains*) shaped Melville's conception of Ahab and even supplied key words in his definition of such a tragic hero, in "The Ship" (chapter 16 of *Moby-Dick*):

And when these things unite in a man of greatly superior natural force, with a globular brain and a ponderous heart; who has also by the stillness and seclusion of many long night-watches in the remotest waters, and beneath constellations never seen here at the north, been led to think untraditionally and independently ... —that man makes one in a whole nation's census—a mighty pageant creature, formed for noble tragedies. Nor will it at all detract from him, dramatically regarded, if either by birth or other circumstances, he have what seems a half wilful over-ruling morbidness at the bottom of his nature. For all men tragically great are made so through a certain morbidness. Be sure of this, O young ambition, all mortal greatness is but disease. (p. 71)

Coleridge's lecture on *Hamlet* contained the dictum which led to this conception of Ahab:

Now one of Shakspeare's modes of creating characters is, to conceive any one intellectual or moral faculty in morbid excess, and then to place himself, Shakspeare, thus mutilated or diseased, under given circumstances. (pp. 204–5)

As Howard stated, "*Moby-Dick* itself indicated that Coleridge's lecture on *Hamlet* came into Melville's mind whenever he stopped to comment on Captain Ahab as an artistic creation" (137, p. 202).[7]

Sometimes Melville went from a book to its sources via its footnotes or quotations, as Hayford's study of *Omoo* (480) shows. But more often Melville simply incorporated them into his text, thus appearing (or making his narrator appear) to be a more learned and widely read scholar than he really was. Habitually Melville did *not* read a whole source, but plucked his borrowings from one section of it. Even some of his major source-works Melville did not read from cover to cover, a fact suggested by the absence of annotations and line-markings in certain plays of Shakespeare and essays of Emerson and perhaps corroborated by his confession in his ecstatic essay on Hawthorne's *Mosses from an Old Manse* that he had not even read that collection through before beginning to write about it. Of course, Melville may have read the unmarked parts of some sources in another copy at an earlier or later date, but there are certain plays of Shakespeare and then-best-known essays of Emerson in his First and Second Series to which Melville never alluded in any surviving writings.

Melville did sometimes synthesize his informational sources, but this was more often true of his inspirational literary sources—Shakespeare, Milton, Shelley, Carlyle—than of those which merely provided facts. With the works of such writers as Bennett, Beale, and Scoresby—what Melville called his "numerous fish documents"—his borrowings tended to be separate or sequential rather than patched together or interspersed. In "The Affidavit" (chapter 45 of *Moby-Dick*), for example, Melville first discussed the sinking of the *Essex*, as had Beale, on whom most of the chapter was based. He next quoted directly from Chase's own *Narrative* in a long footnote; mentioned the loss of the *Union* (but wrote that he had never encountered the particulars of that incident); described Commodore J—'s encounter with a sperm whale, for which no source has yet been found; borrowed a passage from Langsdorff's *Voyages*; quoted from Dampier's *Voyages Round the World*; and finally concluded with the story of the

Pusie Hall, which he had found in Bennett (Vincent pointed out this sequence, 182, pp. 189–91). Thus, Melville evidently went from source-book to source-book, searching out incidents in which whales attacked ships. Sometimes he was more economical, however, so that the belief that in a certain passage Melville showed his wide reading in a subject like geology, for instance, has often been superseded by a later scholar's findings that all the information came from *one* source. Melville's use of *The Penny Cyclopaedia* for his multiple citations in the chapters "Cetology" and "The Fossil Whale" in *Moby-Dick* is a fine example of his dependence on such a single eclectic work.

Whether Melville remembered appropriate passages and returned to them for verification or whether he systematically searched for such passages is hard to answer without external evidence. When Melville inserted factual information from his source-books into his already drafted narrative, he usually took it from books he had at hand. But sometimes he first used bits of information recollected from his wide reading and then sought out its source or sources for verification and more information with which to amplify his original passage.

Source-books used in earlier works sometimes turn up again in later writings, but not, after Melville's first three books, to the extent one might expect. *Typee*, *Omoo*, and the first part of *Mardi* were drawn in narrative outline from his South Sea adventures but increasingly filled out with information and episodes from earlier travel works, Ellis's *Polynesian Researches*, Stewart's *A Visit to the South Seas*, and Wilkes's *Narrative*. But after *Mardi*, the more varied nature of his successive books made such repeated use less possible. Matter from Beale never again appeared after *Moby-Dick*. This was partly due, of course, to the subject matter of the books: what use could be made of the *Natural History of the Sperm Whale* in a story about people traveling downriver on a steamboat? And *King Lear*, which so informed the character of Ahab as Melville wrote *Moby-Dick* in 1850–51, did not shape that of the tragic hero in the book which he wrote in the next few months; instead, it was *Hamlet* that similarly marked *Pierre*.

Melville obtained his source materials in four different ways.[8] The first was to seek out books deliberately in order to enrich real or pseudo-autobiographical narratives with interspersed factual information presented, typically, as Melville's own "observations." Melville was writing at a time when readers and publishers demanded "useful knowledge." Reviewers, too—especially the reviewers of *White-Jacket* and *Moby-Dick*—praised the informational value of Melville's works. It was probably to meet this utilitarian demand that Melville included detailed information about the customs, dress, and language of the South Sea islanders in his works, especially *Typee* and *Omoo*. To supplement his tale in *Typee*, he drew on Charles S. Stewart's *A Visit to the South Seas*, David Porter's *Journal of a Cruise Made to the Pacific Ocean*, William Ellis's *Polynesian Researches*, Georg H. von Langsdorff's *Voyages and Travels*, and the Harper Family Library summary of Pacific narratives called *Historical Account of the Circumnavigation of the Globe*. Melville may have journeyed from his home in upstate Lansingburgh to New York City in January 1845 to find those materials he needed. Even after his brother Gansevoort had taken a manuscript of *Typee* to England with him, Melville continued to search source-books for interesting information. He wrote three additional chapters (20, 21, and 27), derived mostly from Porter, and sent them on to his brother in November. This new material, especially chapter 27, had the effect of helping to make the narrative more authentic by establishing the narrator as a close observer of the Marquesan people. Gansevoort noted this when he sent the three chapters on to the English publisher, John Murray. The new chapters, wrote Gansevoort, "from their subject matter, especially that of Chapter 27, will go far to give a more life-like air to the whole, an[d] parry the incredulity of those who may be disposed to regard the work as an ingenious fiction."[9]

As he gradually exhausted what seemed usable in his stock of early experiences on sea and land, Melville occasionally chanced upon a tale that he recognized could be worked up into an entire book or story. Even before writing *Moby-Dick*, he discovered Henry Trumbull's *Life and Remarkable Adventures of Israel R. Potter*, and from that he later fashioned his own *Israel Potter*. As he explained in its preface, "From a tattered copy [of "Israel Potter's autobiographical story"], rescued by the merest chance from the rag-pickers, the present account has been drawn."[10] Melville worked the same way with Amasa Delano's

Narrative of Voyages and James Hall's *Sketches of History, Life, and Manners in the West*; he became interested in them through an association with a shipmate or a publisher and eventually recognized he could shape parts of them into "Benito Cereno" and the Indian-hater chapters of *The Confidence-Man* (chapters 26–27).

Melville's third way of obtaining source material was when friends, spontaneously or on request, lent or gave him books. Evert A. Duyckinck, at the center of the New York literary circle to which Melville belonged, lent Melville many books during his early years there. In the winter of 1847–48 Melville first borrowed volumes from Duyckinck, including the works of Rabelais and Sir Thomas Browne, *A Narrative of the Sufferings and Adventures of Capt. Charles H. Barnard*, and Esaias Tegner's *Frithiof's Saga*.[11] Melville's comments on Browne caused Duyckinck to write his brother,

By the way Melville reads Old Books. He has borrowed Sir Thomas Browne of me and says finely of the speculations of the Religio Medici that Browne is a kind of "crack'd Archangel." Was ever anything of this sort said before by a sailor?[12]

Melville was working on *Mardi* at the time, and the influence of these authors, especially Browne and Rabelais, is very apparent. Duyckinck's list of "Books Lent" eventually recorded twenty-nine titles lent to Melville (Sealts, p. 16).

Duyckinck continued to supply Melville with books even after Melville left New York to live in Pittsfield, Massachusetts. Through him Melville also received issues of the *Dollar Magazine* (also called *Holden's Dollar Magazine*), of which Duyckinck was the editor. Melville mentioned the magazine in letters to Duyckinck of 12 February and 26 March 1851, and to Hawthorne of [1?] June 1851. In the *Dollar Magazine* Melville read Hawthorne's "Ethan Brand," which Howard P. Vincent and Leo Marx have argued had a profound influence on "The Try-Works" chapter (96) of *Moby-Dick* (182, p. 335, and 279, p. 40). Marx wrote that the "Try-Works" chapter "is quite literally constructed out of the symbols of 'Ethan Brand.' Again it is night, and vision is limited to the lurid light of a 'kiln' or 'furnace.' Fire again is a means of production, rendering the whale's fat, and again it is also the source of alienation" (279, pp. 40–41).

Further evidence of Melville's dependence on Duyckinck for reading material in Pittsfield is found in Melville's letter to Duyckinck of 7 November 1851:

Why didn't you send me that inestimable item of "Herman de Wardt" before? Oh had I but had that pie to cut into! But that & many other fine things doubtless are omitted. All one can do is to pick up what chips he can buy[?] round him. They have no Vatican (as you have) in Pittsfield here.[13]

Melville had only recently finished *Moby-Dick*, a fact which explains his regret at not having the "Herman de Wardt" piece sooner.

Much later, after his move back to New York, Melville continued to borrow books from Duyckinck. On [1?] February 1862, he wrote him:

I want you to loan me some of those volumes of the Elizabethan dramatists. Is Deckar among the set? And Webster? If so, please put them up and let the bearer have them.— Send me any except Marlowe, whom I have read. (*Letters*, p. 213)

(Melville had been laid up with rheumatism and so had not been able to visit and get the volumes in person.)

Family members and other friends also supplied Melville with books. Momentously, on 18 July 1850, an aunt gave him a copy of Hawthorne's *Mosses from an Old Manse* (Sealts #248). This gift, followed by Melville's first meeting with Hawthorne, 5 August 1850, inspired his "Hawthorne and His Mosses"[14] and *Moby-Dick*.

Melville's friendship with Hawthorne, growing from that first meeting, opened up another source of books. On 22 January 1851, Hawthorne presented Melville with a copy of *Twice-Told Tales* (Sealts #259) and on 14 March 1851 with four volumes of *The Mariner's Chronicle*, a collection of narratives of shipwrecks, fires, famines, and other calamities (Sealts #194), which Hawthorne had received from his uncle. As Howard P. Vincent argued, "The gift [of *The Mariner's Chronicle*] suggests that Melville had discussed his plot problems [in the book that became *Moby-Dick*] with his friend and that Hawthorne had given his old volumes . . . in a helping spirit" (182, p. 47).

There is no evidence that Melville used *The Mariner's Chronicle* in *Moby-Dick*, but he did draw on a work provided by his father-in-law, Judge Lemuel Shaw. Judge Shaw secured from Thomas Macy of Nantucket a copy of Owen Chase's *Narrative of the Most Extraordinary and Distressing Shipwreck of the Whale-Ship Essex* (Sealts #134), which he presented to Melville in April 1851. That Melville had asked Judge Shaw to find him a copy is indicated by Thomas Macy's letter of 4 April 1851 to the judge, reporting that this "mutilated copy" was "the only copy" that he had been able to procure (Sealts, p. 20). Melville added eighteen pages of notes to Chase's *Narrative* and used the account of the sinking of the *Essex* by a sperm whale in his conclusion to *Moby-Dick*. Shaw had earlier (in January 1851) received from Macy a copy of Lay and Hussey's *A Narrative of the Mutiny, on Board the Ship Globe* (Sealts #323), which he also gave to Melville. On 7 January 1852, after *Moby-Dick* was published, Thomas Macy inscribed to Melville himself a copy of Obed Macy's *The History of Nantucket* (Sealts #345), of which Melville had already amply used some other unrecorded copy for *Moby-Dick* (see 182, esp. pp. 83–84 and 87–88).

Melville's fourth source of material came through the reading aloud of books in the family circle, through reading he was engaged in for pleasure, and finally through all the literature with which he had come in contact during his life. Melville always read whenever his weak eyes permitted, and what he read stayed with him. His eyes hurt him at night, so he read little then; in late 1850 he spent his evenings, as he wrote Duyckinck on 13 December, "in a sort of mesmeric state in my room—not being able to read—only now & then skimming over some large-printed book" (*Letters*, p. 117). Sometimes during an evening spent with his family one of the women would read aloud, as Elizabeth Melville had earlier recorded (*Log*, p. 266). But during the day Melville could and did read much, and in all his works he made allusions from his extensive reading. An example from Melville's reading of Montaigne's "An Apologie of Raymond Sebond" occurs at the end of chapter 86, "The Tail," in *Moby-Dick*: Melville told the story of an elephant in the flower-market, from Montaigne's "Apologie," as Mansfield and Vincent (229, p. 785) and Shulman (301, p. 198) have pointed out. Melville was also influenced by Montaigne's "Apologie" in the following chapter, "The Grand Armada." This evidence suggests that

Melville was reading Montaigne as he was writing these chapters, not as a direct source—for Frederick Debell Bennett's *A Whaling Voyage Round the Globe* provided Melville with the factual information for chapter 87—but for his own pleasure, and that Montaigne in unforeseen ways affected his writing. Melville's language also reflected his long hours with Shakespeare, Milton, Carlyle, Dante, and the Bible, though there is no evidence that he had any of these open before him as he wrote.

As noted above, it was not until the late 1940s that a few scholars, following the example of Lowes, became interested in questions about Melville's compositional process. In his earliest method of composition, Melville inserted into his running narrative—both as he wrote and in later drafts—facts or description he gleaned from other books. This is his first and most characteristic manner of borrowing, and hence the one which has received the most attention from scholars. These genetic theorists tried to conceive of Melville's acts in temporal succession: at what stages did he get his ideas and source materials, when did he work them into his manuscript, and how did unforeseen additions affect the work in progress?

The Hendricks House edition of *Omoo* offers a good example of early study of Melville's compositional process.[15] As noted earlier, one of its editors, Harrison Hayford, reported that he could find no new sources since Anderson's search had been so thorough. But he added: "With only *Omoo* to account for, however, we have been able to study Melville's use of these books much more closely than the scope of Anderson's work permitted him to do" (480, p. xiv).

Hayford's study made it clear that William Ellis's *Polynesian Researches* had been Melville's major source and that he repeatedly used information from Ellis without ever citing him as an authority. But Melville took only Ellis's facts—not his missionary attitudes toward those facts. Thus Ellis was Melville's major source for information about Tahitian culture presented in chapters 45, 46, 47, and 49 of *Omoo*, but for an interpretation he preferred of this culture Melville went to "the unevangelical Reverend Michael Russell" (480, p. xxviii), whose philosophic reservations about missionary work—and whose topics, quotations, and footnotes—he followed closely. Hayford concluded

from his study of Melville's use of Ellis and Russell that originally chapter 49 had followed chapter 47 and that Melville had later
inserted chapter 48, based on Russell. Melville first quoted Russell's references to Beechey and Kotzebue, then went to their
original works and drew directly from them. As Hayford explained,

Since he made little further use of Kotzebue and Beechey, two report-
ers whose views were close to his own, it seems likely that he did not
have their works to draw upon while he was writing his first draft, but
looked them up later for amplification of what he had found quoted by
Russell. (480, p. 393)

This suggestion is supported by the fact that Judge Shaw with-
drew Kotzebue's volumes from the Boston Athenaeum during a
visit Melville made to the Shaws just before making the last revi-
sions in his manuscript of *Omoo* (Sealts #313).

The same method Hayford used in showing how Melville
used sources in composing *Omoo* has been applied by other
scholars to the composition of *Moby-Dick*.[16] Leon Howard and
James Barbour have extensively studied this work's composition, using Melville's acquisition of sources as major evidence
for hypothesizing various stages of composition. "Second
Growth," chapter 7 in Howard's biography (213, pp. 150–79),
gave in some detail his theory (later several times modified) of
the growth of the book.[17] Barbour's 1970 dissertation, "The Writing of *Moby Dick*" (directed by Leon Howard), a complex compositional study extending and revising Howard's theory, is especially important because of its detail and thoroughness. Barbour
divided the book's composition into three hypothetical stages:
February through August 1850, when Melville wrote a whaling
narrative built up from other whaling narratives; fall and early
winter 1850, when he expanded the work with facts drawn from
Beale's *The Natural History of the Sperm Whale* and Scoresby's
An Account of the Arctic Regions; and spring and summer 1851,
when Melville completed *Moby-Dick* under the influence of
Hawthorne, Shakespeare, and Carlyle's *Sartor Resartus*. In April
1851, Melville received the copy of Chase's *Narrative of the Most
Extraordinary and Distressing Shipwreck of the Whale-Ship Es-
sex* which his father-in-law had found for him, and this book,
Barbour believed, led Melville to change his plans for the final

chapters. Predictions in the early chapters of *Moby-Dick*, according to Barbour, were that deaths among the crew were to occur sequentially, but ultimately all except Ishmael die at once, when a sperm whale, as in Chase's account of *Essex* tragedy, turns on the whaleship itself.

Barbour's work is a clear example of how the analysis of sources can illuminate the process of composition, but it also is vulnerable to some of the possible hazards in this type of study. The unexamined assumption that writers write their chapters in order, from the first to the last, may be a fallacy adopted in genetic study. It is tempting but possibly misleading to assume that if a writer changes his conception in the course of composition the change will show up only in subsequent chapters. This fallacy is evident in those theories which, pointing to Ahab's late appearance in *Moby-Dick*, argue that the character of Ahab was inspired by Melville's rereading of Shakespeare and thus postulate two *Moby-Dicks*, the first written before July/August 1850 (when Melville made his comparison of Hawthorne and Shakespeare in his essay on *Mosses*), the second after.[18] Charles Olson used this type of reasoning, flatly asserting that

> *Moby-Dick* was two books written between February, 1850 and August, 1851.
> The first book did not contain Ahab.
> It may not, except incidentally, have contained Moby-Dick. (164, p. 35)

George Stewart made the same assumption, on different evidence, not emphasizing the influence of Shakespeare as Olson did. Stewart divided *Moby-Dick* as follows:

1) Chapters I–XV. These represent an original story, very slightly revised.
2) Chapters XVI–XXII. These represent the original story with a certain amount of highly important revision.
3) Chapters XXIII–Epilogue. These represent the story as it was written after Melville reconceived it, but may preserve certain passages of the original story, doubtless somewhat revised. (255, p. 417)

Even Barbour, though he put part of his compositional stage three before stage two, accepted to some extent the assumption of linear composition. Thus he referred repeatedly to the published chapters 1–22 as "the early narrative" (see, e.g., 487, pp. 185 and 195) and argued that "the initial and concluding sections of the novel present a continuous narrative, the result, the evidence tells us, of a *seriatim* composition" (487, p. 196).

Until Hayford's "Unnecessary Duplicates: A Key to the Writing of *Moby-Dick*" (1978), all theorizers—including Barbour, Olson, and Stewart—assumed that all the early land chapters (1–21) must have been written first and been part of the original narrative that was "mostly done" in August of 1850. Hayford's argument was based on internal evidence of what he called "unnecessary duplicates"—e.g., two introductory chapters, two whaling ports, two inns, two experienced whaleman "comrades," three captains, and so on. Hayford conjectured that Melville did not proceed in linear fashion from start to finish; he repeatedly went back to revise what he had written and to insert new description, characters, or episodes. Vestigial elements usually survive from the earlier stages of composition, a fact which can help one to follow the compositional process. But the stages Hayford posited were always more complex than most of the "two *Moby-Dicks*" theorists have assumed; these stages of composition did not always break cleanly at the chapter breaks.[19]

A second hazard illustrated by Barbour's work was his inferring dates of composition from the dates when Melville acquired certain books. Barbour dated his stage two as consequent upon Melville's acquisition of his copy of Beale. This copy did not reach Melville until 10 July 1850 (at least if he signed and dated it without delay), and in the month that followed, so Barbour inferred, Melville was too busy with social engagements to work on his manuscript. Therefore, Barbour concluded, Melville could not have begun writing the scientific whaling chapters based on Beale until fall 1850. But the hazard is that the copy of Beale which Melville received in July (Sealts #52) was not necessarily the first copy Melville had used. He may have had access to some other copy of which no record happens to have survived (as was the case with Chase's *Narrative*), or, before his own copy arrived, he may have found and used, at least for some passages, materials from Beale reprinted or summarized in other sources. For some matters Melville used the "Whale" entry in the *Penny Cyclopaedia*, in which passages from Beale are paraphrased and his book is cited (see 628). Perhaps this was how Melville learned about Beale's book, prompting him to ask his bookseller to import it from England, or he could also have learned about it from J. Ross Browne's *Etchings of a Whaling Cruise*, a work we know he had read because he reviewed it for the *Literary World* on 6 March 1847. Browne's appendix contained extensive quotations from Beale, on which Melville could already have been drawing before his copy of Beale arrived. In short, the assumption that Melville's use of a source can be "precisely dated" by Melville's acquisition of a copy of it has the same inherent hazard as does uncritical use of Sealts's *Melville's Reading*. Surviving documentary evidence is always incomplete.

A related hazard is illustrated by Howard's and Barbour's basing their arguments on the chapters as published in *Moby-Dick*. Their unit of analysis is usually the chapter; therefore, if a given chapter derives from or has a central passage drawn from Beale, they argue that it could not have been written before July 1850. And if contiguous chapters depend on that chapter for their sense, they, too, supposedly could not have been written until after July 1850. But, again, Melville could in fact already have gotten Beale material for his passage from somewhere else, and then, after his own copy of Beale arrived, added more from it to his previously written passage. I use the word "passage" because Melville's early divisions were not always his final chapter divisions, as the surviving fragments of *Confidence-Man* manuscript show.[20] In the course of composition, what became Melville's chapters were often expanded from initial sentences or passages which he had returned to amplify. Thus, what began as a brief passage could easily have become expanded into one or more chapters in the final draft. For determining when a given source is used the basic unit cannot strictly be any longer than the identifiable passage based on a source and its *immediate context*—frequently not more than a paragraph or even a sentence.

Melville's first method of composition was to incorporate old facts in new narratives; his second was to refashion an already published narrative, like those of Trumbull, Delano, and Hall. His method in these cases can be reconstructed by closely comparing his source with his final work. "Benito Cereno" was his first work so written, from Delano's *Narrative of Voyages*, but *Israel Potter*, because it has been much less studied, is the example given here.

Evidence that Melville was already thinking of making a book about Israel Potter from Henry Trumbull's *Life and Remarkable Adventures of Israel R. Potter* occurs in his London journal for 18 December 1849:

Looked over a lot of ancient maps of London. Bought one (A.D. 1766) for 3 & 6 pence. I want to use it in case I serve up the Revolutionary narrative of the beggar.[21]

Nothing more is known about Melville's writing this book until 7 June 1854, when he wrote to his publisher, George P. Putnam, to ask about sixty-odd pages of its manuscript he had sent and the terms under which the story was to be published (*Letters*, pp. 169–70). Subsequently, *Israel Potter* was serialized in *Putnam's Monthly Magazine* from July 1854 through March 1855. This is the only hard evidence we have of the book's composition, but much more can be inferred by directly comparing Trumbull's and Melville's versions.

The Northwestern-Newberry edition of *Israel Potter* includes a photographic reproduction of Trumbull's *Life* with marginal page and line numbers (keyed to the NN text) to show where Melville used each passage. The first pages are full of these marginal numbers—Melville followed his source so closely that there are many words and phrases in common—but the later pages have fewer and fewer marginal numbers. As Melville continued writing he invented more and used fewer passages from the original. Trumbull's account of Israel's life became bleaker and less eventful after the Revolution episodes, and Melville evidently found his earlier idea of developing the long London years of Israel's poverty too constraining.

After Trumbull's p. 52 Melville returned to that source only briefly and occasionally. He turned to other sources in order to invent two sets of Revolutionary War experiences for Israel, with Benjamin Franklin in Paris and with John Paul Jones at sea. From four pages in Trumbull Melville built up the humorous sequence on Franklin which became his chapters 7–10, 12. *The Works of Benjamin Franklin*, edited by Jared Sparks (Boston, 1836–40), as Walter E. Bezanson convincingly suggested, provided the grist for these chapters (685, p. 192). From Trumbull's mere mention of John Paul Jones (p. 60), Melville created his own flamboyant Jones chapters (10–11, 14–20). His primary sources for the maritime episodes were Robert C. Sands's *Life and Correspondence of John Paul Jones* (New York, 1830) and James Fenimore Cooper's *History of the Navy of the United States of America* (New York, 1853). As he rewrote material from Sands and Cooper, Melville inserted Israel's name where they wrote of "a sailor" or "one man" doing a gallant deed.

Reshaping a source while keeping the main structure and narrative line of the original was thus Melville's second method of composition. In this manner Melville rewrote Trumbull, Delano, Hall, and, to a lesser extent, Sands and Cooper. Early source-hunters recovered the central sources for *Israel Potter*, "Benito Cereno," and chapters 26–27 of *The Confidence-Man* by investigating the names—Potter, Delano, Hall—which Melville cited along with the words he borrowed.

Both in inserting source materials into his own narrative and in adapting the narratives of others, Melville appropriated blocks of writing whose origin is so clear that the source-hunter can often identify not only Melville's source but also the very edition he used. The "fingerprints" by which scholars make such identifications with confidence include peculiar wording, errors in titles or dates, and misspellings. In chapter 41 of *Moby-Dick*, for instance, Melville misspelled Olafsen as "Olassen" when he referred to Olafsen and Povelsen's representation of the sperm whale as incredibly ferocious and thirsting for human blood. Since Beale made the same reference with the same misspelling, it is clear that Melville got his information from Beale and not directly from Olafsen and Povelsen's *Travels in Iceland*.[22]

Melville's third method of using his sources is much more difficult to document, since it is hardly a "method" at all. As William H. Gilman wrote, "Melville's knowledge was not deep but eclectic. Although he had acquired some familiarity with the classics, he was no more a scholar in his thirties than he had been in his teens. He was a wide reader with a brilliant memory who abstracted with rare perception the quintessence of what he read" (212, p. 223). Melville's allusions to his wide reading and his sometimes shaky recollection of it make up his third method, which I will refer to as recall, to denote those moments when Melville presumably did not have the source-books in front of him as he wrote. The authors Melville drew on in this way were typically among the greatest literary figures—Shakespeare, Milton, Dante, Spenser, Carlyle—because theirs were the works which persisted in his mind and inspired him. These great authors did in fact sometimes contribute to Melville's works more directly. For example, as we have seen, Melville adapted from Spenser almost all the epigraphs to the sketches in "The Encantadas" without identifying his source. Lesser writers may also have received this casual treatment. Thus in Fenimore Cooper's *Homeward Bound* (1838), Captain Truck related an anecdote concerning one Joe Bunk, and Melville may have recalled that name when he had "Joe Bunk" play the Commodore's Cockswain in "The Old Wagon Paid Off," the theatrical advertised in chapter 23 of *White-Jacket*. The danger of this inference is that as a generic sailor name "Joe Bunk" is so close to "Jack Tar" that it may turn out to have been common during the little more than a decade which saw publication of both works.

To sum up, then, Melville acquired his sources in four ways: deliberately seeking out books in order to add factual material to narratives based on his own adventures; chancing upon tales that he could work up into whole books or stories; obtaining source material, either as loan or gift, from friends; and gathering allusions or quotations from works read aloud to him or from reading he was doing apart from his writing. He used these source materials in three ways: inserting facts or descriptions gleaned from source-books into his running narrative; refashioning an already published narrative; and enriching his narratives with language, structures, and characterizations—sometimes even names and events—he recalled from his past reading.

METHOD

The compilation of this two-part checklist was simple in conception, though ambitious in execution. I tried to read everything ever written on Melville—from the contemporary reviews through twentieth-century articles, books, and dissertations—

culling from this mass of commentary all the sources attributed there. Though any study on such a scale is to some extent incomplete, this checklist records all that is essential along with much that is inessential, absurd, and inconsequential. My reading has covered all known reviews and articles published on Melville through 1969 (after which the file of them in the Newberry Library Melville Collection is as yet incomplete) and most though not all published since. In general, I have tried to consult those items published after 1969 whose own titles or citations in other works identify them as source studies. In addition, I have examined all the dissertations in the Newberry Library collection, which lacks only a few relevant ones through 1980.[23] Dissertations offered few problems because not many of them since the early 1960s are full-length or important source studies. If a book was published from a dissertation, as Charles Roberts Anderson's was, I examined the book instead of the dissertation. I have tried to examine all the relevant books published through 1980[24], first searching out those which included discussions of Melville's reading and use of sources rather than beginning with the earliest book on Melville (1921) and working forward. I have sifted sources from all the volumes of the Northwestern-Newberry and Hendricks House editions of Melville's works (a task in itself, especially the 260 dense pages of Explanatory Notes to the Hendricks House edition of *Moby-Dick*). Finally, I read all the *Melville Society Extracts* published to date, because it is a major repository of short source studies.

In sum, I have searched in all these secondary writings for any reference to Melville's reading or any attribution of a source. Whenever I came upon an attributed source, I listed that source, the work Melville used it in, and the writer who made the attribution. I included as attributed sources not only books but also pieces Melville is said to have used from journals or magazines, such as articles, short stories, essays, and book reviews, and I also listed, as cross-references, the periodicals in which such pieces appeared. I read contemporary reviews and listed sources suggested in them, but listed the reviews themselves as sources (though Melville doubtless read many of them) only when someone has suggested he used one as a source. In any case, all the reviews known up to 1975 are listed in Steven Mailloux and Hershel Parker's *Checklist of Melville Reviews* (Los Angeles: The Melville Society, 1975). I also did not list Melville's own works—though critics sometimes suggest that earlier ones may have served as "sources" for later ones (see, for example, Hayford and Sealts's discussion of sources, especially *White-Jacket*, in their edition of *Billy Budd, Sailor*, 345).

Three lists appear below, with sample entries preceding the first two. The first is the "Checklist of Melville's Sources," in alphabetical order by author. It includes all the works which anyone has suggested that Melville used as sources. Since it is not a technically detailed bibliography, it gives only the author's name, the short title, and the publication date. However, if the edition Melville is supposed to have used is specified or is known, either as identified by Sealts or by another scholar, I have marked the entry with an asterisk and specified that edition. If the work is already listed in Sealts's *Melville's Reading*, I have included the Sealts number in brackets. When the edition is not known, I have given the author's name, the title, and the date the work was first published, as supplied (where possible) by one of the Oxford Companions to literature. These reference works were chosen for their simplicity and consistency of reference and because they are readily available. Checking all the entries against the National Union Catalog or a similar listing was not appropriate here, since the inclusion of any more detailed information might be mistaken as suggesting that Melville used that particular edition. Thus, I have gone to the National Union Catalog and the British Museum Catalog only for works not included in the Oxford Companions. By giving the first-publication date in parentheses, I have indicated the earliest possible edition Melville *could* have used—and also whether the source is, for instance, a seventeenth-century work or one written in the 1840s. (For an explanation of my symbols, see the key to symbols and the sample entry that precede the list.)[25]

The second list is the chronological "List of Scholarship."[26] (The first list is cross-referenced to it.) This second list includes contemporary reviews, biographies, works of criticism which mention in passing books read by Melville, and detailed source studies—anything which discusses Melville's reading or his sources. This list is given in chronological order, to make readily apparent when Melville's reading of each work was first suggested. The "List of Scholarship" is immediately followed by an alphabetical "Index of Scholars," with the anonymous contemporary reviews alphabetized under "Review." To avoid confusion, I refer to the numbers for the entries in the "Checklist of Melville's Sources" as "source numbers" and numbers for the entries in the "List of Scholarship" as "reference numbers."

Each discussion in the "List of Scholarship" has also been evaluated. The evaluations are mine and are not meant to suggest any sort of consensus. They are meant simply to provide initial assistance to users of the checklist and are coded as follows: ! = good, ? = questionable, ?? = blunder. These symbols (based on standard chess notation) appear in an entry after the reference number. Items to which no symbol is given seemed to me to require none, being neither very good nor questionable.

I found it difficult to specify for all cases what makes a discussion of a source "good." If the scholar gave convincing parallel passages and "fingerprints," or identified Melville's edition by internal evidence, then the discussion was usually marked "good." But often it was already known that Melville read a particular book because the book with his annotations in it still survives. In such a case, anyone who suggested Melville read that book has taken no chances—a good source study is one that discusses such a known source at length and shows specifically how Melville incorporated it into his work. Many scholars since Anderson in 1935 have referred to Melville's use of Nathaniel Ames's *A Mariner's Sketches* in *White-Jacket*, and they are all listed under Ames. But the best of these discussions—and the only ones marked "!"—are Anderson's in 1939, Matthiessen's in 1941, and Vincent's in 1970. The reader who must limit his research should consult at least these three. The other discussions noted under Ames are not questionable and so do not have "?" after them, but neither are they the most detailed or otherwise outstanding, and so they are simply left without remark.

A reference number followed by "?" means that the scholar's suggestion of a particular work as a source was weak, tenuous—somehow questionable. With the "?" I evaluate the scholar's suggestion, not his discussion—this differs from the "!," which evaluates mainly the scholar's discussion of Melville's use of a particular source. Sometimes a known source is followed by a reference number marked "?": the entry for Amasa Delano's

Narrative of Voyages provides a good example. In 1974 John Harmon McElroy argued unconvincingly (to me) that Delano was a source for *Typee* as well as "Benito Cereno." Thus, his reference number following *Typee* is marked "?," but not his reference number following "Benito Cereno." If an entry in the checklist is followed by only one reference number marked "?," that work (in my judgment) is probably *not* a source. Most reference numbers have no evaluation marks after them, meaning that I agree that Melville could have read the source suggested—the arguments are not conclusive but neither are they so tenuous as to make it questionable that Melville read the work.

Only two other symbols are used. The first is "??," which identifies an out-and-out blunder, where the scholar's attribution is demonstrably wrong. The second is "r," which indicates "rebuttal." An entry marked "000?? [r 000]" means that the first scholar made a blunder and was rebutted by the second. Often, however, there has been an attempted rebuttal even though it is unclear that the earlier scholar did make an outright blunder.

An example of a blunder occurred in William Bysshe Stein's "Melville Roasts Thoreau's Cock" (1959). Stein wrote, "It is possible to trace the inspiration for the work ["Cock-A-Doodle-Doo!"] directly to Thoreau's essay, 'Walking' " (309, p. 218). But, as Sidney P. Moss pointed out in 1968, there was one major problem: "The *essay* 'Walking' was published only posthumously (in June, 1862, in the *Atlantic Monthly*), some nine years after Melville published 'Cock-A-Doodle-Doo!' (in December, 1853, in *Harper's New Monthly Magazine*)" (470, p. 194).

Occasionally a sound article may survive an attempted rebuttal, as in the case of the Foster-Hillway debate over Melville's geological knowledge. In 1945 Elizabeth S. Foster published "Melville and Geology" in *American Literature*. Using chapter 132 of *Mardi* in particular ("Babbalanja regales the Company with some Sandwiches"), in which Babbalanja lectured on fossiliferous strata as "sandwiches," Foster attempted to determine the extent of Melville's geological knowledge. Babbalanja's geological table was "amazingly accurate, so accurate and full indeed" that Foster concluded that Melville was writing with a book or books before him (153, p. 54). Despite a long search, she could not find the specific source-books Melville used "except possibly, and even then with supplementary works, that of Lyell [Charles Lyell, *Elements of Geology*]" (153, pp. 54 and 59, n. 12). Foster also noted that two of Melville's geological references were "pure error": the "onion" theory of the earth's layers mentioned in *Pierre* and the belief that coral islands and atolls are built up from the bottom of the ocean as mentioned in *Omoo*, *Moby-Dick*, and *Pierre* (153, p. 62).

In 1949 Tyrus Hillway "answered" Foster, noting that he would "like to make some additions and to suggest possible sources not named in her article" (190, p. 232). Hillway believed that Melville's coral island theory came from John Reinold Forster's *Observations Made during a Voyage round the World* (1778) and that the onion theory was "taken directly" from Oliver Goldsmith's *Animated Nature*. The theory was also accessible to Melville, he continued, in John Mason Good's *The Book of Nature* (190, p. 234). Using Robert Chambers's *Vestiges of the Natural History of Creation*, Hillway set up a table, as Foster had done with Lyell and *Mardi*, to suggest that Chambers was the source for Babbalanja's lecture on fossiliferous strata.

In 1951 Foster published her point-by-point rebuttal of Hillway's claims, which she thought "overconfident and misleading" (215, p. 479). Foster refuted Hillway's article by showing that there were many other books that could have provided Melville with as much information as the ones Hillway claimed were the sources.

Another exposure of a misattribution was Hershel Parker's 1972 rebuttal of H. Bruce Franklin's 1961 suggestion that William Stirling's *Cloister Life of the Emperor Charles the Fifth* (London, 1853) was a major source for "Benito Cereno." Franklin made a high claim for Stirling's *Cloister Life* when he called it "a source of more ultimate significance than Delano's *Voyages*" (342, p. 462). Even if his claim was extravagant, his article noted many apparent similarities between the environments of "Benito Cereno" and *Cloister Life*, and between the men themselves (Benito Cereno and Charles the Fifth). And Franklin responsibly showed how Melville might have been aware of Stirling's book through reviews published in the same periodicals in which Melville's works were reviewed.

But Franklin's attempt to show Melville's acquaintance with Stirling was not convincing enough for Theodore L. Gaillard, Jr., who wrote in April 1972 that "while England was quite familiar with Stirling's work, it is doubtful that the American public was" (523, p. 482). Gaillard cast other doubts on Franklin's study, but it was Hershel Parker (528) who demolished Franklin's claim, pointing out that editions of Stirling were published only in London during the time Melville was writing "Benito Cereno," and that Franklin did not actually name any of the periodicals which reviewed Stirling. Parker questioned whether these editions and periodicals would have been available to Melville in Pittsfield, and then he dismissed most of the parallels between "Benito Cereno" and *Cloister Life*. Several verbal similarities did remain, but these were details of Charles the Fifth's life that need not have come from Stirling. As Parker wrote, "The evidence proves neither that Melville read Stirling nor that he did not, but it does prove that Stirling was not a major source for 'Benito Cereno' " (528, p. 222).

Such bold assertions and their rebuttals add spice to the study of Melville's sources. More tedious—and frustrating—are the many inconclusive or vague suggestions in Melville scholarship. One example is found in Newton Arvin's discussion of *Billy Budd* in his *Herman Melville* (1950):

For the tale of the Handsome Sailor and his unhappy end has an archetypal depth and scope that no reader can quite mistake; it is Melville's version of a primordial fable, the fable of the Fall of Man, the loss of Paradise. There are vibrations in it of the Book of Genesis, of the *Works and Days*, of Milton; there are other vibrations that are pure Melville. (198, p. 294)

Has Arvin suggested that Melville read the *Works and Days* or not? The Book of Genesis is a simpler case—we know Melville read it—but is it a source for *Billy Budd*? The answer perhaps may be that Arvin does not care, for he was neither citing analogues nor writing source-study. In fairness to Arvin, and to Mansfield and Vincent, whose liberal use of the terms "See" and "Compare" in their 1952 Hendricks House edition of *Moby-Dick* I criticized earlier, they were probably not attempting source-study, but merely pointing out resemblances between Melville's writings and the larger whole of nineteenth-century cultural life. Yet the question remains as to whether these "*vides*" should be included as suggested sources or not. I finally did not include most of them because they were not specifically suggested as sources.

Another difficulty is trying to determine whether in particular attributions a scholar has done original work or is simply incorporating earlier attributions. In "Melville's Education in Science," Tyrus Hillway presented a list of books to which Melville presumably went for scientific information, "though with less than certainty in some cases." Four of these were G. J. Guthrie's *A Treatise on Gun-Shot Wounds*, John Hennen's *Principles of Military Surgery*, William Fergusson's *A System of Practical Surgery*, and John and Charles Bell's *The Anatomy and Physiology of the Human Body*, by John D. Godman (571, p. 422). Hillway was evidently not making an original contribution here, but relying for this list, though he did not say so, upon Vincent's *The Tailoring of Melville's White-Jacket* (491, pp. 131–32). The last of the books with its peculiar citation of two sets of authors points to Vincent as Hillway's source, for the double citation appeared that way in Vincent (with the addition of publisher, date, and edition).

In certain cases it is immediately obvious to anyone acquainted with the topic that a scholar is simply passing along an attribution from one of the major works of Melville scholarship, such as Leon Howard's *Herman Melville: A Biography* (1951). Howard suggested that Nathaniel Fanning's *Narrative of the Adventures of an American Naval Officer* was a primary source for the John Paul Jones section of *Israel Potter*, but no earlier or later scholar who has worked with the sources of *Israel Potter*—W. Sprague Holden, Walter Dickinson Jones, Walter Bezanson—has agreed with him. Howard also suggested Alexander S. Mackenzie's *Life of Paul Jones* as a source (213, pp. 213–14), a suggestion which also has not been supported. (See the discussion of sources in the "Historical Note" to the Northwestern-Newberry edition of *Israel Potter*, 685, especially p. 195.) Thus any scholar who confidently asserts that, "for details concerning Jones, Melville relied on Nathaniel Fanning's *Narrative of the Adventures of an American Navy Officer* (1806) and, to a lesser degree, on Captain Alexander S. Mackenzie's standard *Life* (1841)," as Norman Eugene Hoyle did (317, p. 127), has been betrayed by his sole, uncited reliance on Howard's biography. (That Hoyle had not examined the original books himself is shown by his running together of two of the three items in Howard, who referred both to the standard *Life* of Jones *and* to Mackenzie's biography of him; they are not the same work—213, p. 214.)

And there are other scholars whose wholesale use of earlier source-study is inadequately distinguished (if at all) from their own original attributions. The discussion of sources in the commentary of Harold Beaver's edition of *Moby-Dick* (Penguin, 1972) relies heavily upon Mansfield and Vincent's notes in their Hendricks House edition with only a general acknowledgment. (The same is true of Beaver's textual apparatus, appropriated from the Norton Critical *Moby-Dick*.) Beaver wrote that "any new edition must stand on the backs of previous editors"—an allusion presumably to Isaac Newton's humble admission that he had "stood on the shoulders of giants."[27] But Beaver rides his predecessors as the Old Man of the Sea rode Sindbad.

These few examples point out that many assertions about sources are not based on original research. Nevertheless, Melville *did* rely, for instance, on Ellis in writing *Omoo*, and all the critics who say so are right, even if most of them did not look at Ellis's book itself, but only at Anderson (133), Hayford (480), or Howard's biography (213). Still, given their failure to say so, I cannot always be certain; thus, I have included nearly every discussion of a source unless it was patently no more than a summary of the work of an earlier scholar. I hope that part of what my work shows is the need for more careful and thorough examination, all along, of earlier attributions and for scrupulous citation of earlier scholarship.

POSSIBILITIES FOR FUTURE RESEARCH

What work still remains to be done in the study of Melville's sources? One of the most important study aids needed is a volume of Melville's allusions, covering all his works including the still unpublished manuscripts. Such a volume, to supplement Sealts's *Melville's Reading* and the present *Melville's Sources*, would be invaluable to scholars.

The most obvious need is for a comprehensive study of Melville's use of Shakespeare, whose presence in Melville's writings is so very strong. Although many scholars have mentioned Melville's use of Shakespeare (I have listed 120) and several full-length studies have been undertaken, no book has yet been published. There have been only two full-length dissertations on the subject, Roma Rosen's in 1962 (347) and Raymond Long's in 1965 (396). As one weary old scholar remarked, "That is a cave with many footprints leading in and none coming out."[28] More work eventually can also be done on Melville's use of Milton now that Melville's own copy of *The Poetical Works of John Milton* (Boston: Hilliard & Gray, 1836), heavily marked and annotated, has been discovered, though it is in the hands of a private owner and not now available for study.

Perhaps an even more difficult remaining task is a comprehensive treatment of Melville's use of sources in *Moby-Dick*. Such a work might treat the subject in both a factual and analytical way and could be organized around the chapters of *Moby-Dick*, the separate sources, or the chronology of Melville's composition. The two Scott dissertations with their documentation of the whaling sources and Vincent's *The Trying-Out of Moby-Dick*, which combined a chapter-by-chapter study of the whaling sources with a running literary interpretation, are the only existing books which approach this prescription.

Among Melville's shorter works, the poems and "The 'Gees" also deserve source study. No main source for Melville's portrait of the Cape de Verd [*sic*] islanders ("'Gees") has yet been found. Most scholars have avoided critical discussion of this sketch— perhaps because of its apparent racism—and little study has been made of it other than Carolyn L. Karcher's "Melville's 'The 'Gees': A Forgotten Satire on Scientific Racism" (1975).[29] Despite scattered studies such as Walter E. Bezanson's excellent article on Melville's use of Arnold's poetry (260) and his detailed work on *Clarel* (315), the poems continue to invite further source study.

The following pages present a list of abbreviations of titles, a key to evaluation marks, a sample entry for each of the first two lists, and the three lists themselves: "Checklist of Melville's Sources," "List of Scholarship," and "Index of Scholars."

NOTES

1. Merton M. Sealts, Jr., *Melville's Reading: A Check-List of Books Owned and Borrowed* (Madison: University of Wisconsin Press, 1966). Hereafter

cited in the text as Sealts, p. 00 (for his introduction and notes) and Sealts #000 (for numbered items in his checklist). My own title is patterned on Sealts's to make clear the distinction between the scopes of each checklist. Sealts's standard reference work was first published as a series of articles in the *Harvard Library Bulletin* from 1948 to 1950. Offprinted articles from the *Bulletin* were then issued in single-volume paperback form in 1950. In 1966 the revised checklist was published as a book by the University of Wisconsin Press; two supplementary notes subsequently appeared in the *Harvard Library Bulletin* in 1971 and 1979; and a revised edition is currently in progress.

2. There are several books which do discuss Melville's allusions: Thomas Alexander Little, "Literary Allusions in the Writings of Herman Melville" (Ph.D. dissertation, University of Nebraska, 1948); Julianne Small, "Classical Allusions in the Fiction of Herman Melville" (Ph.D. dissertation, University of Tennessee, 1974); Shigeru Maeno, *The Sources of Melville's Quotations* (Tokyo: Kaibunsha Ltd., 1981); and Gail H. Coffler, compiler, *Melville's Classical Allusions: A Comprehensive Index and Glossary* (Westport, Conn: Greenwood Press, 1985). They are all, except for Coffler's, difficult to obtain, however, because two are dissertations and one is a foreign publication. And Coffler's only covers the classical allusions.

3. All quotations from works that consider Melville's sources are keyed to the numbered "List of Scholarship" below. Hereafter they are cited parenthetically in the text by reference number, followed by page number. The *Examiner* review is 21, p. 195; emphasis added. Typographical errors in reviews are uncorrected and marked [*sic*] only if it seems necessary.

4. My system of documentation and treatment of such matters as italicization within titles in my text is explained in section 3, "Method."

5. Robert S. Forsythe, review of *Melville in the South Seas* by Charles Roberts Anderson, *American Literature*, 11 (March 1939), 85–92.

6. John Livingston Lowes, *The Road to Xanadu: A Study in the Ways of the Imagination* (Boston and New York: Houghton Mifflin, 1927), p. 4.

7. Harrison Hayford and Hershel Parker, eds., *Moby-Dick* (New York: W. W. Norton, 1967), p. 71. Hereafter all citations to *Moby-Dick* are to this edition. Samuel Taylor Coleridge, *The Literary Remains* (London: William Pickering, 1836), pp. 204–5. Leon Howard first suggested Melville's use of Coleridge's lecture in his 1940 article, "Melville's Struggle with the Angel" (137, pp. 202–3), discussed it again in his 1951 biography (213, especially p. 165), and in 1981 used new evidence to date Melville's reading of Coleridge's lecture as 30 December 1850. That date, as recorded in the report of Howard's 1981 lecture, "enabled Professor Howard to make his most startling suggestion—that Melville gave Ahab his ivory leg as a New Year's present on or about the beginning of 1851 and, by a process of revision and back-writing, gave his book its Shakespearean force during the months of intense writing pressure which followed" (677, p. 6). The question of the writing of *Moby-Dick* is discussed on pp. 24–27.

8. See Sealts's introduction, pp. 3–26, for a more detailed and specific account of Melville's acquisition habits.

9. Jay Leyda, *The Melville Log: A Documentary Life of Herman Melville, 1819–1891* (New York: Harcourt, Brace and Company, 1951), vol. I, pp. 200–

201 [The *Log* was reissued in 1969 with a supplement (New York: Gordian Press) and a third edition is forthcoming]. Hereafter cited in the text as *Log*. The information presented here on the writing of *Typee* comes from Leon Howard's "Historical Note" to the Northwestern-Newberry edition of *Typee* (460) and Hershel Parker's "Evidences for 'Late Insertions' in Melville's Works," *Studies in the Novel*, 7 (Fall 1975), 407–24. Parker argues convincingly against Howard's assertion that "Murray insisted that Herman make additions and changes" (460, p. 282).

10. Harrison Hayford, Hershel Parker, and G. Thomas Tanselle, eds., *Israel Potter: His Fifty Years of Exile* (Evanston and Chicago: Northwestern University Press and The Newberry Library, 1982), p. vii. Hereafter all citations to *Israel Potter* are to this edition.

11. See Mansfield's 1936 dissertation (123) for a discussion of Melville's friendship with Duyckinck. The information above comes from p. 40.

12. Evert A. Duyckinck to George L. Duyckinck, 18 March 1848, in the Duyckinck Collection of the New York Public Library, cited by Mansfield (123), p. 195.

13. Merrell R. Davis and William H. Gilman, eds., *The Letters of Herman Melville* (New Haven: Yale University Press, 1960), p. 140. Hereafter cited in the text as *Letters*. The forthcoming Northwestern-Newberry edition is a revised and supplemented version of Davis-Gilman's.

14. Harrison Hayford, in chapter 2 of "Melville and Hawthorne: A Biographical and Critical Study" (152, pp. 40–70), first discussed in detail whether Melville wrote his review before or after meeting Hawthorne and concluded with strong evidence that he wrote it *after*. See also the Northwestern-Newberry edition of *The Piazza Tales and Other Prose Pieces 1839–1860*.

15. This edition was originally completed in 1951 although it was not published until 1969. The 1957 "Editors' Preface" explains the division of work between the two editors (480, p. xvi). Since most of my discussion is based on Hayford's sections I cite "Hayford" rather than "Hayford and Blair."

16. For convenience, in the following discussion the title *Moby-Dick* is used all along, although the evidence is clear that Melville did not assign that title until just before the New York publication in November 1851— too late to change the earlier title, *The Whale*, in the London edition.

17. On the basis of prior publication, Charles Olson is often credited as the first to suggest that *Moby-Dick* was not written as one consecutive narrative. But Olson got the idea from Howard P. Vincent, who also told him about Melville's copy of Owen Chase, which became so central to Olson's book. Vincent's own genetic chapter in *The Trying-Out of Moby-Dick* (182, pp. 35–52) was added after the rest of his book was written, when he read Harrison Hayford's dissertation, "Melville and Hawthorne," especially chapter 6 (152, pp. 174–96), as he acknowledged in general terms (182, pp. [vii], 35, n. 7, and 38, n. 9). Hayford's dissertation, in turn, had cited Leon Howard's "Melville's Struggle with the Angel" (1940), based on a paper delivered at the Modern Language Association meeting in 1939, the first public formulation of the theory which became known (by George Stewart's 1954 title) as the "two *Moby-Dick*s." Stewart (255, p. 419,

n. 2) reported that he had been developing and teaching the theory for years.

18. The character of Ahab was certainly affected by Melville's reading of Shakespeare, as is evident in Ahab's soliloquies, such as the one beginning "I leave a white and turbid wake" in chapter 37, in the dramatic form of such chapters as "The Quarter-Deck" (36), and in the Shakespearean quality of the language. What is questionable is not this fact but the theory it has been called to support.

19. Harrison Hayford, "Unnecessary Duplicates: A Key to the Writing of *Moby-Dick*," in *New Perspectives on Melville*, ed. Faith Pullin (Edinburgh: Edinburgh University Press, 1978), pp. 128–61. Hayford's conjectures about the composition of *Moby-Dick* are supported by what he discovered in his work on the composition of *Omoo*, with Merton M. Sealts, Jr., on *Billy Budd, Sailor*, and on *The Confidence-Man*. For arguments against the "two *Moby-Dicks*" theory or against the whole idea that Melville's works changed as he wrote, see skeptical reviews such as Willard Thorp's of Charles Olson's *Call Me Ishmael*, in *Modern Language Notes*, 63 (Feb. 1948), 141–42; recurrent admonitions by Hershel Parker in *American Literary Scholarship*; Robert Milder's "The Composition of *Moby-Dick*: A Review and a Prospect," in *ESQ* (IV Quarter 1977), 203–16; and Edwin M. Eigner, *The Metaphysical Novel in England and America: Dickens, Bulwer, Melville, and Hawthorne* (Berkeley: University of California Press, 1978).

20. See "Manuscript Fragments," as analyzed by Hayford and MacDougall in *The Confidence-Man: His Masquerade* (Evanston and Chicago: Northwestern University Press and The Newberry Library, 1984), pp. 401–99. The *Billy Budd* manuscript even more fully illustrates this genetic pattern. See the genetic text and commentary in Hayford and Sealts's edition of *Billy Budd, Sailor* (345).

21. Eleanor Melville Metcalf, ed., *Journal of a Visit to London and the Continent by Herman Melville: 1849–1850* (Cambridge: Harvard University Press, 1948), p. 75. See the "Historical Note" to the Northwestern-Newberry edition of *Israel Potter*, especially pp. 173–205, for a thorough discussion of the sources and composition of *Israel Potter*. In the forthcoming Northwestern–Newberry edition of Melville's *Journals*, Howard Horsford shows how Melville's 1849 London journal recorded his exploration of seamy areas of London for use in depicting Israel's life of poverty there. I have referred to the *Life and Remarkable Adventures of Israel R. Potter* as "Trumbull" throughout because Henry Trumbull was its ghost-writer as well as printer. Sealts (#407) lists this work under Potter.

22. Mansfield and Vincent, who pointed out the Olafsen error (229, p. 695), misspelled the other Scandinavian name as "Povelson" (p. 178).

23. I worked through the dissertations in chronological order. Indispensable to this process were the directories published by The Melville Society, *Doctoral Dissertations on Herman Melville: A Chronological Summary (1933–1952)* by Tyrus Hillway (1953), *Directory of Melville Dissertations* by Tyrus Hillway and Hershel Parker (1962), *Melville Dissertations: An Annotated Directory* by Joel Myerson and Arthur H. Miller, Jr. (1972), and John Bryant's *Melville Dissertations, 1924–1980: An Annotated Bibliography and Subject Index* (Westport, Conn.: Greenwood Press, 1983).

24. For this I was guided by my pamphlet, *Books on Melville 1891–1981: A Checklist* (Evanston: Loose-Fish Books, 1982).

25. "MKB," "HH," and "RDM" indicate Mary K. Bercaw, Harrison Hayford, and Robert D. Madison. Information on sources marked with these initials was obtained privately and has not yet been published.

26. For the sake of simplicity and ease of printing I have not used diacritical marks throughout or distinguished italicized words in the original titles.

27. Harold Beaver, ed., *Moby-Dick* (Harmondsworth, Middlesex, England: Penguin Books, 1972), p. 689. In the second and subsequent printings there was (in sole response to the protest of W. W. Norton, publishers) a brief footnote on p. 60, "Harrison Hayford and Hershel Parker together pioneered the textual scholarship of *Moby-Dick*. To facilitate cross-reference to their Norton Critical Edition, these lists, in both format and content, are closely aligned to their original tabulations."

28. In an angry article published in 1951, Edward Dahlberg claimed that Charles Olson discovered the influence of Shakespeare on Melville, as published in "Lear and Moby Dick" (1938) and *Call Me Ishmael* (1947), and that all those scholars who have since written on Shakespeare and Melville have robbed Olson. Dahlberg lambasted scholars throughout his article—"The academic is a bibliographer and not an interpreter of books. Learning has palpably decayed" (p. 188)—but he concentrated the force of his attack on Newton Arvin's *Herman Melville* (1950). With parallel passages, he attempted to show that Arvin took the bulk of his information, especially in reference to Shakespearean influence, from Olson, and some from D. H. Lawrence. Part of the irony of Dahlberg's attack, of course, is that Olson, too, borrowed from other scholars. Dahlberg wrote that "Arvin does not trouble to say that Olson was the first to publish the story of the Essex disaster" (p. 188)—nor does Olson trouble to say that he first heard of the existence of Melville's heavily annotated copy of Owen Chase's *Narrative of the . . . Essex* from Howard P. Vincent and rushed the annotations into print, in *Call Me Ishmael*, before Vincent could. (Edward Dahlberg, "Laurels for Borrowers," *Freeman*, 2 [17 Dec. 1951], 187–90.)

29. A slightly expanded version of this article was included as chapter 6 in Carolyn L. Karcher, *Shadow Over the Promised Land: Slavery, Race, and Violence in Melville's America* (Baton Rouge: Louisiana State University Press, 1980), pp. 160–85. Karcher noted that there were only four published discussions of "The 'Gees": Sidney Kaplan's in 1957 (285, pp. 31–32), Warner Berthoff's prefatory note to "The 'Gees" in *Great Short Works of Herman Melville* (1970), p. 355, R. Bruce Bickley, Jr.'s in 1975 (576, pp. 56–58), and William B. Dillingham's in 1977 (621, pp. 357–59). None of these establishes a source for the sketch.

II

CHECKLIST OF
MELVILLE'S SOURCES

LIST OF ABBREVIATIONS FOR MELVILLE'S WORKS

In order of publication:

F   "Fragments"

F1   "Fragments from a Writing Desk, No. 1," *Democratic Press and Lansingburgh Advertiser* (4 May 1839), 1

F2   "Fragments from a Writing Desk, No. 2," *Democratic Press and Lansingburgh Advertiser* (18 May 1839), 1–2

T   *Typee: A Peep at Polynesian Life* (London: John Murray, 1846; New York: Wiley & Putnam, 1846)

O   *Omoo: A Narrative of Adventures in the South Seas* (London: John Murray, 1847; New York: Harper & Brothers, 1847)

RE   Review of *Etchings of a Whaling Cruise* . . . by J. Ross Browne and *Sailors' Life and Sailors' Yarns* by Captain Ringbolt, *Literary World*, 1 (6 March 1847), 105–6

OZ   "Authentic Anecdotes of 'Old Zack.' [Reported for Yankee Doodle by his Special Correspondent at the Seat of War.]," *Yankee Doodle*, 2 (19 June 1857), p. 101; (17 July 1847), p. 148; (24 July 1847), pp. 152–54; (31 July 1847), pp. 167– 68; (7 Aug. 1847), p. 172; (14 Aug. 1847), p. 188; (21 Aug. 1847), p. 194; (21 Aug. 1847), p. 199; (28 Aug. 1847), p. 202; (4 Sept. 1847), p. 218; (11 Sept. 1847), p. 223; (11 Sept. 1847), p. 229; and (25 Sept. 1847), p. 232

M   *Mardi: and A Voyage Thither* (London: Bentley, 1849; New York: Harper & Brothers, 1849)

RP   "Mr. Parkman's Tour," review of *The California and Oregon Trail* . . . by Francis Parkman, Jr., *Literary World*, 4 (31 March 1849), 291–93

RSL   "Cooper's New Novel," review of *The Sea Lions* ... by J. Fenimore Cooper, *Literary World*, 4 (28 April 1849), 370

R   *Redburn: His First Voyage. Being the Sailor-boy Confessions and Reminiscences of the Son-of-a-Gentleman, in the Merchant Service* (London: Bentley, 1849; New York: Harper & Brothers, 1849)

WJ   *White-Jacket: or The World in a Man-of-War* (London: Bentley, 1850; New York: Harper & Brothers, 1850)

TBB   "A Thought on Book-Binding," review of *The Red Rover* by J. Fenimore Cooper, *Literary World*, 6 (16 March 1850), 276–77

HHM   "Hawthorne and His Mosses. By a Virginian Spending July in Vermont," *Literary World*, 7 (17 August 1850), 125–27, and (24 August 1850), 145–47

MD   *Moby-Dick: or, the Whale* (London: Bentley, 1851; New York: Harper & Brothers, 1851)

P   *Pierre; or, The Ambiguities* (New York: Harper & Brothers, 1852; London: Sampson, Low, Son, and Co., 1852)

B   "Bartleby, The Scrivener. A Story of Wall-Street," *Putnam's*, 2 (Nov. 1853), 546–57, and (Dec. 1853), 609–15

CDD   "Cock-A-Doodle-Doo! Or, The Crowing of the Noble Cock Beneventano," *Harper's*, 8 (Dec. 1853), 77–86

E   "The Encantadas, or Enchanted Isles. By Salvator R. Tarnmoor," *Putnam's*, 3 (March 1854), 311–19, (April 1854), 345–55, and (May 1854), 460–66

PMP   "Poor Man's Pudding and Rich Man's Crumbs," *Harper's*, 9 (June 1854), 95–101

HF   "The Happy Failure. A Story of the River Hudson," *Harper's*, 9 (July 1854), 196–99

IP   "Israel Potter; or, Fifty Years of Exile," *Putnam's*, 4 (July 1854), 66–75, (Aug. 1854), 135–46, (Sept. 1854), 277–90, (Oct. 1854), 371–78, (Nov. 1854), 481–91, (Dec. 1854), 592– 601, 5 (Jan. 1855), 63–71, (Feb. 1855), 176–82, (March 1855), 288–94; and (New York: G. P. Putnam & Co., 1855)

LRM   "The Lightning-Rod Man," *Putnam's*, 4 (Aug. 1854), 131–34

TF   "The Fiddler," *Harper's*, 9 (Sept. 1854), 536–39

PB   "The Paradise of Bachelors and the Tartarus of Maids," *Harper's*, 10 (April 1855), 670–78

BT	"The Bell-Tower," *Putnam's*, 6 (Aug. 1855), 123–30
BC	"Benito Cereno," *Putnam's*, 6 (Oct. 1855), 353–67, (Nov. 1855), 459–73, (Dec. 1855), 633–44
JR	"Jimmy Rose," *Harper's*, 11 (Nov. 1855), 803–7
IMC	"I and My Chimney," *Putnam's*, 7 (March 1856), 269–83
TG	"The 'Gees," *Harper's*, 12 (March 1856), 507–9
ATT	"The Apple-Tree Table; or, Original Spiritual Manifestations," *Putnam's*, 7 (May 1856), 465–75
PT	*The Piazza Tales* (New York: Dix & Edwards, 1856)
TP	"The Piazza," first published in *The Piazza Tales* (New York: Dix & Edwards, 1856)
CM	*The Confidence-Man: His Masquerade* (New York: Dix, Edwards & Co., 1857; London: Longman, Brown, Green, Longmans, & Roberts, 1857)
BP	*Battle-Pieces and Aspects of the War* (New York: Harper & Brothers, 1866)
C	*Clarel: A Poem and Pilgrimage in the Holy Land* (New York: G. P. Putnam's Sons, 1876)
JM	*John Marr and Other Sailors* (New York: The De Vinne Press, 1888)
TIM	*Timoleon etc.* (New York: The Caxton Press, 1891)
BB	*Billy Budd[, Sailor (An Inside Narrative)]* (London: Constable, 1924)
DO	"Daniel Orme," first published in *Billy Budd and Other Prose Pieces* (London: Constable, 1924), pp. 117–22
TT	"The Two Temples," first published in *Billy Budd and Other Prose Pieces* (London: Constable, 1924), pp. 173–91
JG	"Jack Gentian" Sketches: "Portrait of a Gentleman," "To Major John Gentian, Dean of the Burgundy Club," "Jack Gentian," "Major Gentian and Colonel J. Bunkum," "The Cincinnati" [also called "Burgundy Club Sketches"], first published in *Billy Budd and Other Prose Pieces* (London: Constable, 1924), pp. 353–80
WW	*Weeds and Wildings, with A Rose or Two* (London: Constable, 1924)
MG	*The Marquis de Grandvin* (London: Constable, 1924)

MP   Miscellaneous Poems, not included in the above and first published in the Constable edition (London: Constable, 1924)

UP   Unpublished or Uncollected Poems, not included in the above and first published in Howard P. Vincent, ed., *Collected Poems of Herman Melville* (Chicago: Packard and Company, Hendricks House, 1947)

Unspec   Unspecified

In alphabetical order by abbreviation:

ATT   "The Apple-Tree Table"

B   "Bartleby"

BB   *Billy Budd*

BC   "Benito Cereno"

BP   *Battle-Pieces*

BT   "The Bell-Tower"

C   *Clarel*

CDD   "Cock-A-Doodle-Doo!"

CM   *The Confidence-Man*

DO   "Daniel Orme"

E   "The Encantadas"

F   "Fragments"

F1   "Fragments from a Writing Desk, No. 1"

F2   "Fragments from a Writing Desk, No. 2"

HF   "The Happy Failure"

HHM   "Hawthorne and His Mosses"

IMC   "I and My Chimney"

IP   "Israel Potter"

JG   "Jack Gentian" Sketches

JM   *John Marr*

JR   "Jimmy Rose"

LRM	"The Lightning-Rod Man"
M	*Mardi*
MD	*Moby-Dick*
MG	*The Marquis de Grandvin*
MP	Miscellaneous Poems
O	*Omoo*
OZ	"Authentic Anecdotes of 'Old Zack' "
P	*Pierre*
PB	"The Paradise of Bachelors and the Tartarus of Maids"
PMP	"Poor Man's Pudding and Rich Man's Crumbs"
PT	*The Piazza Tales*
R	*Redburn*
RE	Review of *Etchings of a Whaling Cruise* and of *Sailors' Life and Sailors' Yarns*
RP	Review of Parkman's *The California and Oregon Trail*
RSL	Review of *The Sea Lions*
T	*Typee*
TBB	"A Thought on Book-Binding" (Review of *The Red Rover*)
TF	"The Fiddler"
TG	"The 'Gees"
TIM	*Timoleon*
TP	"The Piazza"
TT	"The Two Temples"
Unspec	Unspecified
UP	Unpublished Poems
WJ	*White-Jacket*
WW	*Weeds and Wildings*

KEY TO SYMBOLS

‹   (Preceding a source number): This pointer marks a source which has been suggested for works written prior to Melville's acquisition of the edition given.

*   (Preceding a source number): This asterisk indicates that Melville's edition of this source has been established.

*   (With a reference number in square brackets following a source's publication data): The reference number marked with this asterisk identifies the scholar who suggested the edition listed.

!   (Following a reference number): The exclamation point indicates a good discussion of a source.

?   (Following a reference number): The question mark indicates a questionable suggestion of a source.

??   (Following a reference number): Two question marks signify a blunder.

r   (With a reference number in square brackets): The letter "r" within a bracketed entry indicates a rebuttal of the preceding scholar's suggestion of a source.

SAMPLE ENTRY

┌─Suggested for *Mardi*, which was written before 1856

  ┌───Melville's edition has been identified by scholar 806

  │   ┌────── Source number

‹*589a. Rogers, Stanley, *Flowers of Bermuda* (Halifax: Juvenile Tract Society, 1856). [Sealts #428.1; *806]
M: 821?? [r 823]; C: 806!────────────────────────────────

           └─ Sealts includes the work but does not identify the edition

   └───Scholar 821 has blundered and has been refuted by scholar 823
Scholar 806 has a superior discussion of the work's use in *Clarel*───

CHECKLIST OF MELVILLE'S SOURCES

A

"Abolition of Impressment": see 359.

"About Niggers": see 740.

The Academy and Literature: see 88.

a. Account of a Polar Expedition to Rescue Sir John Franklin (second half), *Literary World*, no. 284 (10 July 1852).
JM: 512b

*1. Adams, William Henry Davenport, *The Buried Cities of Campania; or, Pompeii and Herculaneum, Their Destruction, and Their Remains* (London: Nelson, 1869). [*Sealts #4]
Unspec: 213

2. Addison, Joseph, *Cato: A Tragedy* (1713).
MD: 229, 445; MG: 378

3. Addison, Joseph, *Remarks on Several Parts of Italy* (1705).
BT: 603

3a. Addison, Joseph, *Spectator*, 69 (1714).
CM: 440c
See also 662.

3b. "Adventures in the Pacific—Dr. Coulter and Herman Melville," *Dublin University Magazine*, 28 (August 1846), 127-39. [*MKB]
E: MKB

4. Aeschylus, trans. Rev. R. Potter, in *Classical Library* (New York: Harper, [18—]), vol. 13. [*Sealts #147]
MD: 82, 148a, 407, 590; Unspec: 686b

Aesthetic Papers: see 710.

Afghanistan: see 256a, 322a, 601.

"The African Character": see 126.

Agassiz: see 577.

*5. Akenside, Mark, *The Pleasures of Imagination* (New York: M'Dermut & Arden, 1813). [*Sealts #8]
P: 534c; CM: 254, 534c; Unspec: 488a

Albany Argus: see 51.

Albany Evening Journal: see 263a, 529.

6. Aleman, Mateo, *Guzman de Alfarache* (1603; first translated into English in 1622). [Sealts #9]
Unspec: 236

7. Alger, William Rounseville, *The Poetry of the East* (Boston, 1856). [*315]
C: 315

*8. Alger, William Rounseville, *The Solitudes of Nature and of Man; or, The Loneliness of Human Life*, [3d ed.] (Boston: Roberts, 1867). [*Sealts #11]
Unspec: 139, 179, 183, 198, 254, 315, 369, 536

9. Allen, Ethan, *Narrative of Colonel Ethan Allen's Captivity* (1779).
IP: 108, 146, 213, 317, 346, 440d, 481e, 559, 685!

10. Allen, Ethan, *Reason the Only Oracle of Man* (1784).
P: 229a?; C: 146

11. Allen, Joseph, *Battles of the British Navy* (London, 1852). [*345]
BB: 345

12. Allston, Washington, *Lectures on Art, and Poems* (New York: Baker & Scribner, 1850). [*672]
MD: 672; BB: 672

Almanac: see 12a, 702.

12a. *The American Almanac* (Boston, 1844 and 1845).
M: 576d?

American Magazine: see 649, 747b, 753.

American Magazine of Useful and Entertaining Knowledge: see 216a.

12b. American Peace Society, "Safety of Pacific Principles" [pamphlet, reprinted in *The Book of Peace*, ed. George C. Beckwith (Boston, 1845)]. [*440c]
CM: 440c

American Review [later renamed *American Whig Review*]: see 749.

*13. Ames, Nathaniel, *A Mariner's Sketches, Originally Published in the Manufacturers and Farmers Journal* (Providence, 1830). [*490]
R: 212, 491; WJ: 121, 129, 133!, 139!, 198, 213, 345a, 416, 437, 440b, 490, 491!, 511a, 543, 662a; MD: 182, 229

Amir Khan: see 193.

14. Anacreon, trans. Thomas Bourne, in *Classical Library* (New York: Harper, [18—]), vol. 36. [*Sealts #147]
F: 84; CM: 254

"Ancient Peru": see 665.

Anderson, Robert, *Poets of Great Britain*: see 663.

*15. Andrews, James, *Floral Tableaux* (London: Bogue, 1846). [*Sealts #13]
M: 226; Unspec: 213

16. Anthon, Charles, *A Classical Dictionary* (New York: Harper & Brothers, 1843). [*226]
M: 226, 345a; Unspec: 489, 686b

16a. Anthon, Charles, ed., *Xenophon's Memorabilia of Socrates* (New York, 1848). [*686b]
M: 686b
See also 580a.

The Anti-Slavery Picknick: see 126.

17. Antoninus, Marcus [Aurelius], *The Commentaries of the Emperor Marcus Antoninus*, trans. James Thomson (London, 1747). [*143]
M: 143

Antoninus Pius: see 160a.

18. *Arabian Nights' Entertainments*, trans. Lane (London: Charles Knight, 1841). [*333]
F1: 212, 333; F2: 212, 333, 440e; T: 488c; M: 29, 333!, 488; R: 333; CM: 333

Arabian Nights' Entertainments: see also 598.

19. Aratus, *Phaenomena*.
Unspec: 146

*20. *Arcturus, a Journal of Books and Opinion* (New York, 1841– 42), vol. 1 (1841). [*Sealts #14]
M: 144

*21. *Arichandra, the Martyr of Truth: a Tamil Drama*, trans. Mutu Coomara Swamy (London: Smith, Elder, 1863). [*Sealts #14.1]
BB: 632, 662

The Aristocracy of England: see 375.

22. Aristotle, *Poetics*.
MD: 286; BP: 556; Unspec: 708

23. Aristotle, *The Politics and Economics of Aristotle, Translated, with Notes ... and Analyses. To which are Prefixed, An Introductory Essay and a Life of Aristotle, by Dr. Gillies. By Edward Walford* (London: H. G. Bohn, 1853). [*254]
CM: 254!

*23a. Aristotle, *Aristotle's Treatise on Rhetoric, Literally Translated, with Hobbes' Analysis, Examination Questions, and an Appendix Containing the Greek Definitions. Also, The Poetic of Aristotle, Literally Translated, with a Selection of Notes, an Analysis, and Questions. By Theodore Buckley* (London: Bell & Daldy, 1872). [*Sealts #14b]
TIM: 488a

24. Arnold, Sir Edwin, *The Poems* (New York: Hurst, [1879]). [*Sealts #15]
WW: 333

Arnold, Matthew.
C: 260; BB: 345; Unspec: 146

Arnold, Matthew, *Culture and Anarchy*: see 25a.

*25. Arnold, Matthew, *Essays in Criticism* (Boston: Ticknor & Fields, 1865). [*Sealts #17]
C: 143, 540, 637a, 667; BB: 345; Unspec: 139, 146, 179, 183, 198, 200, 213, 275, 315, 333, 488a, 504a, 580, 705a

25a. Arnold, Matthew, essays in *Every Saturday: A Journal of Choice Reading Selected from Foreign Current Literature* [*Every Saturday* was assimilated by *Littell's Living Age* in 1874], especially series entitled "Culture and Its Enemies" and "Anarchy and Authority" (July 1867–Aug. 1868) [this series was to become Matthew Arnold's *Culture and Anarchy*]. [*637a]
C: 637a

25b. Arnold, Matthew, essays in *Littell's Living Age*, especially "Literature and Dogma" reprint-

ed in *Littell's Living Age*, 110 (26 Aug. 1871), 515–29. [*637a]
C: 637a; Unspec: 637a

*26. Arnold, Matthew, *Literature & Dogma; an Essay towards a Better Apprehension of the Bible* (New York: Macmillan, 1881). [*Sealts #18]
Unspec: 146
See also 25b.

*27. Arnold, Matthew, *Mixed Essays, Irish Essays, and Others* (New York: Macmillan, 1883). [*Sealts #19]
BB: 365a?; Unspec: 139, 146, 200, 504a

*28. Arnold, Matthew, *New Poems* (Boston: Ticknor & Fields, 1867). [*Sealts #20]
C: 179, 211, 260!, 315, 319, 461b, 479c, 499a, 504a, 512b, 540, 652; JM: 489; TIM: 179, 441b; BB: 211; Unspec: 139, 143, 229, 686b, 705a

*29. Arnold, Matthew, *Poems . . . A New and Complete Edition* (Boston: Ticknor & Fields, 1856). [*Sealts #21]
C: 260!, 315; Unspec: 580, 686b, 705a

29a. "Arrest of the Confidence Man," New York *Herald* (8 July 1849), 2.
CM: 479a, 504b, 510b!, 686a

30. "Articles of War" [passed by the Sixth Congress on 23 April 1800], *United States Statutes at Large*, vol. 2, ch. xxxiii. [*490]
WJ: 490

Atlantic Monthly: see 329.

Atlas: see 99.

31. Augustine, St., of Hippo, *The Confessions* (printed in Latin, 1470; in English, 1620).
MD: 229?; CM: 254; Unspec: 143

Aurelius, Marcus: see 17.

B

32. Bacon, Francis, *Essays or Counsels, Civil and Moral* in *The Works of Francis Bacon* (Philadelphia: Hart, 1851). [*519]
P: 181, 519

33. Bacon, Francis, *The Wisdom of the Ancients* in *The Works of Francis Bacon* (Philadelphia, 1844). [*143]
M: 143; MD: 143; P: 143, 181; CM: 254; C: 143

34. Bailey, Philip James, *Festus* (1839).
MD: 229; Unspec: 303

35. Baker, Dr. Louis A., *Harry Martingale; or, Adventures of a Whaleman in the Pacific Ocean* (Boston, 1848). [*182]
MD: 96?, 182?

Balzac, Honore de.
BB: 247; Unspec: 92

*36. Balzac, Honore de, *Bureaucracy: or, A Civil Service Reformer* [trans. Katharine Prescott Wormeley] (Boston: Roberts, 1889). [*Sealts #22]
Unspec: 265, 274

*37. Balzac, Honore de, *The Correspondence of Honore de Balzac; with a Memoir by His Sister, Madame de Surville; Translated by C. Lamb Kenney; with Portrait and Facsimile of the Handwriting of*

Balzac (London: Bentley, 1878). [*Sealts #23]
Unspec: 274, 291b, 441, 442a

*38. Balzac, Honore de, *Eugenie Grandet; or, The Miser's Daughter. From the French of Honore de Balzac. Translated by O. W. Wight and F. B. Goodrich* (New York: Rudd & Carleton, 1861). [*Sealts #28]
Unspec: 247

*39. Balzac, Honore de, *Pere Goriot* [trans. Katharine Prescott Wormeley] (Boston: Roberts, 1885). [*Sealts #33]
Unspec: 274

⟨*40. Balzac, Honore de, *Seraphita. With an Introduction by George Frederic Parsons* [trans. Katharine Prescott Wormeley] (Boston: Roberts, 1889). [*Sealts #34]
P: 163a, 198; Unspec: 274, 442a

*41. Balzac, Honore de, *The Two Brothers* [trans. Katharine Prescott Wormeley] (Boston: Roberts, 1887). [*Sealts #37]
TIM: 213, 247, 377b, 442a, 488a; UP: 377b; Unspec: 274

Balzac, Honore de: see also 739.

42. Bancroft, George, *History of the Colonization of the United States* (1834–38) in *A History of the United States* (1834–75), vols. 1–3.
WJ: 518

43. [Banvard, John], *Description of Banvard's Panorama of the Mississippi River* (Boston, 1847) [pirated nearly verbatim from Timothy Flint's *A Condensed Geography and History of the Western States; or, The Mississippi Valley* (1828)]. [*705]
CM: 254, 705

43a. "A Barber-ous Adventure," *United States Magazine of Science, Art, Manufactures, Agriculture, Commerce and Trade*, 2 (1855), 145–48. [*714]
CM: 714

43b. "A Barberous Drama" in "Editor's Drawer," *Harper's*, 11 (Nov. 1855), 854–55. [Sealts #240; *686a]
CM: 686a

44. Barlow, Joel, *The Columbiad: A Poem* (Philadelphia and Baltimore: Printed by Fry & Kammerer for C. & A. Conrad & Co., 1807). [*569]
CM: 569?

45. Barlow, Joel, *The Vision of Columbus: A Poem in Nine Books* (Hartford: Printed by Hudson & Goodwin for the Author, 1787). [*569]
CM: 569?

46. Barnard, Charles H., *A Narrative of the Sufferings and Adventures of Capt. Charles H. Barnard, in a Voyage round the World* (New York: Bliss [etc.], 1829; *or*, New York: Callender, 1836). [*Sealts #38]
Unspec: 123, 212, 226

46a. Barnum, Phineas Taylor, *Life of P. T. Barnum, Written by Himself* (1855).
CM: 254, 461a, 479a, 504b

46b. "Barnumopsis. A Recitative" [poem], *Literary World*, 7 (14 Sept.

1850), 212–13. [*Sealts #326; *479a]
CM: 479a

⟨*47. Bartlett, William Henry, *Forty Days in the Desert, on the Track of the Israelites; or, A Journey from Cairo, by Wady Feiran, to Mount Sinai and Petra*, 5th ed. (New York: Scribner, [186–?]). [*Sealts #48]
B: 707?; C: 213, 315!, 333!, 687

*48. Bartlett, William Henry, *The Nile-Boat; or, Glimpses of the Land of Egypt*, 5th ed. (New York: Scribner, [186–?]). [*Sealts #49]
C: 213, 315, 333

*49. Bartlett, William Henry, *Walks about the City and Environs of Jerusalem* (London: Virtue, [186–?]). [*Sealts #50]
C: 213, 315!, 333!

*50. Bayle, Pierre, *An Historical and Critical Dictionary*, trans. Jacob Tonson (London: Harper, 1710). [Sealts #51; *633]
M: 227; R: 229a; WJ: 139; MD: 133b, 139, 182, 223!, 227, 229, 229a, 235, 248, 302, 334, 339, 365a, 377c, 397a, 436, 441, 481d, 532, 675, 686b; P: 181, 227, 365a?, 441, 576b, 631, 675; B: 365a?; BT: 547; CM: 254, 435, 459c, 613; C: 227; TIM: 166, 229a, 377b, 489, 512b; BB: 227, 229a, 538; Unspec: 123, 129, 143, 146, 212, 213, 229a, 365a, 534d, 633!, 686b

51. Beale, Thomas, "Method of Taking the Whale" [chapter from *The Natural History of the Sperm Whale* (London, 1839)], *Albany Argus* (27 May 1839). [*212]
Unspec: 212

⟨*52. Beale, Thomas, *The Natural History of the Sperm Whale To Which Is Added a Sketch of a South-Sea Whaling Voyage in Which the Author Was Personally Engaged* [2d ed.] (London: Van Voorst, 1839). [*Sealts #52]
T: 133; MD: 133, 147!, 148, 165, 182!, 198, 199, 201!, 213, 229, 377c, 440e, 473, 487, 602, 720

52a. Beatty, William, *The Death of Lord Nelson; 21 October 1805* (1807).
BB: 172a

*53. Beaumont, Francis, and John Fletcher, *Fifty Comedies and Tragedies* (London: Martyn [etc.], 1679). [*Sealts #53]
P: 181; E: 477; Unspec: 95, 167, 316, 440a!

⟨*54. Beckford, William, *Vathek: An Arabian Tale . . . With Notes, Critical and Expository* with *The Castle of Otranto. By Horace Walpole. The Bravo of Venice* [by Heinrich Zschokke], trans. M. G. Lewis (London: Bentley, 1849), Standard Novels, no. 41. [*Sealts #54]
F2: 84; M: 439a; WJ: 416, 662a; MD: 363; BT: 480a; BP: 512b; C: 315; Unspec: 95, 100, 187a, 303, 333!, 380, 478, 550

Beckwith, George C.: see 12b.

55. Beechey, Captain Frederick W., *Narrative of a Voyage to the Pacific and Bering Straits* (Philadelphia, 1832). [*133]
O: 16, 17, 133, 480!

56. Belcher, Sir Edward, *Narrative of a Voyage round the World 1836–1842* (London, 1843). [*133]
O: 133?

57. "Belisarius,—Was He Blind?," *Blackwood's Edinburgh Magazine*, 61 (May 1847), 606–21. [*226]
M: 226

58. Bell, John and Charles, *The Anatomy and Physiology of the Human Body*, by John D. Godman, M.D., 5th American ed. (New York: Collins & Co., 1827). [*491]
WJ: 491?; Unspec: 571?

59. Belzoni, Giovanni, *Narrative of the Operations and Recent Discoveries within the pyramids, temples, tombs, and excavations, in Egypt and Nubia* (1820).
M: 488; P: 333; IMC: 333

60. Bennett, Frederick Debell, *Narrative of a Whaling Voyage round the Globe, from the Year 1833 to 1836* (London, 1840). [*201]
O: 133, 480; M: 127!, 133, 182, 213, 218, 226!, 228, 345a, 488; MD: 84, 147!, 148, 165, 182!, 199, 201, 213, 228, 229, 239, 487; Unspec: 176a

60a. Bentham, Jeremy, *Deontology, or the Science of Morality* (1834).
B: 619a?

*61. Beranger, Pierre-Jean de, *The Songs of Beranger, in English. With a Sketch of the Author's Life* (Philadelphia: Carey & Hart, 1844). [*Sealts #58]
C: 319; MP: 295, 377b; Unspec: 213

62. *Berkshire County Eagle* (1855, 1856). [*254]
CM: 254

‹*63. Bible, *The Holy Bible . . . Together with the Apocrypha* (Philadelphia: Butler, 1846). [*Sealts #62; see also Sealts #60–61, 63–65]
All Works: 136a, 183!; O: 480!; R: 136a, 212, 504c; WJ: 662a; MD: 92b, 128a, 146, 148a, 165, 182, 229, 229a, 256, 280, 311, 318, 334, 339, 347a, 360, 371, 377c, 386, 440e, 552, 595, 601, 623, 651a, 695; P: 181!, 229a, 318, 439a, 651a; B: 651a; CDD: 350; E: 654?; IP: 440d; BT: 594; BC: 271?, 342, 365a; PT: 173; TP: 331; CM: 213, 254!, 334, 375a, 434, 440c, 440d, 487a, 503a, 504b, 641, 651a, 705; BP: 508a; C: 146, 315!, 441b, 461b, 512b; TIM: 512b; BB: 217, 345, 440d, 637c; WW: 440f; UP: 305; Unspec: 139!, 146, 178, 194, 297, 318, 440e, 686b
King James Bible: Unspec: 178, 297, 440a
Old Testament: MD: 182; Unspec: 400
Genesis: M: 534b; R: 178; MD: 178, 181a, 298a, 300; P: 178; LRM: 520; BC: 495; CM: 178; BP: 441b; JM: 377b; TIM: 377b, 441b, 489; BB: 198; WW: 489
Exodus: MD: 542, 642; BP: 166; C: 377b; TIM: 377b
Numbers: T: 512c; BP: 166; JM: 441b
Deuteronomy: JM: 441b
Joshua: C: 377b
Judges: MD: 681; HF: 621; BT: 594, 618, 621; TIM: 377b, 441b
I Samuel: C: 461b; BB: 172a
II Samuel: BC: 271, 495; C: 461b, 512b; Unspec: 316
I Kings: MD: 128a, 178, 289, 300, 334, 397a, 642; P: 194; C: 377b; Unspec: 178
II Kings: O: 511a; BC: 557a
III Kings: O: 439a; MD: 289

Esther: BT: 594
Job: M: 499c; R: 375, 499c; WJ:
    375, 499c; MD: 128a, 229a, 232,
    273a, 273b, 291b, 297, 300, 311,
    334, 339, 361, 375, 397a, 408,
    439a, 499c, 539, 558, 595, 597,
    623, 651a; P: 481b, 499c; B:
    180a, 421a, 499c, 586, 604, 711;
    E: 499c; CM: 499c; BP: 512b; C:
    377b; JM: 441b, 489; TIM: 377b,
    489; BB: 476, 499c; Unspec: 297
Psalms: M: 33
Ecclesiastes: M: 377a, 511a;
    MD: 148a, 168, 623; P: 547a,
    551a, 576c; IMC: 179, 325, 663;
    BP: 512b; C: 461b, 512b; Un-
    spec: 194
Song of Solomon: M: 33; BC:
    560; WW: 489
Jeremiah: MD: 300, 654; E: 654
Ezekiel: PMP: 621; BC: 271
Daniel: M: 576d; BP: 377b; DO:
    151
Jonah: MD: 334, 339, 408; BB:
    377b
Wisdom of Solomon: Unspec:
    183
Ecclesiasticus: CM: 146
*The New Testament ... The
    Book of Psalms* (New York:
    American Bible Society, 1844)
    [*Sealts #65]: Unspec: 146!,
    183, 623
Matthew: MD: 334, 439a; P:
    365a, 481b; B: 365a, 497; IMC:
    663; CM: 434, 441a; C: 377b;
    TIM: 489; WW: 489
Mark: MD: 256; CM: 434; C: 377b
Luke: BC: 439a; CM: 434; C:
    377b; BB: 508c; MG: 489
John: MD: 256, 423; BC: 342,
    618; CM: 434, 439a; C: 377b;
    JM: 489; TIM: 377b; BB: 646a;
    WW: 489
Acts: C: 377b; BB: 345, 554

I Corinthians: MD: 383; CM:
    383, 544, 562, 618, 686a, 705;
    Unspec: 139
II Corinthians: CM: 544; WW:
    489
Galatians: C: 652
II Thessalonians: C: 377b; BB:
    229a, 377b
I Timothy: CM: 629
II Timothy: JM: 489
James: TIM: 377b, 489
Jude: HHM: 291a; MD: 291a,
    334a, 501
Revelation: MD: 556a!, 595; ATT:
    453; CM: 219, 334, 459c; BP:
    377b; C: 512b; JM: 193, 377b,
    441b, 489; BB: 439a; WW: 489;
    MG: 489

"The Big Bear of Arkansas": see
713a.

63a. Bigelow, Jacob, *Nature in Disease* (1854).
CM: 504b

Bigelow, Jacob: see also 579a.

64. Bird, Robert Montgomery,
*Nick of the Woods; or, The Jib-
benainosay* (1837).
CM: 254

*Blackwood's Edinburgh Maga-
zine*: see 57, 204, 205, 522a.

65. Blake, Andrew, *Delirium
Tremens* (1830).
R: 156?

66. Blake, William.
C: 77; Unspec: 139
See also 290.

*66a. Boaden, James, *An Inquiry
into the Authenticity of Various
Pictures and Prints, Which, from
the Decease of the Poet to Our
Own Times, Have Been Offered to*

the *Public as Portraits of Shakespeare* (London: Triphook, 1824). [*Sealts #71]
Unspec: 440a

67. Boccaccio, Giovanni, *The Decameron* (1349–51).
PB: 621; C: 315

68. Boccaccio, Giovanni, *Life of Dante* (1477).
P: 188?

69. *The Book of Common Prayer, and Administration of the Sacraments; and Other Rights and Ceremonies of the Church, According to the Use of the Protestant Episcopal Church in the United States of America: Together with the Psalter, or Psalms of David* (New York: Harper, 1845, or later edition). [*Sealts #409; see also Sealts #410]
MD: 552; CM: 686a?

70. *The Book of Mormon*, trans. Joseph Smith, Jr. (1830).
M: 424?

The Book of Peace: see 12b.

71. Borrow, George, *Lavengro, the Scholar—the Gypsy—the Priest* (1851).
P: 181; Unspec: 92

Boston Pearl and Literary Gazette: see 156b.

72. Boswell, James, *The Life of Samuel Johnson, LL.D.*, ed. John Wilson Croker (London: Murray, 1835), 10 vols. [*HH; Sealts #84]
MD: 229!; CM: 254; BB: 345; Unspec: 213

*73. Bougainville, Louis-Antoine de, Comte, *A Voyage round the World. Performed . . . in the Years 1766, 1767, 1768, and 1769, Translated from the French by John Reinhold Forster, F.A.S.* (London: Nourse [etc.], 1772). [*Sealts #85]
M: 480; Unspec: 213, 226, 228

74. Bradford, Alexander W., *American Antiquities and Researches into the Origins of the Red Race* (New York: Wiley & Putnam, 1841). [*561]
T: 561; MD: 561

74a. Brandt, Sebastian, "The Ship of Fools" [published first as *Das Narrenschiff* in 1494].
CM: 330a?

75. Brewer, Ebenezer Cobham, *Brewer's Dictionary of Phrase and Fable* (1870).
Unspec: 489?

76. Brewster, David, *The Life of Sir Isaac Newton* (New York, 1831). [*571]
O: 571; MD: 571

76a. Bridge, Horatio, *Journal of an African Cruiser*, edited by Nathaniel Hawthorne (1845).
WJ: 291a?; MD: 291a?

77. Briggs, Charles Frederick, *The Adventures of Harry Franco* (1839).
R: 274a; WJ: 274a, 490

77a. Briggs, Charles Frederick, "Letter to John Waters from Hezediah Starbuck, Third" by Harry Franco [pseud.], *Knickerbocker* (Aug. 1840). [*274a]
MD: 274a
See also 747b.

77b. Briggs, Charles Frederick, "Letters of Ferdinand Mendez

Pinto," *Weekly Mirror* (1846–47). [*274a]
OZ: 274a, 557

*78. Briggs, Charles Frederick, *The Trippings of Tom Pepper; or, The Results of Romancing. An Autobiography*, by Harry Franco [pseud.] (New York: Burgess, Stringer, 1847), vol. 1 only. [*Sealts #86a]
CM: 313

78a. Briggs, Charles Frederick, *Working a Passage* (1844).
R: 274a, 334a; WJ: 274a

*79. A British Seaman, *Life on Board a Man-of-War; Including a Full Account of the Battle of Navarino* (Glasgow: Blackie, Fullarton, & Co., 1829). [*490, *491]
WJ: 490, 491!

Brooklyn Daily Eagle: see 757.

"Brought to the Gangway": see 441.

*80. Broughton, Thomas Duer, *Selections from the Popular Poetry of the Hindoos. Arranged and Translated by Thomas Duer Broughton* (London: Martin, 1814). [*450; *Sealts #87a]
TIM: 512b; Unspec: 450

Brown, Charles Brockden.
E: 64

81. Brown, Charles Brockden, *Wieland; or, The Transformation* (1798).
R: 359 [r 384]

*82. Browne, John Ross, *Etchings of a Whaling Cruise, with Notes of a Sojourn on the Island of Zanzibar. To Which Is Appended a Brief*

History of the Whale Fishery (New York: Harper, 1846). [*Sealts #88]
RE: 182, 213, 226, 394, 557, 614, 694; M: 226; R: 212, 394, 614; WJ: 416, 662a; MD: 84, 133, 147, 163a, 165, 178, 182!, 198, 201, 213, 228, 229, 345a, 377c, 382!, 487, 602, 718

*83. Browne, Sir Thomas, *Sir Thomas Browne's Works, Including His Life and Correspondence*, ed. Simon Wilkin (London: Pickering, 1835–36) and *The Works . . . With Alphabetical Tables* [1st collected ed.] (London: Basset [etc.], 1686). [*Sealts #89 and 90]
R: 181a; M: 21, 80a, 129, 133, 143, 186, 213, 226, 227, 301, 318, 345a, 441, 481f, 623, 686b; MD: 48, 85, 139, 143, 149, 165, 168, 199, 201, 229, 301!, 334, 377c, 397a, 441, 473, 481d, 481f, 486, 542; P: 181?; B: 711?; BT: 603; Unspec: 92, 95, 100, 122, 123, 146, 163a, 178, 212, 229a, 378

83a. Browne, William, [*Brittania's Pastorals*, vols. 1 and 2 of] *The Works* (London: Davies, 1772), 3 vols. [now bound together]; or, *Brittania's Pastorals* (London: Clarke, 1845). [*Sealts #91]
MD: 686b

*84. Browning, Elizabeth Barrett, *The Poems . . . A New Edition* (New York: Francis, 1860). [*Sealts #93]
C: 488a; Unspec: 200, 265, 488a

Browning, Robert.
C: 488a; WW: 488a

84a. Browning, Robert, "Childe Roland to the Dark Tower Came" (1855).
C: 512b

84b. Browning, Robert, *Pippa Passes* (1841).
BP: 488a

85. Browning, Robert, *The Return of the Druses* (1843).
C: 315, 674

86. Brownson, Orestes Augustus, *The Spirit-Rapper: An Autobiography* (1854).
ATT: 508; CM: 394, 440c, 653

*87. Bruce, James, *Interesting Narrative of the Travels of James Bruce, Esq. into Abyssinia, to Discover the Source of the Nile* (Boston, 1798). [*333]
M: 228, 333!

*87a. Bryant, William Cullen, *Poems . . . Collected and Arranged by the Author* (New York: Appleton, 1863). [*Sealts #94]
WW: 440f

*88. Buchanan, Robert, "Socrates in Camden," *The Academy and Literature* (London), 28 (15 August 1885). [*Sealts #1]
Unspec: 139, 691

Buddha: see 469a.

89. Buffon, Georges-Louis Leclerc, Comte de.
T: 7

90. Bulkeley, John, and John Cummins, *A Voyage to the South Seas, in the years 1740–41* (1793).
WJ: 543?

91. Bulwer-Lytton, Edward George Earle Lytton, First Baron, *The Last Days of Pompeii* (1834).
R: 688?; MD: 213, 302, 439a; Unspec: 137, 688

91a. Bulwer-Lytton, Edward George Earle Lytton, First Baron, *The Last of the Barons* (1843).
T: 512c

*91b. Bulwer-Lytton, Edward George Earle Lytton, First Baron, *The Pilgrims of the Rhine*, new ed. (London: Tilt, 1840). [*Sealts #333]
CM: 686a

92. Bulwer-Lytton, Edward George Earle Lytton, First Baron, *Zanoni* ([New York: Harper, 1842?]). [*Sealts #334]
P: 504 [r 651b], 511c!, 576b

93. Bunyan, John, *The Pilgrim's Progress* [1830 ed. with biography by Robert Southey?]. [Sealts #95; *229]
MD: 128a, 229, 377c; P: 181, 551a; CM: 219!, 254, 334, 440c, 705; Unspec: 229a

94. Burckhardt, John Lewis, *Travels in Syria and the Holy Land* (London, 1822).
C: 315?

*95. Burke, Edmund, *A Philosophical Inquiry into the Origin of Our Ideas of the Sublime and Beautiful with an Introductory Discourse concerning Taste* (Philadelphia: Johnson, 1806). [*Sealts #97]
HHM: 606; MD: 606, 609, 680; MG: 512b; Unspec: 369, 600c

96. Burke, Edmund, *Reflections on the Revolution in France* (1790).
F1: 212, 503; M: 368!; MD: 503; C: 503; BB: 369, 503, 559

97. Burney, James, *Chronological History of the Discoveries in the South Sea or Pacific Ocean*

(London: G. & W. Nicol, 1803). [*109]

E: 109!, 173, 180a, 213, 571

*98. Burns, Robert, *The Poetical Works ... With Memoir, Critical Dissertation, and Explanatory Notes, by the Rev. George Gilfillan* (Edinburgh: Nichol, 1856). [*Sealts #101]

CM: 440c; Unspec: 200

99. Burritt, Elijah Hinsdale, *Atlas, Designed to Illustrate the Geography of the Heavens* ([New York: F. J. Huntington, c. 1835?]). [*658; Sealts #101a]

Unspec: 658

‹*100. Burton, Robert, *The Anatomy of Melancholy* (New York: Wiley, 1847). [*Sealts #102; see also Sealts #103]

F: 291b; F1: 123, 178, 212; M: 28, 143, 146, 178, 213, 226, 227, 488, 576d; R: 143, 146; MD: 48, 49, 129, 139, 146, 163a, 178, 182?, 301, 397a, 486; P: 143, 146, 181, 481c, 576b; CDD: 173, 621; BC: 459b, 572; CM: 254, 330a, 459c, 487a, 613, 686a, 705; JM: 512b; Unspec: 84, 92, 122, 143

101. Butler, Joseph, *The Analogy of Religion, Natural and Revealed, to the Constitution and Course of Nature* (1736).

M: 146?; C: 534c; Unspec: 534c

101a. Butler, Bishop, *Three Sermons upon Human Nature* (1834).

P: 345a?

*102. Butler, Samuel, *Hudibras. The First [—Third and Last] Part. Written in the Time of the Late Wars. Corrected and Amended.*

With Several Additions and Annotations (London: Baker, 1710). [*Sealts #104; see also Sealts #105]

O: 480; P: 481c; C: 163a, 181a, 315, 499a, 504a; Unspec: 95, 100

103. Byron, George Anson, Lord, *Voyage of H.M.S. Blonde to the Sandwich Islands, in the Years 1824–1825* (London, 1826). [*133]

O: 133, 480; MD: 202; Unspec: 571

104. Byron, George Gordon Noel Byron, Sixth Baron, *The Bride of Abydos* (1813). [Sealts #107a]

F: 209, 212; F2: 333

*105. Byron, George Gordon Noel Byron, Sixth Baron, *Don Juan* (London: Murray, 1837). [*Sealts #108]

F2: 212; M: 226

*106. Byron, George Gordon Noel Byron, Sixth Baron, *Dramas* (London: Murray, 1837). [*Sealts #109]

   Cain: A Mystery: MD: 229a, 302; P: 181, 511c!; Unspec: 229a
   Sardanapalus: P: 181

*107. Byron, George Gordon Noel Byron, Sixth Baron, *Life of Lord Byron: With His Letters and Journals*, by Thomas Moore, and *The Poetical Works* (Boston: Little, Brown, [1853?]). [*Sealts #369 and 112]

F: 100, 238, 380; F1: 212!, 333; F2: 212!; T: 8; RE: 229, 433; M: 213, 226, 440, 488; RP: 212; R: 212, 229, 433; WJ: 181, 433; MD: 165, 229, 229a, 292, 433, 481e; P: 181!, 409, 481b, 511c!, 551a, 576b; C: 238, 315, 499a, 504a; TIM: 377b, 489; Unspec: 238!, 440e, 686b

*108. Byron, John, *The Narrative of the Honourable John Byron Containing an Account of the Great Distresses Suffered by Himself and His Companions on the Coast of Patagonia, from the Year 1740, till Their Arrival in England, 1746. With a Description of St. Jago de Chili, and the Manners and Customs of the Inhabitants. Also a Relation of the Loss of the Wager, Man of War, One of Admiral Anson's Squadron. Written by Himself,* 2d ed. (London: Baker & Leigh, 1768). [*Sealts #113]
T: 7; Unspec: 571

C

*109. Calderon de la Barca, Pedro, *Three Dramas of Calderon, from the Spanish. Love the Greatest Enchantment, The Sorceries of Sin, and The Devotion of the Cross,* by Denis Florence MacCarthy (Dublin: Kelly, 1870). [*Sealts #114]
Unspec: 236, 266, 303 110.

Callot, Jacques.
P: 59?

111. Camoens, Luis de, *The Lusiad; or Discovery of India,* trans. William Mickle [*651] (1776). In Alexander Chalmers, *The Works of the English Poets from Chaucer to Cowper,* vol. 21 (London, 1810). [*182]
WJ: 100, 166, 182, 198, 229, 229a, 345, 416, 419, 651; MD: 182, 198, 229, 297, 651; TIM: 377b; BB: 166; MP: 100, 166, 198, 229a, 377b; Unspec: 100; see also 112. below.
See also 498b.

*112. Camoens, Luis de, *Poems, from the Portuguese of Luis de Camoens. With Remarks on His Life and Writings. Notes, etc. etc.,* by Lord Viscount Strangford, new ed. (London: Carpenter, 1824). [*Sealts #116]
C: 488a; BB: 166, 345; MP: 651; Unspec: 213, 651; see also 111. above.

112a. Campbell, John, *Lives of the British Admirals; The Naval History continued to the year 1777 by Dr. Birkenhout. A New Edition revised and corrected by Henry Redhead Yorke, Esq.,* 8 vols. (London, 1812–17). [*172a]
BB: 172a

112b. Campbell, Thomas, "Battle of the Baltic," in *The Poetical Works of Thomas Campbell,* ed. W. A. Hill (London, 1854), pp. 111–14. [*633a]
BB: 633a

112c. Campbell, Thomas, "Death-Boat of Heligoland" (1828).
MD: 141a?

*113. Campbell, Thomas, *The Pleasures of Hope, and Other Poems* (New York: Longworth, 1811). [*Sealts #118]
F1: 212

Carlyle, Thomas.
M: 18, 27, 30, 139, 181a, 366; R: 576a; WJ: 45, 576a; MD: 48, 49, 50, 51, 93, 139!, 172b, 181, 576a; P: 57, 124, 139, 172b, 181, 283, 504, 576a; CM: 576a; Unspec: 92, 146, 251, 283, 366, 499b

113a. Carlyle, Thomas, *Critical and Miscellaneous Essays,* vol. 5 of *The Modern British Essayists*

([Philadelphia: Carey & Hart, 1847–49?]). [*Sealts #359]
WJ: 576a; MD: 297a; Unspec: 440e

114. Carlyle, Thomas, essays in *Edinburgh Review*: "Jean Paul Friedrich Richter" (1827, no. 91); "The State of German Literature" (1827, no. 92); "Burns" (1828, no. 96); "Signs of the Times" (1829, no. 98); "Characteristics" (1831, no. 108). [*366]
WJ: 576a; PB: 576a; BT: 576a; Unspec: 366, 576a

115. Carlyle, Thomas, *The French Revolution, A History* (1837).
WJ: 416, 576a; MD: 165, 172b, 229, 229a, 345, 345a, 366, 576a; P: 104a; CM: 229, 345, 576a; C: 315; BB: 229, 345, 576a

*116. Carlyle, Thomas, trans., *German Romance: Specimens of Its Chief Authors; with Biographical and Critical Notices* (Boston: Munro, 1841). [*Sealts #121]
Unspec: 187a, 303

116a. Carlyle, Thomas, *Life of Schiller* (1823–24, 1825).
Unspec: 705a?

117. Carlyle, Thomas, *On Heroes, Hero-Worship, and the Heroic in History. Six Lectures: Reported, with Emendations and Additions by Thomas Carlyle* (New York: Appleton, 1841; or New York: Wiley & Putnam, 1846). [*Sealts #122]
MD: 211, 229, 229a, 449, 576a; P: 181?, 211, 229; B: 421b?; CM: 229a, 254; BB: 211

118. Carlyle, Thomas, *Past and Present* (1843).
R: 366

‹119. Carlyle, Thomas, *Sartor Resartus: The Life and Opinions of Herr Teufelsdrockh* (Boston: Munroe, 1840; or New York: Wiley & Putnam, 1847). [*Sealts #123]
M: 28, 139, 211, 226, 265, 318, 366!, 440, 576a; R: 211, 366, 576a; WJ: 229a, 366, 491, 567, 576a; HHM: 229, 366, 406, 576a; MD: 139, 172b, 213, 229, 229a, 265, 292, 318, 345a, 366!, 366a, 375, 377c [r 501], 440!, 462c, 481c, 487, 493, 505, 534c, 576a, 602, 615, 665, 669; P: 104a, 139, 181, 213, 265, 366, 440!, 511c!, 665; B: 421b, 440, 576a; CDD: 440; IP: 440; CM: 440, 576a; C: 211, 213; TT: 576a; Unspec: 146, 229a, 686b

Carlyle, Thomas: see also 723b.

120. Carteret, Philip, *An Account of a Voyage round the World, in the years MDCCLXVI, MDCCLXVII, MDCCLXVIII, and MDCCLXIX* (1773).
T: 7

Cary, Henry: see 747a, 747b.

121. Cellini, Benvenuto, *The Life of Benvenuto Cellini by Himself* (1730).
MD: 534; BT: 534

‹*122. Cervantes Saavedra, Miguel de, *Don Quixote de la Mancha. Translated from the Spanish of Miguel de Cervantes Saavedra, by Charles Jarvis, Esq. Carefully Revised and Corrected. With Numerous Illustrations by Tony Johannot* (Philadelphia: Blanchard & Lea, 1853). [*Sealts #125; see also Sealts #124]
T: 488c; M: 488c; WJ: 167; MD: 167, 229, 236, 488c, 512a; P: 486a, 576b, 622a; BC: 167; TP: 167, 488c, 621;

CM: 213, 254, 334, 442a, 686a!, 705; C: 315; MP: 167, 377b, 686a; Unspec: 100, 164, 229, 236, 266, 621

Chalmers, Alexander: see 111, 498b.

*123. Chambers, Ephraim, *Cyclopaedia: or, An Universal Dictionary of Arts and Sciences* (London: Knapton [etc.], 1728). [*Sealts #128; see also Sealts #128b]
M: 213, 226!, 441, 670; WJ: 670; MD: 481d, 657a, 670; C: 670; BB: 670; Unspec: 223

124. Chambers, Robert, *Vestiges of the Natural History of Creation*, Fourth Edition, from the Third London Edition, Greatly Amended by the Author (New York: Wiley & Putnam, 1846). [*215]
M: 148, 190 [r 215 [r 571?], 226], 215, 459a, 571

124a. Chambers, Robert and William, *Chambers's Edinburgh Journal* (London, 1833–44; Edinburgh, 1844–54) [Melville's holding: vol. 5, no. 121 (25 April 1846) only?]. [*Sealts #128a]
Unspec: 459a

124b. *Chambers's Miscellany of Useful and Entertaining Knowledge* (Boston, [1847–48?]). [*273b]
MD: 273b?

*125. Chamisso, Adelbert von, *Peter Schlemihl . . . Translated by Sir John Bowring . . . With Plates by George Cruikshank*, 3d ed. (New York: Denham, 1874). [*Sealts #129]
Unspec: 139, 303, 442a

126. Channing, William Ellery, "The African Character" in *The Anti-Slavery Picknick: A Collection of Speeches, Poems, Dialogues and Songs; Intended for Use in Schools and Anti-Slavery Meetings*, ed. John A. Collins (Boston, 1842), pp. 56–58. [*482]
BC: 482

*127. Channing, William Ellery, *The Works . . . Eighth Complete Edition, with an Introduction* (Boston: Munroe, 1848). [*Sealts #130]
Unspec: 200

*128. Chapone, Hester Mulso, *Letters on the Improvement of the Mind. Addressed to a Lady* (Boston: Wells & Wait, 1809). [*Sealts #132]
Unspec: 200

129. "Characters in Bleak House," *Putnam's Monthly Magazine*, 2 (Nov. 1853), 558–62. [Sealts #413; *660]
CM: 660!

*130. Chase, Owen, *Narrative of the Most Extraordinary and Distressing Shipwreck of the Whale-Ship Essex, of Nantucket; Which Was Attacked and Finally Destroyed by a Large Spermaceti-Whale, in the Pacific Ocean; with an Account of the Unparalleled Sufferings of the Captain and Crew* (New York: Gilley, 1821). [*Sealts #134; see also Sealts #133]
MD: 84, 96, 120!, 133d, 147, 164, 165, 176a, 182, 198, 201, 229, 246, 254a, 291a, 345a, 377c, 395, 440e, 487, 507, 674a!; B: 674a?; C: 176a, 246, 291a, 315, 377b, 674a!; Unspec: 133, 164, 213, 214, 440e, 674a!, 686b

130a. Chateaubriand, Francois-Auguste-Rene de, Vicomte, *Rene: A Tale Translated from the French of Mons. F. A. De Chateaubriand* (Boston: Cummings & Hilliard, 1815) [first American translation]. [*711]
B: 711?

131. Chateaubriand, Francois-Auguste-Rene de, Vicomte, *Travels in Greece, Palestine, Egypt, and Barbary, During the Years 1806 and 1807*, trans. F. Shobert (New York, 1814). [*315]
C: 315!, 333, 441b

*132. Chatterton, Thomas, *The Poetical Works . . . With Notices of His Life, History of the Rowley Controversy, a Selection of His Letters, and Notes Critical and Explanatory* (Cambridge: Grant, 1842). [*Sealts #137]
R: 35; Unspec: 200, 213, 442a
   "The Mynstrelle Songe from Aella": E: 109, 134, 173, 213, 379, 428

‹*133. Chaucer, Geoffrey, *Poetical Works . . . Edited with a Memoir by Robert Bell* (London: Parker, 1854–56). [*Sealts #138; see also Sealts #139–41]
WJ: 254; CDD: 316a; CM: 254; C: 148a, 213a, 315, 377a; see also 134. below

*134. Chaucer, Geoffrey, *The Riches of Chaucer, in Which His Impurities Have Been Expunged, His Spelling Modernised . . . Obsolete Terms Explained. Also Have Been Added a Few Explanatory Notes, and a New Memoir of the Poet*, by C. C. Clarke (London: Wilson,

1835). [*Sealts #141; see also Sealts #138–40]
LRM: 520; C: 315; WW: 440f; see also 133. above

135. Cheesebrough, Caroline, "Magnetic Influences," *Knickerbocker*, 37 (May 1851), 430–41. [*512]
P: 512?

136. Cheever, Henry T., *The Whale and His Captors; or, The Whaleman's Adventures, and the Whale's Biography, as Gathered on the Homeward Cruise of the "Commodore Preble"* (New York: Harper & Brothers, 1849 or 1850). [*RDM; *182]
MD: 123 [r 200], 147, 182, 189, 198, 199, 201!, 229, 487, 510

137. Chesterfield, Philip Dormer Stanhope, Fourth Earl of, *Letters Written by the Late Right Honourable Philip Dormer Stanhope Earl of Chesterfield to His Son; with Some Account of His Life* (New York: C. A. Hinkley, 1824). [*212]
F1: 212

*138. Chesterfield, Philip Dormer Stanhope, Fourth Earl of, *Principles of Politeness, and of Knowing the World . . . Methodised and Digested under Distinct Heads, with Additions, by the Rev. Dr. John Trusler . . . To Which Is Now First Annexed a Father's Legacy to His Daughters: By the Late Dr. Gregory, of Edinburgh* (Portsmouth, N.H.: Printed by Melcher & Osbourne, 1786). [*Sealts #142]
F: 100; F1: 212

*139. Child, Francis James, ed., *English and Scottish Ballads* (Boston: Little, Brown, 1854–57). [*Sealts #143]
BP: 304; Unspec: 315, 382
   "Sir Patrick Spens": JM: 441b, 489

Childers, R. C.: see 469a.

140. *The China Aster, or Youth's Book of Varieties* (Portland, Maine: S. H. Colesworthy, 1845–51). [*629]
CM: 629

Chowder Controversy: see 77a, 747a, 747b.

Chretien de Troyes: see 720.

141. Churchill, John and Awnsham, *Collection of Voyages and Travels* (London, 1732). [*530]
M: 530?; MD: 530?, 532?

142. Cicero, Marcus Tullius, *De divinatione* [in *Classical Library*, vols. 8–10, The Orations Translated by Duncan, the Offices by Cockman, and the Cato and Laelius by Melmoth (New York: Harper, [18—])?]. [*Sealts #147]
MD: 445; B: 619a?

Circumnavigation of the Globe: see 357.

143. Clark, Lewis G., "Editor's Table," *Knickerbocker*, 33 (March 1849), 267–68. [*452]
MD: 452

143a. Clarke, Adam, *Commentary*, 8 vols. (1810–26; reprinted in 6 vols., 1851). [*503a]
CM: 503a

143b. Clarke, Adam, *The New Testament of our Lord and Saviour Jesus Christ*, with a Commentary and Critical Notes by Adam Clarke (New York: Carlton & Porter, 1832). [*503a]
CM: 503a

144. Clarke, Marcus Andrew Hislop, *For the Term of His Natural Life* ([London: Bentley, 1885?]). [*Sealts #146]
BB: 247

Clemens, Samuel Langhorne: see Mark Twain.

145. Clough, Arthur Hugh.
C: 78

145a. *Cocke Lorell's Bote* (sixteenth century).
CM: 330a?

*146. Codman, John, *Sailors' Life and Sailors' Yarns, by Captain Ringbolt* [pseud.] (New York: Francis, 1847). [*Sealts #149]
RE: 212, 334a, 614, 699!; R: 212 [r 699], 377b, 614; WJ: 662a; JM: 377b?

Coleridge, Samuel Taylor.
F: 100; M: 301; WJ: 146, 283; MD: 146, 283; BB: 146, 283; Unspec: 283

147. Coleridge, Samuel Taylor, *Biographia Literaria; or, Biographical Sketches of My Literary Life and Opinions*, from the Second London Edition (New York: Wiley & Putnam, 1847 or 1848). [*Sealts #154]
WJ: 143, 252; MD: 252, 675; P: 675; C: 315; TIM: 336, 377b; Unspec: 213, 226, 378, 440a, 600c, 675

147a. Coleridge, Samuel Taylor, "The Eolian Harp" (1796).
P: 561b

148. Coleridge, Samuel Taylor, "Kubla Khan, a Vision in a Dream" (1816).
BP: 441b, 556; WW: 489?

‹*149. Coleridge, Samuel Taylor, *Notes and Lectures upon Shakespeare and Some of the Old Poets and Dramatists; with Other Literary Remains*, ed. Mrs. H. N. Coleridge (London: Pickering, 1849). [*Sealts #155]
MD: 137!, 213, 249, 345a, 487, 602, 677; P: 172b; CM: 686a; Unspec: 314, 378, 440a

150. Coleridge, Samuel Taylor, "The Rime of the Ancient Mariner" (1798).
M: 20; WJ: 491!; MD: 53, 182, 229, 291b, 314, 334, 445, 465, 590, 618!; E: 503; BC: 314; CM: 71; JM: 512b

151. Coleridge, Samuel Taylor, *Specimens of the Table-Talk of S. T. Coleridge* (New York, 1835). [*143]
P: 143

152. Coleridge, Samuel Taylor, "To Genevieve" (1794).
F1: 212

Collingwood, G. L. Newnham: see 397.

Collins, John A.: see 126.

‹*153. Collins, William, *The Poetical Works* (Boston: Little, Brown, 1854). [*Sealts #156; see also Sealts #464]
E: 109, 134, 173, 213, 379, 428

*154. Colnett, Captain James, *A Voyage to the South Atlantic and round Cape Horn into the Pacific Ocean, for the Purpose of Extending the Spermaceti Whale Fisheries, and other Objects of Commerce, by ascertaining the Ports, Bays, Harbours, and Anchoring Births, in Certain Islands and Coasts in those Seas at which the Ships of the British Merchants might be Refitted.* (London: W. Bennett, 1798). [*MKB]
MD: 109, 147!, 165, 182, 201!, 229, 696; E: 109!, 133, 134!, 173, 213, 387, 392, 421, 696!

Colt Murder Case: see 237a.

155. Colton, George H., *Tecumseh* (1842). [*229]
R: 229; MD: 229

*156. "The Compensation Office," *Putnam's Monthly Magazine*, 5 (May 1855), 459-68. [*Sealts #413]
CM: 213

Comstock, Samuel: see 156c, 157.

156a. Comstock, William, abridgement of *A Voyage to the Pacific* in *Evangelical Magazine and Gospel Advocate* [Utica, NY], 15 (19 April 1841), 124–25. [*605]
MD: 605, 720

156b. Comstock, William, "The Art of Whaling," *Boston Pearl and Literary Gazette*, 4 (18 July 1835), 359; (25 July 1835), 369–70; and "Whaling in the Pacific," *Boston Pearl and Literary Gazette*, 4 (1 Aug. 1835), 377–79; (8 Aug. 1835), 384–85; (15 Aug. 1835), 392–93; (22 Aug. 1835), 400–401; (29 Aug. 1835), 408–9; and (5 Sept. 1835), 415. [*720]
MD: 720

156c. Comstock, William, *The Life of Samuel Comstock, the Bloody*

Mutineer (Boston: Blanchard, 1845). [*461d]
MD: 461d

157. Comstock, William, *The Life of Samuel Comstock, the Terrible Whaleman. Containing an Account of the Mutiny, and Massacre of the Officers of the Ship Globe, of Nantucket; with His Subsequent Adventures, and His Being Shot at the Mulgrave Islands. Also, Lieutenant Percival's Voyage in Search of the Survivors* (Boston: James Fisher, 1840). [*461d]
MD: 147, 461d

158. Comstock, William, *A Voyage to the Pacific, Descriptive of the Customs, Usages, and Sufferings on Board of Nantucket Whale-Ships* (Boston: Oliver L. Perkins, 1838). [*605]
MD: 605, 720
See also 156a.

Comstock, William, "Whaling in the Pacific": see 158a.

158a. Comstock, William, "Whaling in the South Pacific. Encounter with a White Whale," *Nantucket Daily Telegraph*, 1 (7 Aug. 1843), 1. [*461d]
MD: 461d, 720

Confidence Man: 29a, 373a, 529, 754.

" 'The Confidence Man' on a large Scale," *New York Herald* (11 July 1849): see 373a.

159. Cook, Captain James A., *A Collection of Voyages round the World . . . Containing a Complete Historical Account of Captain*

Cook's Voyages (London, 1790). [*201]
T: 5, 7; O: 15, 133, 201; M: 29, 32, 201; MD: 201; Unspec: 228; see also 160. below

159a. Cook, Captain James A., *Journals* (1773, 1777, 1784).
M: 576d?

160. Cook, Captain James A., *A Voyage to the Pacific for Making Discoveries in the Northern Hemisphere [1776–1780]*, 2d ed. (London, 1785). [*229]
MD: 229

160a. Cooke, George, engravings of Hadrian and Antoninus Pius from *Historic Gallery of Portraits and Paintings*, vol. 3 (London, 1807–11). [*377b]
TIM: 377b

*161. Cooke, Philip Pendleton, *Froissart Ballads, and Other Poems* (Philadelphia: Carey & Hart, 1847). [*Sealts #158]
M: 213, 226

Cooper, James Fenimore.
T: 251; O: 9; RSL: 129; MD 249; P: 551a; CM: 254; Unspec: 100, 129, 212, 251

162. Cooper, James Fenimore, *Afloat and Ashore; or the Adventures of Miles Wallingford* (1844).
R: 511; P: 181?; BC: 537?

*163. Cooper, James Fenimore, *The History of the Navy of the United States of America* (New York: G. P. Putnam, 1853), 3 vols. in 1. [*682]
IP: 108, 346, 682, 685!

164. Cooper, James Fenimore, *Homeward Bound: Or, The Chase. A Tale of the Sea* (1838).
MD: 413?; CM: 244?, 395a?

164a. Cooper, James Fenimore, *The Littlepage Manuscripts* [*Satanstoe* (1845), *The Chain-bearer* (1845), and *The Redskins* (1846)].
P: 481b, 576b

165. Cooper, James Fenimore, *The Monikins* (1835).
M: 18, 481c

166. Cooper, James Fenimore, *The Pathfinder; or, The Inland Sea* (1840).
MD: 394?

167. Cooper, James Fenimore, *The Pilot; A Tale of the Sea* (1824).
MD: 110, 229; Unspec: 110?

167a. Cooper, James Fenimore, *The Pioneers; or, The Sources of the Susquehanna* (1823).
CM: 487a; BB: 441b

168. Cooper, James Fenimore, *The Prairie; A Tale* (1827). [Sealts #158a]
MD: 229, 420; Unspec: 181, 499b

169. Cooper, James Fenimore, *Proceedings of the Naval Court Martial in the Case of Alexander Slidell Mackenzie, A Commander in the Navy of the United States, &c. Including the Charges and Specifications of Charges, Preferred Against Him by the Secretary of the Navy. To Which is Annexed, An Elaborate Review* (New York: Langley, 1844).
WJ: 216, 490; BB: 138, 172a, 481b, 511

‹*170. Cooper, James Fenimore, *The Red Rover. A Tale* (New York: Putnam, 1849). [*Sealts #159]
T: 511?; O: 10; WJ: 440e, 511; TBB: 110, 123, 212, 213, 334a, 511; MD: 213, 334a, 345a, 440e, 481b, 487, 511; IP: 345a?; BB: 345; Unspec: 212, 213, 440e

‹*171. Cooper, James Fenimore, *The Sea Lions; or, The Lost Sealers* (New York: Stringer & Townsend, 1849). [*Sealts #160]
T: 481c; RSL: 110, 123, 129, 146, 334a, 511!, 651b; WJ: 416; MD: 146, 334a!, 511; P: 481b; Unspec: 499b

172. Cooper, James Fenimore, *The Two Admirals. A Tale* (1842).
BB: 345

173. Cooper, James Fenimore, *The Wing-and-Wing, or Le Feu-Follet; A Tale* (1842).
BB: 345

173a. Cooper, James Fenimore, *Wyandotte, or The Hutted Knoll* (1843).
P: 481b

Cooper, James Fenimore: see also 181a.

174. Corcoran, Denis, *Pickings from the Portfolio of the Reporter of the New Orleans "Picayune"* (Philadelphia: Peterson, 1846). [*548]
CM: 548

Cornhill Review: see 458b.

Cosmopolitan Magazine: see 320.

175. Coulter, John, *Adventures in the Pacific* (Dublin, 1845).
E: 109, 379, 428

Coulter, John: see also 3b.

176. Cowley, Captain [Ambrose], "Cowley's Voyage Round the Globe" in William Hacke's *A Collection of Original Voyages* (London, 1699), pp. 1–[48]; also appeared in John Harris's *Navigantium atque iterantium bibliotheca* (London, 1744), 1, 77–84. [*201]; or "Captain Ambrose Cowley's 'Voyage Round the Globe [1683–1686],' " in *A Collection of Voyages* (London: J. & J. Knapton, 1729), vol. 4. [*229]
E: 109, 134, 201, 213, 421, 571; MD: 201, 229

177. Cowper, William, *Poems* (1782). [Sealts #161]
MD: 202, 229, 552
> "The Castaway" (written shortly before Cowper's death in 1800): MD: 202, 229

178. Crevecoeur, J. Hector St. John de, *Letters from an American Farmer* (1782).
MD: 229?

179. Croly, George, *Salathiel* (1829).
C: 652?

*180. Cruchley, George Frederick, *Cruchley's Picture of London, Comprising the History, Rise, and Progress of the Metropolis to the Present Period ... A Route for Viewing the Whole in Seven Days: To Which Is Annexed a New and Superior Map*, 11th ed. (London: Cruchley, 1847). [*Sealts #166]
PMP: 500b; Unspec: 685

181. *A Cruise in a Whale-Boat* (1849).
MD: 147

181a. *The Cruise of the Somers: Illustrative of the Despotism of the Quarter-Deck; and of the Unmanly Conduct of Captain Mackenzie* (New York, 1844) [mistakenly attributed to James Fenimore Cooper]. [*172a]
BB: 172a, 229a

182. Cuffe, Paul, *Narrative of the Life and Adventure of Paul Cuffe, a Pequot Indian: During Thirty Years Spent at Sea, and in Travelling in Foreign Lands* (Vernon, N.Y., 1839). [*210]
MD: 210?

Cummins, John: see 90.

183. Cunningham, Allan, *The Songs of Scotland, Ancient and Modern* (1825).
CM: 254, 440c, 487a

183a. Curtis, George William, "Easy Chair" editorial essays, *Harper's*. [*461a; Sealts #240]
CM: 461a, 705

184. Curzon, Robert, *Visit to the Monasteries of the Levant* (1849).
C: 315

185. Cuvier, Frederick, *De l'histoire naturelle des cetaces, ou recueil et examen des faits dont se compose l'histoire naturelle de ces animaux* (Paris, 1836). [*182]
MD: 148?, 182?

‹*186. Cuvier, Georges, Baron, *The Animal Kingdom Arranged in Conformity with Its Organization, by the Baron Cuvier ... With Additional Descriptions of All the Species Hitherto Named, and of Many Not Before Noticed, by Edward Griffith ... and Others* (London:

Whittaker, 1827–43), vol. 10.
[*Sealts #171]
T: 7, 148; M: 148?, 571?; MD: 148,
165, 182?, 201!, 229

187. Cyrano de Bergerac,
Savinien, *The Comical History of
the States and Empires of the
Worlds of the Moon and Sun,
Newly Englished by A. Lovell*
([London: Rhodes, 1687?]).
[*Sealts #172]
MD: 229?

D

187a. Dampier, William, *A Collection of Voyages* (London, 1729).
[*693a]
MD: 693a

188. Dampier, William, *A New Voyage round the World* (London,
1697).
E: 421

188a. Dampier, William, *Voyages
and Descriptions* (London, 1699).
MD: 182, 201

188b. Dana, Richard Henry, Jr.,
The Seaman's Friend (1841).
R: 709!

*189. Dana, Richard Henry, Jr.,
*Two Years before the Mast. A Per-
sonal Narrative of Life at Sea* (New
York: Harper, 1840). [*Sealts #173]
T: 3; O: 11, 382, 394?; R: 35, 312!;
WJ: 46, 47, 126, 133, 250!, 312!, 416,
440e, 490, 491!; MD: 182, 229, 394?,
440e; JM: 250; BB: 312; Unspec: 80,
80a [r 84, 126], 81, 100 [r 126], 133c,
198, 212, 213, 291b, 440e, 481c

189a. Dana, Richard Henry, Jr.,
Two Years before the Mast, rev.
ed. (1869). [*250]
BB: 250!, 345

*190. Dante Alighieri, *The Vision;
or Hell, Purgatory, and Paradise*,
trans. Rev. Henry Francis Cary
(London: Henry G. Bohn, 1847).
[Sealts #174; *719]
M: 113, 188, 226, 229a, 273b, 340,
380, 417, 576d, 686b; R: 196; WJ:
188; MD: 148a, 188, 229, 340, 377c;
P: 95, 146, 172b, 179, 181, 188!, 196
[r 205], 205, 229a, 321!, 324!, 340,
367, 380, 417, 439a, 457, 463b, 504,
551a, 576b, 576e; E: 379, 428, 619;
IP: 181a; PB: 621; C: 179, 188, 196,
315, 441b, 461b, 512b; BB: 188;
WW: 489; Unspec: 213, 719!

190a. Darwin, Charles, *The Descent of Man* (1871).
MP: 512b

‹*191. Darwin, Charles, *Journal of
Researches into the Natural History and Geology of the Countries
Visited during the Voyage of
H.M.S. Beagle round the World,
under the Command of Capt. Fitz
Roy, R.N.* (New York: Harper,
1846). [*Sealts #175]
T: 228?; M: 218?; MD: 148, 201, 229,
451, 475b, 571; E: 148, 228, 379, 421,
428, 451!, 459a!, 475b, 604; C: 148,
228, 315; Unspec: 226

Darwin, Charles: see also 271.

*192. D'Avenant, Sir William, *The
Works* (London: Herringman,
1673). [*Sealts #176]
MD: 229

193. Davidson, Lucretia Maria,
*Amir Khan and Other Poems: The
Remains of Lucretia Maria David-*

son, who died at Plattsburgh, N.Y. August 27, 1825, aged 16 years and 11 Months. With a Biographical Sketch by Samuel F. B. Morse (New York, 1829). [*333]
F2: 333

194. Day, Jeremiah, *The Mathematical Principles of Navigation and Surveying* (1817).
Unspec: 627

195. "The Dead-Letter Office," *Washington National Intelligencer* (9 Oct. 1852). [*515]
B: 515

Dead Letters: see 195, 573, 731.

Decameron: see 67.

Defoe, Daniel, *The Fortunate Mistress*: see 197.

196. Defoe, Daniel, *The Life and Strange Surprising Adventures of Robinson Crusoe* (1719).
T: 2, 4, 13, 53, 512c; O: 13, 15, 100; M: 19, 21, 25, 301; R: 35, 39, 40, 41, 43, 44; E: 66

197. Defoe, Daniel, *Roxana, or the Fortunate Mistress* (1724). [Sealts #177]
Unspec: 213

Defoe, Daniel: see also 588.

198. DeForest, John William, *Oriental Acquaintance: in a Series of Letters from Asia Minor* (1856).
C: 315

199. Dekker, Thomas, *Old Fortunatus* (1600).
WJ: 513

*200. Delano, Amasa, *A Narrative of Voyages and Travels, in the Northern and Southern Hemi-

spheres: Comprising Three Voyages Round the World; Together with a Voyage of Survey and Discovery, in the Pacific Ocean and Oriental Islands* (Boston: Printed by E. G. House, for the Author, 1817). [*98]
T: 572?; WJ: 421; E: 134, 379, 421, 428; BC: 98!, 100, 129, 172!, 173, 180a, 198, 213, 224 [r 240], 240, 249a, 257a, 285, 299, 329, 358, 404, 415!, 421, 481e, 511b, 557a, 559, 572, 576, 610, 621, 642a, 646, 662b, 697; CM: 504b

Delirium Tremens: see 65.

Democratic Press, and Lansingburgh Advertiser: see 770.

Democratic Review: see *United States Magazine, and Democratic Review*.

201. Denon, Vivant, *Travels in Upper and Lower Egypt*, trans. from French (New York, 1803). [*229]
MD: 165, 229

202. De Quincey, Thomas, *Autobiographic Sketches* (1834–53).
P: 181

203. De Quincey, Thomas, *Confessions of an English Opium Eater* (1822). [Sealts #180]
MD: 95, 229, 291b, 397a?, 422, 534c, 680; P: 104a, 181, 481c; IP: 345a; C: 377b; Unspec: 100, 123, 211, 213, 261, 550

204. De Quincey, Thomas, "The English Mail-Coach, Or The Glory of Motion," *Blackwood's Edinburgh Magazine*, 66 (Oct. 1849). [*261]
MD: 261?

De Quincey, Thomas, *Suspiria de Profundis*: see 203 [bound in with *Confessions of an English Opium Eater*].

205. De Quincey, Thomas, "The Vision of Sudden Death," *Blackwood's Edinburgh Magazine*, 66 (Dec. 1849), 741–55; "Childhood's Dream of Terror" passage from above quoted in *Literary World*, 6 (5 Jan. 1850), 13.
MD: 229?, 261?

206. De Sacy, Antoine-Isaac Silvestre, "Memoire sur la Dynastie des Assassins, et sur l'Etymologie de leur Nom," in *Memoire de l'Institut Royal, Classe d'histoire et de litterature ancienne* (Paris, 1818), 4, 1–84. [*273]
MD: 273? [r 478]

de Sevigne, Marie: see Sevigne, Marie (de Rabutin-Chantal), Marquise de.

de Stael, Madame: see Stael-Holstein, Anne-Louise-Germaine (Necker), Baronne de.

206a. de Tocqueville, Alexis Charles Maurice Henri Clerel, *Democracy in America* (1835, 1840).
C: 461b?, 512b?

207. D'Holbach, Paul Henri, Baron.
M: 31

208. Dibdin, Charles, Songs.
R: 192; WJ: 369, 419, 503, 545; BB: 192, 369, 377b, 503

209. Dick, A. L., steel engraving from a painting called "The Ruins of Carthage" by William Linton, published in the New York *Mirror* (2 Jan. 1841). [*621]
B: 621?

Dickens, Charles.
M: 92a; R: 139; MD: 92a, 139; P: 139, 504, 511c; B: 63, 265, 468

210. Dickens, Charles, *American Notes* (1842).
R: 531?; M: 143, 531; MD: 133, 294; P: 531?; CM: 531, 705

211. Dickens, Charles, *Bleak House* (1852–53).
B: 671, 674b?; MG: 512b
See also 129.

212. Dickens, Charles, *The Life and Adventures of Martin Chuzzlewit* (1843–44).
P: 181, 504b, 511c; CM: 95 [r 213a], 219, 440c, 487a, 504b, 705

212a. Dickens, Charles, *Nicholas Nickleby* (1838–39).
P: 511c

*213. Dickens, Charles, *The Personal History and Experience of David Copperfield, the Younger* (New York: Putnam, 1850). [*Sealts #181]
P: 418

‹214. Dickens, Charles, *The Posthumous Papers of the Pickwick Club* (1836–37). [Sealts #182]
WJ: 481e?, 568; MD: 92b; Unspec: 123, 213

Dictionary: see 16, 50, 75, 123, 124b, 223a, 344, 380a, 400, 421, 544, 585, 622a, 651a, 687, 715, 751, 763.

215. Di Lucca, Signor Gaudentio, *The Memoirs of Signor Gaudentio di Lucca* (1737).
M: 226

215a. Diodorus Siculus, *The Historical Library of Diodorus the Sicilian*, trans. G. Booth (London, 1814), 2 vols. [*365a]
MD: 365a?

*216. Diogenes Laertius, *The Lives and Opinions of Eminent Philosophers . . . Literally Translated by C. D. Yonge, B.A.* (London: Bohn, 1853). [*Sealts #183a]
MD: 165, 229; CM: 254, 481c; Unspec: 441, 557b

216a. "Dirt-Eating," *American Magazine of Useful and Entertaining Knowledge*, 2 (May 1836), 372. [*440c]
CM: 440c

"Discursive Thoughts on Chowder": see 747a.

Disraeli, Benjamin.
M: 32; P: 181

217. Disraeli, Benjamin, *Alroy* (1833).
P: 181, 511c

218. Disraeli, Benjamin, *Contarini Fleming, a Psychological Romance* (1832).
P: 181, 511c

219. Disraeli, Benjamin, *Henrietta Temple* (1837).
P: 181, 511c

220. Disraeli, Benjamin, *Venetia* (1837).
P: 181, 511c

221. Disraeli, Benjamin, *Vivian Grey* (1826–27).
P: 181, 511c

‹*222. Disraeli, Isaac, *Curiosities of Literature . . . A New Edition,* Edited, with Memoir and Notes, by His Son, the Right Hon. B. Disraeli (London: Routledge [etc.], 1859). [*Sealts #186]
B: 500a?; Unspec: 183, 200, 504a

*223. Disraeli, Isaac, *The Literary Character; or, The History of Men of Genius, Drawn from Their Own Feelings and Confessions; Literary Miscellanies; and An Inquiry into the Character of James the First . . . A New Edition,* Edited by His Son, the Right Hon. B. Disraeli (London: Routledge [etc.], 1859). [*Sealts #187]
Unspec: 183, 265

223a. *Dobson's Encyclopaedia* (Philadelphia, 1798). [*273b]
R: 273b?; Unspec: 273b?

224. Doddridge, Philip, *The Rise and Progress of Religion in the Soul* (1745).
PMP: 621

Dodge, Abigail R. [also referred to as Mary Abigail Dodge]: see 320.

‹*224a. Dodsley, Robert, ed., *A Select Collection of Old Plays: A New Edition: With Additional Notes and Corrections, by the Late Isaac Reed, Octavius Gilchrist, and the Editor* (London: Prowett, 1825–27). [*Sealts #188]
R: 440a; WJ: 440a; Unspec: 440a

Dollar Magazine: see 330.

225. *Don Juan*, by Wolfgang A. Mozart [opera].
M: 192?; WJ: 192?

225a. Donizetti, Gaetano, *Lucia di Lammermoor* [opera] (1835).
P: 651b; CDD: 180a

225b. Donizetti, Gaetano, *Lucrezia Borgia* [opera] (1833).
P: 651b

226. Donne, John, "Devotion XVII" in *Devotions upon Emergent Occasions* (1624).
MD: 229; Unspec: 158

227. Donne, John, "The Ecstasy" (1633).
MD: 300

228. Draper, John William, *History of the Conflict Between Religion and Science* (1875).
TIM: 489?

‹*229. Dryden, John, *The Poetical Works ... with Illustrations by John Franklin*, 2d ed. (London: Routledge, 1854). [*Sealts #191]
   "Absalom and Achitophel":
   MD: 542

230. Dryden, John, *The State of Innocence, and Fall of Man* (1677).
Unspec: 139?

Dublin University Magazine: see 3b.

231. Dumas, Alexandre, *The Count of Monte Cristo* (1844–45).
CM: 254, 440c, 504b

Duncan, Archibald: see 476.

Duncan, James F.: see 577a.

Duyckinck, Evert A.: see 754.

232. Dwight, Timothy, *Travels in New England and New York* (1821–22).
HHM: 581, 621; MD: 229; ATT: 135!, 503, 581, 621

E

*233. Eastlake, Sir Charles L., *Contributions to the Literature of the Fine Arts* (London: Murray, 1848). [*Sealts #198]
MD: 574

234. Eastlake, Sir Charles L., *Goethe's Theory of Colours* (London: Murray, 1840). [*574]
MD: 574?

"Easy Chair" editorial essays: see 183a.

235. Eckermann, Johann, *Conversations with Goethe in the last years of His Life*, translated from the German of Eckermann by Margaret Fuller (Boston, 1839). [*182]
MD: 146, 178, 182, 229, 407, 705a; P: 172b; Unspec: 303, 665, 705a

Edinburgh Encyclopedia: see 380a.

Edinburgh Journal: see 124a.

‹236. *Edinburgh Review, or Critical Journal* (Edinburgh [etc.], 1803–1929), vol. 41 (1824–25), vol. 47 (1828). [*Sealts #200]
Unspec: 212
See also 114, 359, 397, 577.

237. "Editorial Notes.—American Literature," *Putnam's Monthly Magazine*, 4 (Sept. 1854), 338–44. [Sealts #413]
CM: 625

237a. Editorial *re*: the Colt Murder Case, *Harper's*, 6 (1852–53), 127. [Sealts #240; *534a]
B: 534a

238. Edmonds, John Worth, and George T. Dexter, *Spiritualism* (New York, 1853, 1855). [*512]
ATT: 512

239. Edwards, Jonathan, *A Careful and Strict Enquiry into the Modern Prevailing Notion, of that Freedom of Will which is supposed to be Essential to Moral Agency, Vertue and Vice, Reward and Punishment, Praise and Blame* (1754).
MD: 300; P: 181; B: 328, 483, 534a, 619a

240. Edwards, Jonathan, *Future Punishment of the Wicked* (1741).
MD: 501

240a. Edwards, Jonathan, "The Nature of True Virtue" in *Two Dissertations* (1765).
B: 619a

241. Edwards, Jonathan, "Personal Narrative" (written c. 1740).
LRM: 412

242. Edwards, Jonathan, "Sinners in the Hands of an Angry God" (1741).
LRM: 267, 520

Ellens, Charles: see Ellms, Charles.

*245. Ellis, William, *Polynesian Researches, During a Residence of Nearly Eight Years in the Society and Sandwich Islands*, "Harper's Stereotype Edition" (New York: J. & J. Harper, 1833). [*480]
T: 127, 133, 133c, 178, 213, 228, 460, 512c; O: 17, 83, 127, 133!, 178, 183, 213, 228, 439a, 461, 480!; M: 127!, 133, 178, 198, 213, 226!, 228, 287, 365a, 488, 576d; Unspec: 571

245a. Ellms, Charles, *The Pirates' Own Book* (1837).
R: 212

245b. Ellms, Charles, *Shipwrecks and Disasters at Sea* (1836).
R: 212

246. *Elton's Songs and Melodies for the Multitude; or Universal Songster* (New York, c. 1840). [*165]
MD: 165?

Emerson, Ralph Waldo.
M: 18, 129, 226, 365, 385a; MD: 50, 229, 291b, 300, 345a, 385a, 407, 427, 661; P: 129, 172b, 181, 365; CM: 254, 265; BP: 75; JM: 385a; BB: 385a, 646a; Unspec: 139, 146, 251, 291b, 378, 398, 541, 686b

246a. Emerson, Ralph Waldo, "The American Scholar" (1837).
P: 486a

‹*247. Emerson, Ralph Waldo, *The Conduct of Life*, 2d ed. (London: Smith, Elder, 1860). [*Sealts #203]
P: 181; Unspec: 128!, 179, 251, 333, 365, 580, 686b, 705a

248. Emerson, Ralph Waldo, "Divinity School Address" (1838).
P: 576c, 634

‹*249. Emerson, Ralph Waldo, *Essays*, [4th ed.] (Boston: Munroe, 1847). [*Sealts #204]
M: 669; MD: 229, 402, 444, 669; P: 172b, 576c, 669; CM: 133b, 161, 249, 254, 440c, 499, 504b, 705; BP: 251; Unspec: 128!, 133c, 161, 183, 229, 251, 365, 442a, 504a, 669

‹*250. Emerson, Ralph Waldo, *Essays: Second Series*, 3d ed. (Boston: Munroe, 1844). [*Sealts #205]
P: 481b, 669; TP: 352; CM: 504b,

629, 669; WW: 440f; Unspec: 128!, 133c, 139, 161, 254, 334, 504a, 541, 580, 629, 669

250a. Emerson, Ralph Waldo, "The Heart."
P: 504d?

250b. Emerson, Ralph Waldo, "Lectures on the Times" (1842–43).
P: 504d

250c. Emerson, Ralph Waldo, "Natural History of Intellect" (first mentioned as a topic by Emerson in 1848, delivered as a lecture in 1870, and published in 1893).
P: 504d??

251. Emerson, Ralph Waldo, *Nature* (1836).
M: 576d; MD: 661; P: 504d; PMP: 514; CM: 161 [r 499], 265

*252. Emerson, Ralph Waldo, *Poems*, 7th ed. (Boston: Phillips, Sampson, 1858). [*Sealts #206]
BP: 669; C: 461b, 669; WW: 213, 440f; MP: 213

253. Emerson, Ralph Waldo, "The Problem," quoted in review of *Poems*, by R. W. Emerson, *Literary World*, 1 (3 April 1847), 197. [*669]
TP: 566, 669

254. Emerson, Ralph Waldo, *Representative Men* (1850).
MD: 229, 669; IP: 559; CM: 365a, 440c; BB: 646a; Unspec: 686b, 693b

255. Emerson, Ralph Waldo, "The Transcendentalist" (1843).
MD: 686b; P: 576c, 622a; B: 496, 563; TIM: 525

Emerson, Ralph Waldo: see also 579.

256. "The Enchanted Mule," *Putnam's Monthly Magazine*, 2 (Aug. 1853), 147–50. [Sealts #413]
TP: 331?

Encyclopedia: see Dictionary.

Encyclopedia Britannica: see 622a.

"The English Mail-Coach": see 204.

256a. "The English in Afghanistan," *North American Review*, 55 (July 1842), 45, 70–71. [*475a]
MD: 475a?

The English Reader: see 513.

257. Epictetus, *Discourses* (published in Greek, 1535; in English, 1758).
P: 143; CM: 143, 254; C: 143

258. *Epitome of the History of Philosophy*, translated from the French by C. S. Henry, in *Harper's Family Library* (New York: Harper, 1842). [Sealts #211; *143]
Unspec: 143

258a. Erasmus, Desiderius, *The Praise of Folly* (1509).
MP: 377b

"An Excursion to Canada": see 709.

Evangelical Magazine and Gospel Advocate: see 156a.

*258b. Evans, John, *Shakspeare's Seven Ages: or, The Progress of Human Life; Illustrated by a Series of Extracts in Prose and Poetry, Introduced by a Brief Memoir of Shakspeare and His Writings . . .

Embellished with Eight Copper-plate Engravings (London: Arnold, 1831). [*Sealts #209]
Unspec: 440a

Every Saturday: A Journal of Choice Reading Selected from Foreign Current Literature: see 25a.

259. "An Execution at Sea. A Sketch," *Knickerbocker*, 8 (March 1836), 285–88; reprinted in other periodicals, including *Yeoman's Gazette* (Concord, Mass., 23 April 1836), 1. [*277]
BB: 277?

259a. "Execution at the Yard Arm," *New York Tribune*, with editorial comment from the *Lynn News* (Lynn, Mass.), vol. 2, no. 44 (30 Oct. 1846), 2. [*517a]
BB: 517a?

F

*260. "Facts and Opinions" [anecdote about the Duke of Wellington, Lord Warden of the Cinque Ports], *Literary World*, 6 (29 June 1850), 642. [*Sealts #326]
MD: 182!, 229

261. Falconer, William, *The Shipwreck* (1762).
MD: 143; TIM: 377b

262. Fanning, Edmund, *Voyages round the World* (New York, 1833).
T: 133, 133c, 213

263. Fanning, Nathaniel, *Narrative of the Adventures of an American Navy Officer Who Served During Part of the American Revolution under the Command of* Captain John Paul Jones, Esq. (New York, 1806). [*685]
IP: 213 [r 346, 685!], 317, 440d, 481e, 498a, 557?, 559

Faust: see 300, 477.

263a. "A Female Robinson Crusoe," *Albany Evening Journal* (3 Nov. 1853), 1, or *Springfield Sunday Republican*, vol. 10, no. 275 (22 Nov. 1853), 1. [*648a]
E: 648a, 686b

264. Fenelon, Francois de Salignac de La Mothe-, *The Adventures of Telemachus, Son of Ulysses* (1699). [Sealts #212]
MD: 229

265. Fergusson, William, F.R.S.E., *A System of Practical Surgery*, 3d American ed. from the last English ed. (Philadelphia: Lea & Blanchard, 1848). [*491]
WJ: 491?; Unspec: 571?

*266. Field, David Dudley, ed., *A History of the County of Berkshire, Massachusetts; in Two Parts. The First Being a General View of the County; the Second, an Account of the Several Towns. By Gentlemen in the County, Clergymen and Laymen* (Pittsfield: Printed by S. W. Bush, 1829). [*Sealts #216]
ATT: 135!, 180a, 213, 257, 621; IP: 213, 317, 685!

266a. Fielding, Henry, *The Life of Jonathan Wild the Great* (1743).
CM: 479a, 481c

266b. Fielding, Henry, *Tom Jones, a Foundling* (1749).
P: 551a; CM: 481e

267. "Fines for Swearing," *Sailors' Magazine* (Jan. 1837). [*481]
R: 481

Fingal: see 467.

*268. FitzGerald, Edward, *Polonius: A Collection of Wise Saws and Modern Instances* (London: Pickering, 1852). [*Sealts #218]
BB: 183?; Unspec: 143, 442a

*269. FitzGerald, Edward, *Rubaiyat of Omar Khayyam, the Astronomer-Poet of Persia. Rendered into English Verse*, 1st American from the 3d London ed. (Boston: Houghton, Osgood, 1878). [*Sealts #391; see also Sealts #392–93]
TIM: 512b; WW: 333!, 377b, 440f; MG: 489

*270. FitzGerald, Edward, *Works ... Reprinted from the Original Impressions, with Some Corrections Derived from His Own Annotated Copies* (Boston: Houghton, Mifflin, 1887). [*Sealts #217]
WW: 333

271. Fitzroy, Captain Robert, *Narrative of the Surveying Voyages of H.M.S. Adventure and Beagle ... 1826–1836* (London, 1839) [Vol. III is *Journal and Remarks* by Charles Darwin]. [*133]
O: 133; E: 133

272. Flaxman, John, *Compositions of John Flaxman from the Divine Poem of Dante Alighieri* (London, 1807). [*188]
P: 188

272a. Flaxman, John, *Oeuvre complete de Flaxman, Recueil des ses compositions gravees au trait* (Paris: Librairie Plon, 1833). [*340]
M: 321, 340, 380; MD: 321, 340; P: 321!, 340, 380; Unspec: 188

273. "Fling Out the Banner! Let it Float" [hymn] (1842). [*489]
TIM: 489

274. Flint, Timothy, *A Condensed Geography and History of the Western States; or, The Mississippi Valley* (Cincinnati, 1828) [or in one of its later retitled (*The History and Geography of the Mississippi Valley*) and slightly variant editions]. [*705]
CM: 370!, 461a, 705
See also 43.

Flint, Timothy, *The History and Geography of the Mississippi Valley*: see 274.

275. Flint, Timothy, *The Life and Adventures of Arthur Clenning* (1828).
R: 212

276. Flint, Timothy, *Recollections of the Last Ten Years in The Mississippi Valley* (1826).
CM: 370!, 705

"Flogging in the Navy": see 452.

276a. Forbes, James, *Oriental Memoirs* (1813).
MD: 273b?

277. Ford, John, *'Tis Pity She's a Whore* (1633).
P: 181

Fore-Top-Man: see 498.

Foreign Quarterly Review: see *Westminster Review and Foreign Quarterly Review*.

278. Forster, John Reinold, *Observations Made during a Voyage round the World* (London, 1778). [*190]
T: 148, 190 [r 215]; O: 148, 190 [r 215]; P: 148, 190 [r 215]

*279. Forsyth, Joseph, *Remarks on Antiquities, Arts, and Letters during an Excursion in Italy, in the Years 1802 and 1803*, 3d ed. (London: Murray, 1824). [*Sealts #219]
Unspec: 200

Fouque, la Motte-: see 432.

Franco, Harry: see 77, 77a, 78.

*280. Franklin, Benjamin, *The Works of Benjamin Franklin*, ed. Jared Sparks (Boston, 1836–40). [*685]
R: 557; IP: 108, 346, 507a, 559, 685!; CM: 504b

Franklin, Sir John: see a.

281. Fraser, James B., *Historical and Descriptive Account of Persia*, in *Harper's Family Library* series (New York: Harper, 1842). [Sealts #211; *532]
MD: 532

Frithiof's Saga: see 693.

Froissart, *Ballads*: see 161.

282. Froissart, Jean, *Chronicles of England, France and Spain*, trans. John Bourchier, Lord Berners (1523–25); illus. ed. (New York, 1854). [*432]
MD: 165, 377c; BC: 432

*283. Fuller, Thomas, *The Holy State, and the Profane State. A New Edition. With Notes*, by James Nichols (London: Tegg, 1841). [*Sealts #221]
WJ: 229, 301, 593; MD: 201, 229, 299, 301!, 364, 593; CM: 440c; Unspec: 123, 146

284. Fuller, Thomas, *A Pisgah-sight of Palestine* (1650).
P: 181?

G

G., W. A., *Ribs and Trucks*: see 752b.

286. Gay, John, *The Beggar's Opera* (1728).
F: 175; Unspec: 440e

287. Gessner, Konrad, *Historia animalium* (Latin text, 1558; German text, 1563; woodcuts with brief captions, 1560). [*564]
MD: 564?

288. Gessner, Salomon, *The Death of Abel ... Translated from the German ... By Mrs. Collyer* (London: Ridgway, 1843). [*Sealts #223a]
Unspec: 303

‹289. Gibbon, Edward, *The History of the Decline and Fall of the Roman Empire* (1776, 1781, 1788). [Sealts #223b]
M: 143; MD: 436; CM: 254; C: 315; TIM: 143, 166, 326, 377b, 393, 488a; Unspec: 532

*290. Gilchrist, Alexander, *Life of William Blake, "Pictor Ignotus". With Selections from His Poems and Other Writings, by the Late Alexander Gilchrist ... Illustrated from Blake's Own Works, in Facsimile by W. J. Linton, and in Pho-*

tolithography; with a Few of Blake's Original Plates (London: Macmillan, 1863). [Sealts #224; *119]
C: 119; TIM: 512b; Unspec: 119
See also 66.

291. Gill, John, *Exposition of the Old Testament* (London, 1762–65; Philadelphia, 1815–18). [*506]
MD: 506

292. Gillies, Robert Pearse, *Tales of a Voyager to the Arctic Ocean* (London, 1826). [*147]
MD: 147, 229

Gladwin, Francis: see 597.

293. Glanvill, Joseph, *The Vanity of Dogmatizing* (1661).
CM: 262?

Gliddon, George R.: see 388.

294. Gobat, Samuel, *Journals of Three Years' Residence in Abyssinia* ([New York: Dodd, 1850?]). [*Sealts #224a]
Unspec: 333

God in Disease: see 577a.

Godman, John D.: see 58.

*295. Godwin, William, *The Adventures of Caleb Williams, or, Things as They Are ... Revised and Corrected. With a Memoir of the Author* (London: Bentley, 1849). [*Sealts #225]
P: 181, 511c, 693b; BB: 187a, 438; Unspec: 187a, 380

Goethe, Johann Wolfgang von.
MD: 103; P: 178, 181, 705a; Unspec: 178, 259, 283, 303, 637a

‹*296. Goethe, Johann Wolfgang von, *The Auto-Biography of Goe-*

the. *Truth and Poetry: From My Own Life*, trans. John Oxenford [*Letters from Italy*, trans. A. J. W. Morrison, are pp. 237–450 of vol. 2] (London: Bohn, 1848–49). [*HH; Sealts #228]
M: 178; MD: 181, 182, 213, 229, 345a, 397a, 407, 440e, 686b, 705a; P: 172b, 181, 345a, 631, 705a; WW: 440f; MG: 705a; Unspec: 100, 146, 303, 440e, 504d, 637a, 665, 705a??

297. Goethe, Johann Wolfgang von, "Die Braut von Corinth" [poem] (c. 1780).
M: 226?, 303?

298. Goethe, Johann Wolfgang von, *Egmont* (published in German, 1788; in English, 1841).
P: 181?, 303?

299. Goethe, Johann Wolfgang von, *Faust* (1808, 1832).
WJ: 146, 178, 253, 303, 705a; MD: 50, 131a, 139, 178, 229, 229a, 241, 253, 303, 334, 339, 476, 665, 705a; IP: 705a; BC: 285, 299; CM: 705a; BB: 476; Unspec: 705a

*300. Goethe, Johann Wolfgang von, *Iphigenia in Tauris. A Drama in Five Acts ... Translated from the German. By G. J. Adler, A.M.* (New York: Appleton, 1850). [*Sealts #229]
Unspec: 303, 665?, 705a

301. Goethe, Johann Wolfgang von, *Italian Journey* (published in German, c. 1858; in English, 1892).
Unspec: 665?, 705a?

Goethe, Johann Wolfgang von, *Letters from Italy*: see 296.

302. Goethe, Johann Wolfgang von, *The Sorrows of Young Werther* (1774).
P: 56, 440; CM: 254, 303, 440c

*303. Goethe, Johann Wolfgang von, *Die Wahlverwandtschaften* in *Goethe's Werke ... Originalausgabe* (Vienna: Kaulfuss & Armbruster, 1816–21), vol. 14. [*Sealts #227]
Unspec: 303?

304. Goethe, Johann Wolfgang von, *Wilhelm Meister's Aprenticeship and Travels* (translated into English by Carlyle in 1824). [Sealts #230]
P: 645?; Unspec: 146, 178, 303, 705a

Goethe, Johann Wolfgang von: see also 235.

*305. Goldsmith, Oliver, *The Deserted Village* (New York: Cassell, Petter, & Galpin, [187–?]). [*Sealts #231]
BB: 345

306. Goldsmith, Oliver, *Goldsmith's Natural History*, abridged for the use of schools, by Mrs. Pilkington (Philadelphia, 1829). [*229]
MD: 229

307. Goldsmith, Oliver, *History of the Earth and Animated Nature* (London, 1774); *Goldsmith's History of the Earth and Animated Nature*, abridged ed. (London, 1807). [*201]
T: 148, 571; M: 218; MD: 148, 199, 201, 229, 481d, 571; Unspec: 190 [r 215!]

307a. Goldsmith, Oliver, "The Traveller" (1764).
MD: 377c

308. Good, John Mason, *The Book of Nature* (1826).
T: 481d; O: 481d; M: 148, 190 [r 215], 481d; R: 384!; WJ: 148, 384, 481d, 571; MP: 148?

Gray, Thomas.
M: 24

309. Gray, Thomas, "The Bard" (1757).
P: 181

310. Gray, Thomas, *Correspondence of Thomas Gray* in Thomas James Mathias, ed., *The Works of Thomas Gray with Memoirs of His Life and Writings by William Mason* (London, 1814), or John Mitford, ed., *The Works of Thomas Gray* (London, 1835–43). [*392]
E: 392

"The Great Nation of Futurity": see 531.

310a. Green, Jonathan H., *An Exposure of the Arts and Miseries of Gambling* (1843).
CM: 479a

310b. Green, Jonathan H., *Gambling Unmasked! or the Personal Experience of J. H. Green, the Reformed Gambler* (1844).
CM: 479a

Greylock, Godfrey: see 650.

310c. Griswold, Rufus, obituary for Edgar Allan Poe, *New-York Daily Tribune*, vol. 9, no. 156 (9 Oct. 1849), 2. [*551a]
P: 551a?

The Gulistan: see 597.

311. Guthrie, G. J., *A Treatise on Gun-Shot Wounds, on Injuries of Nerves, and on Wounds of the Extremities Requiring the Different Operations of Amputation, in which The Various Methods of performing these Operations are shown, together with their After-treatment; and Containing an account of The Author's successful Case of Amputation at the Hip-joint*, 2d ed. (London: Burgess & Hill, 1820). [*491]
WJ: 491; Unspec: 571

Guzman de Alfarache: see 6.

H

*311a. Habington, William, *Habington's Castara, with a Preface and Notes, by Charles A. Elton* (Bristol: Gutch, [1812]). [*Sealts #236]
WW: 440f

Hadrian: see 160a.

312. Hafiz, Shams-Ed-Din Muhammad.
C: 77; MG: 295; MP: 295

313. Hakluyt, Richard, *Principall Navigations, Voiages, and Discoveries of the English Nation* (1589, 1598–1600).
MD: 182, 201

313a. Hall, James, *The Harpe's Head: A Legend of Kentucky* (1833).
CM: 705

314. Hall, James, *Legends of the West* (1832).
CM: 254

315. Hall, James, *Letters from the West* (1828).
CM: 254

315a. Hall, James, *Notes on the Western States* (1838).
CM: 504b

316. Hall, James, *The Romance of Western History* (1857).
CM: 228?

317. Hall, James, *Sketches of History, Life, and Manners in the West* (1834).
CM: 179, 245!, 254!, 394, 440c, 487a, 504b, 664, 705

318. Hall, James, *Wilderness and the Warpath* (1846).
CM: 291a, 368

319. Halyard, Harry, *The Doom of the Dolphin: or, The Sorceress of the Sea. A Tale of Love, Intrigue, and Mystery* (1848).
MD: 182?

319a. Halyard, Harry, *Wharton the Whale-Killer! Or, The Pride of the Pacific. A Tale of the Ocean* (1848).
MD: 147, 229

320. Hamilton, Gail [pseud. of Abigail R. Dodge], "The Murder of Philip Spencer," *Cosmopolitan Magazine*, in three installments beginning 7 (June 1889), 134. [*138]
BB: 138, 172a, 213, 441b, 458

321. Hamilton, Robert, *Mammalia. Whale, &c.* (Edinburgh, 1843) in Sir William Jardine, ed., *The Naturalist's Library*, vol. 8. [*182]
MD: 182?

Hammerlein or Hammerken, Thomas: see 417.

Hampden, John, Jr.: see 375.

Hardenberg: see 737.

322. Harington, James, *The Commonwealth of Oceana* (1656).
M: 32

322a. Harlan, Josiah, *A Memoir of India and Avghanistaun* (1842).
MD: 475a?

Harper's Family Library: see 258, 281, 357, 594.

Harper's New Monthly Magazine: see 43b, 183a, 237a, 579a, 665, 714.

323. Harris, John, *Navigantium atque itinerantium bibliotheca; or, a Compleat Collection of Voyages and Travels* (London, 1705). [*693a]
M: 226, 693a; MD: 165, 182, 201, 229, 333, 693a!; Unspec: 333, 530
See also 176.

Harry Martingale: see 35.

325. Hart, Joseph C., *Miriam Coffin; or, The Whale-Fishermen* (1834).
MD: 96, 118!, 133!, 147, 159, 182, 201, 229, 274a, 334a, 345a, 487; CM: 487a, 544

*326. Hart, Joseph C., *The Romance of Yachting: Voyage the First* (New York: Harper, 1848). [*Sealts #242]
WJ: 419; Unspec: 123, 212, 226, 229, 274a!

*327. Hartley, David, *Observations on Man, His Frame, His Duty, and His Expectations. In Two Parts* [including vol. 3, *Notes and Additions to Dr. Hartley's Observations on Man; by Herman Andrew Pis-*

torius] (London: Johnson, 1801). [*Sealts #243; *226]
M: 226, 301, 318, 607; P: 181; Unspec: 129 [r 226], 143, 213, 686b

Hawser Martingale: see 647.

Hawthorne, Nathaniel.
HHM: 302; MD: 163a, 302, 666; P: 58, 163a; B: 576; JR: 163a; IMC: 163a; ATT: 163a; PT: 69, 666; CM: 163a; Unspec: 686b

*328. Hawthorne, Nathaniel, *The Blithedale Romance* (Boston: Ticknor, Reed, & Fields, 1852). [*Sealts #245]
P: 129, 139, 181, 481b; B: 487b; E: 621?; IP: 288; TIM: 587?; Unspec: 213

329. Hawthorne, Nathaniel, "Chiefly About War Matters, by a Peaceable Man," *Atlantic Monthly* (July 1862). [*502]
BP: 405, 441b, 502, 679; JM: 441b

*330. Hawthorne, Nathaniel, "Ethan Brand; or, The Unpardonable Sin," *Dollar Magazine*, 7 (May 1851), 193–201. [*Sealts #189]
MD: 139, 182, 220, 229, 269, 279!, 302; P: 576c; B: 503; IP: 503; BT: 173?, 503; CM: 503?; Unspec: 99??, 100?? [r 102, 105, 242], 241

*331. Hawthorne, Nathaniel, *The House of the Seven Gables, a Romance* (Boston: Ticknor, Reed, & Fields, 1851). [*Sealts #246]
WJ: 494; MD: 241, 481b, 487; P: 101, 139, 481b, 487b, 600; MG: 512b; Unspec: 129, 139, 152, 213, 291b, 343, 440e, 576

*332. Hawthorne, Nathaniel, *The Marble Faun: or, The Romance of*

Monte Beni (Boston: Ticknor & Fields, 1860). [*Sealts #247]
C: 315; BB: 172a, 291a; WW: 440f; Unspec: 139, 213

*333. Hawthorne, Nathaniel, *Mosses from an Old Manse* (New York: Wiley & Putnam, 1846). [*Sealts #248]
HHM: 123, 129, 152!, 158, 181a, 182, 213, 213a, 236a, 242, 269, 291a, 291b, 334, 406, 440e, 447, 475, 487, 487b, 498, 511b, 534b, 581, 621, 661; MD: 182, 213, 229, 241!, 269, 291a, 334, 345a, 347a, 397a, 440e, 487, 487b, 567, 612; P: 139, 181, 265, 576e, 622a, 693b; B: 447, 487b; E: 487b, 503?, 621; HF: 621?; LRM: 487b; PB: 517; BT: 487b, 503, 517, 576; BC: 230, 316a; IMC: 236a, 498, 517, 576; ATT: 498, 576; TP: 475, 487b, 493a, 511b, 517, 566; CM: 219!, 254, 265, 334, 487a, 504b, 591, 641, 705; TIM: 377b; BB: 139, 172a, 345; TT: 517; WW: 440f, 512b; MP: 512b; Unspec: 532, 567

*334. Hawthorne, Nathaniel, *Our Old Home. A Series of English Sketches* (Boston: Ticknor & Fields, 1863). [*Sealts #249]
Unspec: 315

*335. Hawthorne, Nathaniel, *Passages from the American Note-Books* (Boston: Ticknor & Fields, 1868). [*Sealts #250]
C: 315?

*336. Hawthorne, Nathaniel, *Passages from the English Note-Books* (Boston: Fields, Osgood, 1870). [*Sealts #251]
C: 315

*337. Hawthorne, Nathaniel, *Passages from the French and

Italian Note-Books (Boston: Osgood, 1872). [*Sealts #252]
C: 315

‹*338. Hawthorne, Nathaniel, *The Scarlet Letter, a Romance* (Boston: Ticknor, Reed, & Fields, 1850). [*Sealts #253]
MD: 139, 229, 241, 269; P: 481b, 600, 651b, 693b; E: 487b, 503; TF: 621?; CM: 291, 503; C: 315?; BB: 345, 646a; MP: 512b; Unspec: 145, 291b, 661

‹*339. Hawthorne, Nathaniel, *The Snow-Image, and Other Twice-Told Tales* (Boston: Ticknor & Fields, 1865). [*Sealts #255]
P: 401? [r 446]; TF: 316a; TIM: 512b

*340. Hawthorne, Nathaniel, *Tanglewood Tales, for Girls and Boys; Being a Second Wonder-Book* (Boston: Ticknor, Reed, & Fields, 1853). [*Sealts #256]
BT: 547

*341. Hawthorne, Nathaniel, *Twice-Told Tales* (Boston: American Stationers Co., 1837). [*Sealts #258; see also Sealts #259–60]
WJ: 416, 481b; MD: 229, 241, 410, 440e, 551; P: 203, 622a; E: 503; BT: 503; CM: 443, 487a, 504b, 544, 705; C: 315; BB: 410; TT: 576, 621; Unspec: 152, 162

*342. Hawthorne, Nathaniel, *A Wonder-Book for Girls and Boys With Engravings by Baker from Designs by Billings* (Boston: Ticknor, Reed, & Fields, 1852). [*Sealts #261]
HF: 621?

Hawthorne, Nathaniel: see also 76a, 525a.

*343. Haydon, Benjamin Robert, *Life of Benjamin Robert Haydon, Historical Painter, from His Autobiography and Journals. Edited and Compiled by Tom Taylor* (New York: Harper, 1853). [*Sealts #262]
IP: 180a, 346, 685; IMC: 180a; TP: 180a; Unspec: 637

*344. Haydon, Benjamin Robert, *Painting, and the Fine Arts: Being the Articles under Those Heads Contributed to the Seventh Edition of the Encyclopaedia Britannica, by B. R. Haydon . . . and William Hazlitt* (Edinburgh: Black, 1838). [*Sealts #263]
Unspec: 637

*344a. Hazlitt, William, *Criticisms on Art: and Sketches of the Picture Galleries of England . . . With Catalogues of the Principal Galleries . . . Edited by his Son* (London: John Templeman, 1843). [*719]
Unspec: 719

345. Hazlitt, William, *The Life of Napoleon Buonaparte* (1828–30).
Unspec: 299

*346. Hazlitt, William, *The Round Table: A Collection of Essays on Literature, Men, and Manners* (Edinburgh: Constable, 1817). [*Sealts #265]
Unspec: 175, 440a, 440f, 580

347. Hazlitt, William, *The Spirit of the Age* (1825).
BB: 637; Unspec: 637

*347a. Hazlitt, William, *Table Talk; or, Original Essays on Men and Manners*, 2d ed. (London: Col-

burn, 1824). [*Sealts #266; see also Sealts #266a]
Unspec: 440a

Hazlitt, William: see also 344, 502, 721a.

348. Hegel, Georg Wilhelm Friedrich.
M: 31; BB: 211?

*349. Heine, Heinrich, *The Poems of Heine, Complete: Translated in the Original Metres. With a Sketch of Heine's Life. By Edgar Alfred Bowring* (London: Bohn, 1861). [*Sealts #268]
Unspec: 303

350. Hennen, John, *Principles of Military Surgery, Comprising Observations on the Arrangement, Police, and Practice of Hospitals, and on the History, Treatment, and Anomalies Variola and Syphilis. Illustrated with Cases and Dissections*, 3d ed. (London and Edinburgh: John Wilson, Princes Street, Soho; and Adam Black, 1829). [*491]
WJ: 491; Unspec: 571

351. Herbert, George, *The Temple . . . The Priest to the Temple* (Philadelphia: Hazard, 1855 or 1857). [*Sealts #270]
WW: 512b; Unspec: 213, 378, 686b

352. Herodotus, trans. William Beloe, in *Classical Library* (New York: Harper, [18—]), vols. 29–31. [*Sealts #147]
MD: 229, 365a

*353. Herrick, Robert, *Hesperides: or The Works Both Humane and*

Divine of Robert Herrick (Boston: Little, Brown, 1856). [*Sealts #271] WW: 213, 432a, 489

354. Hesiod, *Theogony* (Hesiod's works published in English in 1728). JM: 296

355. Hillard, George S., *Six Months in Italy* (1844). [*637] Unspec: 637?

356. Hine, Ephraim Curtiss, *The Haunted Barque, and Other Poems* (Auburn and New York: M. H. Newman & Co., 1848). [*491] WJ: 221, 491; Unspec: 213

Historic Gallery of Portraits and Paintings: see 160a.

357. *Historical Account of the Circumnavigation of the Globe, and of the Progress of Discovery in the Pacific Ocean* in *Harper's Family Library* (New York: Harper, 1837), vol. 82. [Sealts #211; *461] T: 133, 178, 213, 460, 480, 571; O: 461, 480!; WJ: 419

"The History of a Cosmopolite": see 496.

A History of the County of Berkshire, Massachusetts: see 266.

358. Hobbes, Thomas, *The Leviathan, or the Matter, Form, and Power of a Commonwealth, Ecclesiastical and Civil* (1651). O: 146, 480; MD: 146, 229, 480; P: 146, 480; IP: 146, 480; Unspec: 229a, 283

*359. Hodgskin, Thomas, "Abolition of Impressment," *Edinburgh*

Review, 41 (October 1824), 154–81. [*Sealts #200; *327] WJ: 327!, 490, 491, 662a

360. Hoffman, Charles Fenno, "Sparkling and Bright," first published in *New York American* (8 May 1830), reprinted in Hoffman's *The Vigil of Faith, and Other Poems* (1842), and included in various anthologies. [*229] MD: 229, 377c

361. Hoffman, Charles Fenno, *A Winter in the West* (1835). CM: 394

362. Hoffman, David, *Chronicles Selected from the Originals of Cartaphilus, the Wandering Jew* (London: Thomas Bosworth, 1853). [*652] C: 652?

362a. Hoffmann, Ernst Theodor Amadeus, *Nachtstucke, Herausgegeben von dem Verfasser der Fantasiestucke in Callot's Manier* (Berlin: Realschulbuchhandlung, 1817 [1816–17]). [*Sealts #274] BT: 480a?

363. Hogarth, William. O: 380!, 480; R: 380!, 480; WJ: 380!, 480; MD: 480

Holbach, Paul Henri, Baron d': see 207.

364. Holden, Horace, *A Narrative of the Shipwreck, Captivity, and Sufferings of Horace Holden and Benj. H. Nute: Who Were Cast Away in the American Ship Mentor, on the Pelew Islands, in the Year 1832: And For Two Years Afterwards Were Subjected to Unheard of Sufferings Among the*

Barbarous Inhabitants of Lord North's Island (Boston: Weeks, Jordan, 1839; also, Boston: Russell, Shattuck & Co., 1836). [*573]
T: 573; Unspec: 573

Holden's Magazine: see *Dollar Magazine*.

*365. Hole, Samuel Reynolds, *A Book about Roses, How to Grow and Show Them*, 7th ed., rev. (New York: Gottsberger, 1883). [*Sealts #275a]
WW: 430, 440f

*366. Homer, *Homer's Batrachomyomachia, Hymns, and Epigrams. Hesiod's Works and Days. Musaeus' Hero and Leander. Juvenal's Fifth Satire. Translated by George Chapman. With Introduction and Notes, By Richard Hooper* (London: Smith, 1858). [*Sealts #276]
Unspec: 198

*367. Homer, *The Iliads of Homer, Prince of Poets. Never Before in Any Language Truly Translated, with a Comment on Some of His Chief Places. Done According to the Greek by George Chapman. With Introduction and Notes, by Richard Hooper* (London: Smith, 1857). [*Sealts #277]
Unspec: 139, 200, 206, 213, 263, 580

‹*368. Homer, *The Odysseys of Homer, Translated According to the Greek, by George Chapman. With Introduction and Notes by Richard Hooper* (London: Smith, 1857). [*Sealts #278]
CM: 254; C: 315; Unspec: 139, 146, 206, 213, 263, 440a, 686b

369. Homer, trans. Alexander Pope, in *Classical Library* (New York: Harper, [18—]), vols. 32–34. [*Sealts #147]
M: 139; MD: 139, 206, 307, 377c, 509, 683; CM: 254; TIM: 377b; MP: 377b; Unspec: 263

369a. Hood, Thomas, "The Dream of Eugene Aram" (1829).
MD: 510a

370. Hood, Thomas, "Miss Norman" in *Hood's Own: Selected Papers With Comic Illustrations* (G. P. Putnam & Co., March, 1852). [*529]
B: 529?

‹*371. Hood, Thomas, *The Poetical Works* [with a Memoir of the Author by Richard Monckton Milnes] (Boston: Little, Brown, 1860). [*Sealts #279]
M: 33; Unspec: 315

*372. Hope, Thomas, *Anastasius; or, Memoirs of a Greek* (London: Murray [etc.], 1836). [*Sealts #282; see also Sealts #281]
MD: 229, 347a, 532; C: 315; Unspec: 100, 181a, 208, 333!, 478

373. Horace, trans. Philip Francis, in *Classical Library* (New York: Harper, [18—]), vols. 18–19. [*Sealts #147]
LRM: 267?; CM: 254; C: 461b, 512b; JG: 295; MP: 295

373a. Houston, George, " 'The Confidence Man' on a large Scale," *New York Herald* (11 July 1849), 2. [*479a; *487a]
CM: 479a, 487a, 510b, 686a, 705

*374. Howell, James, *Instructions for Forreine Travell*, in Edward

Arber, ed., *English Reprints* (London, 1869). [*Sealts #285b]
BB: 345

375. Howitt, William, *The Aristocracy of England: A History for the People. By John Hampden, Junr.* [pseud.], [2d ed. (London: Wilson, 1846)?]. [*Sealts #288; *181]
P: 181!

Hudibras: see 102.

376. Hudson, Henry Norman, *Lectures on Shakespeare* (New York, 1848). [*537]
BC: 537; BB: 537

*376a. Hugo, Victor-Marie, Comte, *The Literary Life and Poetical Works of Victor Hugo. Translated into English by Eminent Authors . . . Now First Collected and Edited by Henry Llewellyn Williams* (New York: Hurst, [1883]). [*Sealts #290]
WW: 512b

377. Hume, David [including his essay "Of Suicide" in *Essays on Suicide and the Immortality of the Soul* (1783)].
M: 377a; R: 146, 254; CM: 254, 441, 481d; Unspec: 146, 441

377a. Hume, David, *The Natural History of Religion* (1757).
MD: 365a

378. Hunt, James Henry Leigh, *Bacchus in Tuscany, A Dithyrambic Poem from the Italian of Francesco Redi* (1825).
CM: 254, 440c, 504b

379. Huxley, Thomas Henry, "A Liberal Education" (1870).
BB: 571?

Hymns: see 273, 569, 748, 764.

I

"Iconoclasm in German Philosophy": see 533a.

380. "An Illustrated Criticism," New York *Tribune* (6 Feb. 1849), 2. [*669]
Unspec: 669!

"Incense of the Heart": see 737a.

India: see 322a, 380a.

380a. "India" in *Edinburgh Encyclopedia*, American ed. (1832), 11, 284. [*365a]
CM: 365a?

380b. "Indian Traditions of Monument Mountain," Pittsfield *Sun* (31 Oct. 1833). [*461c]
T: 461c?; P: 461c?

Irving, Washington.
O: 12; HHM: 129; Unspec: 129, 213

381. Irving, Washington, *Bracebridge Hall; or, The Humorists: A Medley* (1822).
PB: 576

*382. Irving, Washington, *A History of New York, from the Beginning of the World to the End of the Dutch Dynasty by Diedrich Knickerbocker* [pseud.] (New York: Van Winkle, 1824). [*Sealts #292]
OZ: 226; R: 504c; WJ: 265, 676; Unspec: 439

383. Irving, Washington, *History of the Life and Voyages of Christopher Columbus* (1828).
BC: 659?

384. Irving, Washington, "The Little Man in Black" in *Salmagundi; or, the Whim-Whams and Opin-*

ions of Launcelot Langstaff, Esq. and Others (1808).
R: 496; B: 576; CM: 461a

385. Irving, Washington, *The Sketch Book*, by Geoffrey Crayon, Gent. [pseud.] (1819–20).
R: 481, 640; MD: 334a; PMP: 514; PB: 576!; JR: 576!; ATT: 488b, 508b; TP: 566; TT: 576!
    "Rip Van Winkle": E: 497b?; HF: 621?; IMC: 576; WW: 100, 316, 440f, 489

386. Irving, Washington, *Tales of a Traveller* (1824).
B: 576; TF: 576

⟨*387. Irving, Washington, *Works* (Philadelphia: Lea & Blanchard, 1840). [*Sealts #292a]
T: 576; O: 576; M: 576; R: 576; WJ: 576; B: 576; WW: 440f

388. "Is Man One Or Many?" review of *Types of Mankind*, by J. C. Nott, M.D., and George R. Gliddon, *Putnam's Monthly Magazine*, 4 (July 1854), 1–14. [Sealts #413]
BC: 299; TG: 599?

J

*389. Jacobs, Thomas Jefferson, *Scenes, Incidents, and Adventures in the Pacific Ocean; or The Islands of the Australasian Seas, during the Cruise of the Clipper Margaret Oakley, under Capt. Benj. Morrell* (New York: Harper, 1844). [*Sealts #293]
M: 226; Unspec: 212, 226

390. James I, King of Great Britain, *Daemonologie* (1597).
MD: 397a; BC: 486

391. James, Henry, *Moralism and Christianity; or Man's Experience and Destiny* (1850).
P: 181?

392. James, William, *The Naval History of Great Britain, from the Declaration of War by France in 1793, to the Accession of George IV ... A New Edition* (London, 1826 [or later edition]). [*Sealts #294a]
BB: 172a, 213, 229a, 345!, 546

393. Jameson, Anna Brownell Murphy, *Legends of the Madonna* (1852).
BC: 560?

394. "Jaques Le Laid," *The Token*, ed. S. G. Goodrich (Boston, 1838), especially pp. 203–5. [*582]
WJ: 582?

*395. Jarves, James Jackson, *The Art-Idea: Part Second of Confessions of an Inquirer* (New York: Hurd & Houghton, 1864). [*Sealts #296]
Unspec: 527

Jean-Paul: see Richter.

Jefferson, Thomas.
MD: 320

396. Jefferson, Thomas, "First Inaugural Address" (1801).
BP: 320

*397. Jeffrey, Francis, review of *A Selection from the Public and Private Correspondence of Vice-Admiral Lord Collingwood*, by G. L. Newnham Collingwood (1828), *Edinburgh Review*, 47 (May 1828), 385– 418. [*Sealts #200; *327]
WJ: 327!, 490, 491, 662a; BB: 345

398. Jerrold, Douglas William, *Black-ey'd Susan* (1829).
BB: 270, 284, 345

398a. Jerrold, Douglas William, *The Housekeeper* (1825).
P: 651b

399. Jerrold, Douglas William, *The Mutiny at the Nore. A Nautical Drama, in Two Acts* in *Lacy's Acting Edition of Plays* (London: Lacy, [18—]), vol. 78. [*Sealts #297]
BB: 213, 270

400. Johnson, Samuel, *A Dictionary of the English Language* (1755).
MD: 49

‹*401. Johnson, Samuel, *The History of Rasselas Prince of Abyssinia* (Philadelphia: Lippincott, 1869). [*Sealts #300]
T: 7, 397, 481c; P: 576b

402. Johnson, Samuel, "Life of Addison" in *The Lives of the Poets* (1779–81).
P: 603?

Johnson, Samuel: see also 449.

403. Johnston, David Claypoole, "A Lesson in Seamanship" [cartoon] in *Scraps* (Boston, 1840). [*212]
R: 212

404. Jones, Sir William, *The Works of Sir William Jones* (1799).
MD: 530; Unspec: 618, 662

*405. Jonson, Ben, *The Works of Ben Jonson, Which were formerly Printed in Two Volumes, are now Reprinted in One. To which is added A Comedy, Called The New Inn. With Additions never before Published* (London: Herringman [etc.], 1692). [*Sealts #302]
WJ: 416; WW: 440f; Unspec: 95, 100, 213, 440a, 442a
  Bartholomew Fair: CM: 291b
  The Gipsies Metamorphosed: CM: 330a?
  Masque of Blacknesse: JM: 193, 668!
  Masque of Queenes: JM: 441b
  "An Ode to Himself": TIM: 160; MP: 441b
  Volpone: CM: 479a; Unspec: 100

406. Josephus, Flavius, *The Works of Flavius Josephus*, trans. Whiston (New York, 1853); or, *The Works of Josephus*, trans. Robert Traill (London, 1847–51). [*315]
C: 315

*407. Judd, Sylvester, *Margaret. A Tale of the Real and Ideal, Blight and Bloom; Including Sketches of a Place Not Before Described, Called Mons Christi* (Boston: Jordan & Wiley, 1845). [*Sealts #303]
P: 101 [r 124], 139, 159, 265, 504, 511c; Unspec: 123, 146

K

408. Kant, Immanuel.
R: 283, 441; M: 283, 441; MD: 283, 303, 441, 686b; P: 283, 303, 441; Unspec: 283

409. Kant, Immanuel, *The Critique of Pure Reason* (1781).
MD: 211, 713; P: 211; BB: 211

Keats, John.
MD: 407; Unspec: 686b

409a. Keats, John, "La Belle Dame sans Merci" (1820).
M: 511a

410. Keats, John, *Endymion* (1818).
M: 213, 226, 345a, 488; P: 181; CM: 504b

411. Keats, John, "Lamia" (1820).
M: 226; P: 181; TIM: 326

412. Keats, John, Letter to Benjamin Bailey (23 January 1818) in *The Letters of John Keats*, ed. John Gilmer Speed (New York, 1883), 1, 162; or, *The Poetical Works and Other Writings of John Keats*, ed. Harry Buxton Forman (London, 1883), 3, 106. [*374]
BB: 374?

413. Keats, John, Letter to John Hamilton Reynolds (3 May 1818).
P: 181

414. Keats, John, "Ode on Melancholy" (1820).
P: 181, 555, 561b

414a. Keats, John, "Ode to a Nightingale" (1820).
BP: 441b

415. Keats, John, "On First Looking into Chapman's Homer" (1816).
C: 315

416. Keats, John, "To Sleep" (1838).
P: 555

417. Kempis, Thomas a, *Imitation of Christ* [*De imitatione Christi*] (translated into English c. 1450).
JM: 489?

417a. "The King of the Southern Sea" [song], *Sailors' Magazine*, 16 (Dec. 1843), 129. [*718]
MD: 718

418. Kinglake, Alexander William, *Eothen* (1844).
C: 228, 315; Unspec: 228, 273b

Kipling, Rudyard.
JM: 441b

419. Kipling, Rudyard, *The Light That Failed*, authorized ed. (New York: United States Book Co., [c. 1890]). [*Sealts #309]
Unspec: 478

*420. Kirkland, Caroline Matilda Stansbury, *Holidays Abroad; or, Europe from the West* (New York: Baker & Scribner, 1849). [*Sealts #311]
Unspec: 622

421. Kitto, John, *Cyclopaedia of Biblical Literature* (1845).
MD: 165, 182!, 229, 248, 334, 339, 377c, 436, 481c, 506, 532, 651a; B: 517; CM: 459c, 503a; C: 315; WW: 512b; Unspec: 223, 534d, 651a

421a. Kitto, John, *Daily Bible Illustrations* (1st ed., 1852; New York: Robert Carter, 1860), vol. 6 [out of eight; commentary on the Book of Isaiah]. [*503a]
CM: 503a

The Knickerbocker, or New-York Monthly Magazine: see 77a, 135, 143, 259, 582, 747a, 747b.

*422. Knight, Charles, ed., *London* (London: Knight, 1841–44), 6 vols. in 3. [*HH; Sealts #312]
MD: 229; PMP: 500b; IP: 448; PB: 576; Unspec: 213

423. Knight, Charles, ed., *Mind Among the Spindles, A Selection from the Lowell Offering* (London: C. Knight, 1844). [*524]
PB: 524

423a. Knox, John, *A New Collection of Voyages* (1767).
MD: 377c

424. Knox, Robert, *An Account of the captivity of Capt. Robert Knox, and other Englishmen, in the island of Ceylon* (1681).
R: 273b; WJ: 273b, 491; Unspec: 100

*425. Kotzebue, Otto von, *A New Voyage round the World, in the Years 1823, 24, 25, and 26* (London: Colburn & Bentley, 1830). [*Sealts #313]
T: 7; O: 10, 16, 17, 133, 133c, 475b, 480

425a. Kotzebue, Otto von, *Voyage of Discovery in the South Sea*, etc. (London, 1821) in Phillips's *Collection of Voyages*, vol. 6. [*182]
MD: 182

426. Krusenstern, Adam Ivan, *Voyage round the World, in the Years 1803–1806* (London, 1813). [*229]
MD: 229?

L

*427. La Bruyere, Jean de, *The Works of M. De La Bruyere. In Two Volumes. To Which Is Added the Characters of Theophrastus. Also the Manner of Living with Great Men; Written after the Manner of Bruyere, by N. Rowe* (London: Bell, 1776). [*Sealts #314]
Unspec: 175!, 213, 265

428. Lacepede, Etienne de, *Oeuvres du Comte de Lacepede* (Paris, 1836). [*148]
MD: 148?

Laertius, Diogenes: see 216.

Lalla Rookh: see 504.

429. Lamartine, Marie-Louis-Alphonse de, *Pilgrimage to the Holy Land* (1835).
C: 315, 333

*430. Lamb, Charles, *Specimens of English Dramatic Poets, Who Lived about the Time of Shakspeare. With Notes. By Charles Lamb* (New York: Wiley & Putnam, 1845). [*Sealts #318]
MD: 82a; P: 576b; Unspec: 213, 440a, 440e, 477

*431. Lamb, Charles, *The Works . . . A New Edition* (London: Moxon, 1848). [*Sealts #316; see also Sealts #315]
R: 212; TBB: 317; HHM: 513; MD: 48, 51, 213, 229; B: 463, 517; PB: 576; CM: 365a, 440c, 487a, 503a; BB: 521?; Unspec: 92, 100

Lamb, Charles: see also 686.

*432. la Motte-Fouque, Friedrich Heinrich Karl, Freiherr de, *Undine, and Sintram and His Companions. From the German* (New York: Wiley & Putnam, 1845). [*Sealts #319]
M: 213, 226!, 283, 345a, 481c, 488; WW: 283; Unspec: 303

Landor, Walter Savage.
TIM: 441b?

432a. Landor, Walter Savage, "Past Ruined Ilion" (1831).
TIM: 441b?

Langdon, E. G.: see 598.

433. Langsdorff, George H. von, *Voyages and Travels in Various Parts of the World . . . 1803–1807* (London, 1813). [*480]
T: 86, 133!, 213, 228, 460; O: 461, 480, 557; MD: 133, 182, 201

433a. Lanier, Sidney, *The Science of English Verse* (1880).
JM: 488a

434. La Perouse, Jean-Francois de.
Unspec: 228

‹*435. La Rochefoucauld, Francois, Duc de, Prince de Marcillac, *Reflections and Moral Maxims . . . With an Introductory Essay by Sainte-Beuve and Explanatory Notes* (London: Hotten, [187-]). [*Sealts #321]
HHM: 254; CM: 254

"The Last of the Boatmen": see 516.

‹436. Lavater, Johann Caspar, *Essays on Physiognomy* (published in German, 1775–78; in English, 1789–98). [Sealts #322]
OZ: 130, 189; M: 130, 148, 189, 283; R: 148, 283; WJ: 189; MD: 130, 182, 189, 229, 283, 344, 474; P: 148, 189, 283; CM: 189, 283; C: 283; BB: 344; Unspec: 571

Lavengro: see 71.

The Lawyer's Story: see 469b.

*437. Lay, William, and Cyrus M. Hussey, *A Narrative of the Mutiny, on Board the Ship Globe, of Nantucket, in the Pacific Ocean, Jan. 1824. And the Journal of a Residence of Two Years on the Mulgrave Islands; with Observations on the Manners and Customs of the Inhabitants* (New London, Conn.: Lay & Hussey, 1828). [*Sealts #323]
T: 461d?; MD: 147, 229, 461d

438. *Lazarillo de Tormes* (1553). [Sealts #324]
IP: 265; Unspec: 236

439. Ledyard, John.
BC: 173?
See also 661.

440. Leech, Samuel, *Thirty Years from Home, or A Voice from the Main Deck, being the Experience of Samuel Leech, who was for Six Years in the British and American Navies: Was Captured in The British Frigate Macedonian: Afterwards Entered the American Navy, and Was Taken in the United States Brig Syren, by the British Ship Medway* (Boston: Charles Tappan, 1843). [*491]
R: 212; WJ: 133, 312, 345a, 419, 437, 490, 491!, 543, 684

441. Leggett, William, "Brought to the Gangway," New York *Mirror*, 11 (19 April 1834), 329–31; collected in *Naval Stories* (New York, 1834). [*207]
WJ: 207 [r 429], 334a, 437, 490

441a. Leggett, William, "Merry Terry," in *Naval Stories* (1834).
BB: 334a

442. Leggett, William, "A Watch in the Main-Top," first collected in *Tales and Sketches by a Country Schoolmaster* (1829), and reprinted in the second edition of *Naval Stories* (1835). [*429]
WJ: 429

Leigh Hunt's Journal: A Miscellany: see 723b.

443. Leonard, Levi W., *The Literary and Scientific Class Book, Embracing the Leading Facts and Principles of Science* (Keene, N.H., 1825 [or later edition]). [*Sealts #325a]
Unspec: 455, 571

Leopardi, Giacomo: see 722, 729.

444. Lesage, Alain-Rene, *The Adventures of Gil Blas of Santillane* (1715–35).
MD: 165, 182, 229

444a. Lesage, Alain-Rene, *Le diable boiteux* (1707).
CM: 440c

Lewes, G. H.: see 578.

445. Lewis, Matthew Gregory, *The Monk* (1796).
P: 187a, 198

Life in a Man-of-War: see 498.

Life on Board a Man-of-War: see 79.

446. Linnaeus, Carolus, *Systema naturae* (1776). [*148]
MD: 148?, 201

Linton, William: see 209.

446a. *Literary World* articles, *Literary World*, 1 (Feb. 1847).
HHM: 512b; JM: 512b; TIM: 512b

Literary World: see also a, 46b, 205, 253, 260, 446a, 507, 578, 579, 580, 598, 701, 754.

Littell's Living Age: see 25a, 25b, 577a.

447. Little, George, *Life on the Ocean* (1843).
R: 212

448. Livy, *The History of Rome*, trans. George Baker, in *Classical Library* (New York: Harper, [18—]), vols. 24–28. [*Sealts #147]
CM: 245

449. Lobo, Father Jerome, *A Voyage to Abyssinia* (translated into English in 1735 by Samuel Johnson).
MD: 268

450. Locke, John, *Essay concerning Human Understanding* (1690).
M: 143, 226; MD: 371; B: 619a?

451. Lockhart, John Gibson, *Reginald Dalton* ([New York: Duyckinck, 1823?]). [*Sealts #327a]
F: 209; P: 209

452. Lockwood, John A., "Flogging in the Navy," *United States Magazine, and Democratic Review*, 25 (August 1849), 97–115 [first of five articles, August through Dec. 1849]. [*327; *490]
WJ: 327!, 490, 662a

*453. *The London Carcanet. Containing Select Passages from the Most Distinguished Writers. From the Second London Edition* (New York: Peabody, 1831). [*Sealts #331]
F: 213; Unspec: 163, 169, 175, 200, 212, 440a, 440e, 488a

454. Longfellow, Henry Wadsworth, "The Building of the Ship" (1849).
WJ: 338?; MD: 338

*454a. Longfellow, Henry Wadsworth, *Evangeline, a Tale of*

Acadie, 5th ed. (Boston: Ticknor, 1848). [*Sealts #332]
E: 499b?

454b. Longfellow, Henry Wadsworth, *Hiawatha* (1855).
CM: 440c

455. Longfellow, Henry Wadsworth, *Hyperion* (1839).
P: 104a [r 104b], 338?

456. Longfellow, Henry Wadsworth, *Kavanagh* (1849).
P: 104a, 181, 338; C: 338?

457. Longfellow, Henry Wadsworth, "The Village Blacksmith" (1841).
MD: 171, 338

458. Lowell, James Russell, *A Fable for Critics* (1848).
P: 499; CM: 161, 254, 265, 499

Lucca, Signor Gaudentio di: see 215.

458a. *Lucian of Samosota from the Greek with the Comments and Illustrations of Wieland and Others*, trans. William Tooke (London: Longman, Hurst, Rees, Orme, & Brown, 1820), 2 vols. [*481c]
MD: 143, 481c

458b. "Lucian," *Cornhill Review*, 36 (Sept. 1877), 336–48. [*148b]
Unspec: 148b?

459. Lyell, Sir Charles, *Elements of Geology*, 2d ed. (London, 1841). [*153]
M: 153

460. Lyell, Sir Charles, *Geological Evidences of the Antiquity of Man* (1863).
MP: 180, 512b

460a. Lyell, Sir Charles, *The Principles of Geology* (1830–33).
M: 459a

461. Lyell, Sir Charles, *A Second Visit to the United States of North America* (1849).
MD: 583?; Unspec: 583?

Lynn News: see 259a.

Lytton, Edward George Earle Lytton Bulwer-Lytton, First Baron: see Bulwer-Lytton.

M

‹462. Macaulay, Thomas Babington Macaulay, First Baron, *Essays, Critical and Miscellaneous* in *The Modern British Essayists* ([Philadelphia: Carey & Hart, 1847–49]), vol. 1. [*Sealts #359]
M: 32; CM: 254

*463. Macaulay, Thomas Babington Macaulay, First Baron, *The History of England from the Accession of James II* (New York: Harper, 1849–61), vols. 1 and 2. [*Sealts #335; see also Sealts #336–37]
BC: 342, 365a, 504b; Unspec: 213

*464. Macgregor, John, *The Rob Roy on the Jordan, Nile, Red Sea, and Gennesareth, &c. A Canoe Cruise in Palestine and Egypt, and the Waters of Damascus . . . With Maps and Illustrations* (New York: Harper, 1870). [*Sealts #340]
C: 333

464a. Machiavelli, Niccolo, *The Prince* (1513; first published English translation, 1640).
Unspec: 708?

*465. Mackay, Charles, ed., *Songs of England. The Book of English Songs* (London: Houlston & Wright, [1857]). [*Sealts #342]
BB: 172a; Unspec: 146, 315, 382

466. Mackenzie, Alexander Slidell, *The Life of Paul Jones* (1841).
IP: 213 [r 685], 317, 440d, 481e

*467. Macpherson, James, *Fingal, an Ancient Epic Poem, in Six Books: Together with Several Other Poems, Composed by Ossian the Son of Fingal. Translated from the Galic Language, by James Macpherson*, 2d ed. (London: Becket & De Hondt, 1762). [*Sealts #343]
M: 30, 32, 200, 226, 345a; R: 212, 380; MD: 87; Unspec: 213

*468. Macpherson, Robert, *Vatican Sculptures, Selected, and Arranged in the Order in Which They Are Found in the Galleries, Briefly Explained* (London: Chapman & Hall, 1863). [*Sealts #344]
Unspec: 527

‹*469. Macy, Obed, *The History of Nantucket; Being a Compendious Account of the First Settlement of the Island by the English, together with the Rise and Progress of the Whale Fishery; and Other Historical Facts Relative to Said Island and Its Inhabitants. In Two Parts* (Boston: Hilliard, Gray, 1835). [*Sealts #345]
MD: 84, 133!, 147, 165, 176a, 182, 229, 274a, 377c; C: 179, 213; Unspec: 176a, 213, 214

"Magnetic Influences": see 135.

469a. *Maha-Parinibbana-Sutta*, ed. R. C. Childers (London, 1878). [*512b]
JM: 512b?

469b. Maitland, James A., *The Lawyer's Story; Or, The Wrongs of the Orphans. By a Member of the Bar*, chapter 1 published as an advertisement in the New York *Times* (18 Feb. 1853) or the New York *Tribune* (18 Feb. 1853). [*599a]
B: 599a!, 674b

470. *Making a Passage, or Life in a Liner* (1844). [*228]
R: 228?

471. Malory, Sir Thomas, *Le Morte Darthur* (1485).
B: 503?

472. Malthus, Thomas Robert, *An Essay on the Principle of Population* (1798; 2d ed., rewritten and augmented, 1803).
M: 185, 226; PB: 524

473. Malthus, Thomas Robert, *An Inquiry into the Nature and Progress of Rent* (1815).
PMP: 524

474. Malthus, Thomas Robert, *Observations on the effects of the Corn Laws, and of a rise or fall in the price of Corn on the agriculture and general wealth of the country* (London: J. Johnson, 1814); 3d ed. published in 1815, with *The grounds of an opinion on the policy of restricting the importation of foreign corn*, as an appendix. [*524]
PMP: 524; PB: 524

Man-of-War's-Man: see 476a.

*475. Mangan, James Clarence, *Poems . . . With Biographical Introduction by John Mitchel* (New York: Haverty, 1859). [*Sealts #347]
BP: 488a; JM: 488a; Unspec: 143, 243, 275, 315

‹*476. *The Mariner's Chronicle; Being a Collection of the Most Interesting Narratives of Shipwrecks, Fires, Famines, and Other Calamities Incident to a Life of Maritime Enterprise*, by Archibald Duncan (Philadelphia: Humphreys, 1806). [*Sealts #194]
R: 162; Unspec: 162, 182, 229

476a. *Maritime Scraps . . . by a Man-of-War's-Man* (1838).
WJ: 334a

477. Marlowe, Christopher, *Plays*. [*Sealts #348]
MD: 229, 266a, 377c; P: 576b; UP: 213; Unspec: 95, 100, 139, 440a
   The Tragical History of Doctor Faustus (1604): MD: 131a, 139, 148a, 229, 253, 311, 397a; Unspec: 303

Marryat, Frederick.
R: 36, 37, 44; MD: 51; Unspec: 213

477a. Marryat, Frederick, *Frank Mildmay* (1829).
M: 576d?

478. Marryat, Frederick, *Jacob Faithful* (1834).
R: 359 [r 384]

479. Marryat, Frederick, *The King's Own* (1830).
WJ: 508c?; BB: 270?

480. Marryat, Frederick, *Mr. Midshipman Easy* (1836).
T: 391?; R: 481c; WJ: 141, 700; BB: 391

481. Marryat, Frederick, *Peter Simple* (1834).
R: 34, 37, 38, 212!, 481c

481a. Marryat, Frederick, *The Phantom Ship* (1839).
M: 500c?; R: 500c, 508c; WJ: 500c?; MD: 500c?; BB: 500c?, 508c?

482. Marryat, Frederick, *Poor Jack* (1840).
Unspec: 703

482a. Marston, John, *The Malcontent* (1604).
WJ: 456

482b. Marston, John, "To everlasting *Oblivion*" (1598).
MP: 441b

483. Martial, Marcus Valerius Martialis, *Epigrams*, trans. Cowley (London: Bohn, 1865 *et seq.*). [*345]
P: 479b; BB: 345, 710

Marvel, Ik [or Ike]: see 501.

‹*484. Marvell, Andrew, *The Poetical Works . . . With a Memoir of the Author* (Boston: Little, Brown, 1857). [*Sealts #351]
MD: 300; BP: 488a; C: 488a; TIM: 441b; BB: 138, 345!, 441b, 466, 488a, 584; WW: 488a; Unspec: 378

485. Mather, Cotton, *Magnalia Christi Americana* (1702).
MD: 345a; LRM: 180a, 213, 334, 345a, 621; ATT: 135, 334, 512, 621; CM: 254, 334, 375a, 479a, 705

486. Mather, Increase, *An Essay for the Recording of Illustrious*

Providences [*Remarkable Providences*] (1684).
MD: 334?

*487. Mathews, Cornelius, *Behemoth: A Legend of the Mound Builders* (1839), reprinted in *The Various Writings* (New York: Harper, 1863 [i.e., 1843]). [*Sealts #352]
MD: 274a, 308!

488. Mathews, Cornelius, *Chanticleer: A Thanksgiving Story of the Peabody Family* (1850).
CDD: 470

489. Mathews, Cornelius, *Motley Book* (New York, 1838). [*301]
MD: 301?

489a. Maturin, Charles Robert, *Melmoth the Wanderer* (1820).
P: 187a, 576b; IP: 576b

490. Maundeville, John de.
M: 22

490a. Maurice, John Frederick Denison, *Theological Essays* (1853).
CM: 503a

491. Maurice, Thomas, *History of the Hindostan* (1795–99).
M: 365a; MD: 365a; Unspec: 365a, 662

492. Maurice, Thomas, *Indian Antiquities: or, Dissertations, Relative to the Ancient Geographical Divisions of Hindostan* (1793–1800).
M: 365a, 375; MD: 182!, 273b, 365a, 530; P: 365a; B: 365a?; CM: 365a; Unspec: 365a, 618, 662

493. Maury, Matthew F., *Explanations and Sailing Directions to Accompany the Wind and Current Charts* (Washington, 1851). [*201]
MD: 182, 201!

*494. Mayo, Sarah Carter Edgarton, *The Flower Vase; Containing the Language of Flowers and Their Poetic Sentiments* (Lowell, Mass.: Powers & Bagley, 1844). [*Sealts #353]
M: 226

495. Mayo, William Starbuck, *Kaloolah; or, Journeyings to the Djebel Kumri* (1849).
M: 481c?; MD: 229, 274a, 362!

496. McCloud, Donald, "The History of a Cosmopolite," review of *Fifty Years in both Hemispheres, or Reminiscences of the life of a former Merchant*, by Vincent Nolte, *Putnam's Monthly Magazine*, 4 (Sept. 1854), 325–30. [Sealts #413]
CM: 702?

*497. McNally, William, *Evils and Abuses in the Naval and Merchant Service Exposed: With Proposals for Their Remedy and Redress* (Boston: Published by Cassady & March, For the Author, at No. 8 Wilson's Lane, 1839). [*293; *490]
R: 212, 416; WJ: 293!, 345, 416, 419, 490, 491!; BB: 345, 416

*497a. Melville, Sir James, *The Memoires of Sir James Melvil of Hal-Hill . . . Now Published from the Original Manuscript. By George Scott* (London: Boulter, 1683). [*Sealts #355]
Unspec: 440a

*497b. *The Men of the Time; or, Sketches of Living Notables* (New

York: Redfield, 1852). [*Sealts #356]
Unspec: 686b

*498. Mercier, Henry James, [and William Gallop], *Life in a Man-of-War, or Scenes in 'Old Ironsides' during Her Cruise in the Pacific*, By a Fore-Top-Man (Philadelphia: Bailey, 1841). [*Sealts #357a]
WJ: 154!, 182, 212, 213, 221, 228, 334a, 416, 419, 437, 490, 491!; MD: 182?, 491?

498a. *The Mermaid Series. The Best Plays of the Old Dramatists* (London: Vizetelly or Unwin, 1887–19[–?]). [*Sealts #358]
Unspec: 80a

"The Metaphysics of Bear Hunting": see 749.

"Method of Taking the Whale": see 51.

498b. Mickle, William Julius, "Inquiry into the Religious Tenets and Philosophy of the Brahmins," supplement to the translation of Camoens's *Lusiad* in Alexander Chalmers, ed., *The Works of the English Poets* (London, 1810), vol. 21, pp. 713–33. [*273b]
MD: 273b

Mickle, William: see also 111.

Military and Naval Magazine: see 752a.

498c. Milton, John, *Areopagitica: a Speech of Mr. John Milton for the Liberty of Unlicensed Printing to the Parliament of England* (1644).
M: 200; TBB: 200; P: 200; C: 200

‹*499. Milton, John, *The Poetical Works of John Milton. With Notes, and a Life of the Author*, A New Edition (Boston: Hilliard, Gray, & Co., 1836). [*706]
F: 100, 200; T: 200, 310!, 577, 592; O: 200, 480; RE: 200; M: 200!, 226, 375, 686b; RP: 200; R: 200!, 229a, 375, 439a, 504c; WJ: 200, 229a, 375, 416, 662a; TBB: 200; MD: 146, 200!, 225, 229, 229a, 273a, 291b, 347a, 375, 377c, 552, 558, 595, 616, 648; P: 181, 200, 229a, 403; CDD: 200; E: 200!, 387; IP: 200; PB: 200; IMC: 200; TP: 200; CM: 200!, 229a, 254, 334, 355, 440c, 487a, 504b, 598?, 686a, 705; BP: 139, 200, 304, 377b, 441b, 508a, 512b, 617; C: 200, 315, 461b; JM: 512b; TIM: 200, 229a, 377b, 439a, 441b; BB: 139, 172a, 198, 200, 213a, 217, 222, 229a, 263, 274, 345, 366a, 377b, 390, 440d, 458, 472, 476, 641a, 686b; TT: 200; WW: 377b, 440f; MG: 200; UP: 213; Unspec: 146, 200!, 229a, 375, 621, 706, 711a

499a. Milton, John, *Of Education* (1644).
WJ: 200

500. *A Miraculous, and Monstrous, but yet most true, and certayne discourse, of a Woman (now to be seene in London) of the age of threescore yeares, or there abouts, in the midst of whose forehead (by the wonderfull worke of God) there groweth out a crooked Horne, of foure ynches long* (London: imprinted by Thomas Orwin to be sold by Edward White, dwelling at the little North dore of Paules Church, at the Signe of the Gun, 1588). [*456]
WJ: 456?

501. Mitchell, Donald Grant [Ik Marvel, pseud.], *Reveries of a*

Bachelor; or, A Book of the Heart (1850).
IMC: 656?

"Mocha Dick": see 143, 582.

*502. Montaigne, Michel Eyquem de, *The Complete Works of Michael de Montaigne; Comprising; The Essays (Translated by Cotton); The Letters; The Journey into Germany and Italy; Now First Translated; A Life, by the Editor; Notes from all the Commentators; The Critical Opinions of Eminent Authors on Montaigne; The Eloges of Mm. Jay and Villemain; A Bibliographical Notice of all the Editions; and Copious Indexes*, by William Hazlitt (London: John Templeman, 1842). [Sealts #366; *441; *462]
M: 146, 178, 227, 381, 441; R: 441; WJ: 146, 178, 229a; MD: 146, 178, 229 [r 441], 229a, 301!, 381, 441, 481d; P: 146, 227, 381; IMC: 178; CM: 660; JM: 377b; BB: 146, 166, 178, 229a, 345, 348, 381!, 441; MP: 146, 166, 178, 301, 377b, 381, 660; Unspec: 213, 226, 229a, 441!, 462!, 686b

502a. Montaigne, Michel Eyquem de, *Essays*, trans. John Florio (1603).
Unspec: 440a

*502b. Montalembert, Charles Forbes Rene de Tryon, Comte de, *The Life of Saint Elizabeth, of Hungary, Duchess of Thuringia . . . Translated by Mary Hackett. The Introduction Translated by Mrs. J. Sadlier* (New York: Sadlier, 1870). [*Sealts #368]
Unspec: 504a

503. Montgomery, James, *World Before the Flood* in *The British Poets of the Nineteenth Century* (1828).
MD: 143

Montreal *Pilot*: see 676.

Moore, Thomas, *Life of Lord Byron*: see 107.

‹*504. Moore, Thomas, *The Poetical Works . . . Collected by Himself . . . With a Memoir* (Boston: Little, Brown, 1856 [1854?]). [*Sealts #370]
F1: 212; M: 32; MD: 478
   Lalla Rookh (1817): F1: 212, 333; F2: 84; M: 116, 333, 478, 488, 530; MD: 128a, 478, 532
   The Loves of the Angels (1823): M: 226; WJ: 478

505. More, Sir Thomas, *Utopia* (1516).
UP: 166, 377b, 686b

506. Morgan, Joseph, *A Complete History of Algiers* (1728).
WJ: 491; Unspec: 100

*507. Morgan, Lewis H., *League of the Ho-de-no-sau-nee or Iroquois* (Rochester, 1851), Advance excerpt from Book 2, chapter 2, "New Year's Festivities of the Iroquois," published in *Literary World*, 7 (28 Dec. 1850), 521–23. [*Sealts #326; *229]
MD: 229!

*508. Morgan, Sydney Owenson, Lady, *The Wild Irish Girl; a National Tale*, 4th American ed. (New York: Scott, 1807). [*Sealts #371]
Unspec: 187a, 380

*509. Morrell, Benjamin, *A Narrative of Four Voyages to the South Sea, North and South Pacific Ocean, Chinese Sea, Ethiopic and Southern Atlantic Ocean, Indian and Antarctic Ocean. From the Year 1822 to 1831* (New York: Harper, 1832). [*Sealts #372]
E: 648a; Unspec: 212, 226

Morrell, Benjamin: see also 389.

Mozart, Wolfgang A.: see 225.

510. Muller, Johannes, and Friedrich Henle, *Systematische Beschreibung der Plagiostomen . . . mit sechzig Steindrucktafeln* (Berlin: Verlag von Veit & Comp., 1841). [*226]
M: 148, 226

"The Murder of Philip Spencer": see 320.

511. Murray, John, *A Handbook for Travellers in Syria and Palestine* (London: John Murray, 1858). [*315]
C: 315!

512. Murray, Lindley, *English Grammar* (1795).
MD: 165, 182

513. Murray, Lindley, *The English Reader: or, Pieces in Prose and Poetry, Selected from the Best Writers* ([2d Canandaigua ed., 1819]). [*Sealts #380]
F: 213; M: 479c, 488a; MD: 479c; CM: 254; WW: 440f; Unspec: 143, 146, 200, 440a, 440e, 464, 479c, 488a, 557b

513a. Murrell, John A., *Pictorial Life and Adventures of John A. Murrell* [numerous mid-nineteenth-century printings by T. B. Peterson & Brothers of Philadelphia among their cheap editions "Suitable for the Parlor, Library, Sitting-Room, Railroad or Steamboat reading"]. [*705]
CM: 705

514. Mushet, Robert, *The Book of Symbols*, 2d ed. (London, 1847). [*143]
M: 143; MD: 143; P: 143

"The Mutiny of the *Somers*": see 681.

"The Mutiny on the Somers": see 649.

N

514a. Nabbes, Thomas, "Upon excellent strong Beere which he drank at the Towne of Wich in Worcester shire where Salt is made" [seventeenth-century song].
R: 504c

514b. *Napoleon's Dream Book* [pamphlet] (1843).
R: 576d?; Unspec: 576d?

Nature in Disease: see 579a.

515. Neale, W. J., *History of the Mutiny at Spithead and the Nore; with an Enquiry into its Origin and Treatment* (London, 1842). [*419]
WJ: 419?

516. Neville, Morgan, "The Last of the Boatmen," *The Western Souvenir* (Cincinnati, 1828). [*191]
MD: 191

New-England Magazine: see 573, 752a.

*517. *The New England Primer; Containing the Assembly's Catechism; the Account of the Burning of John Rogers; a Dialogue between Christ, a Youth, and the Devil; and Various Other Useful and Instructive Matter. Adorned with Cuts. With a Historical Introduction, by Rev. H. Humphrey* (Worcester: Howland, [183–?]). [*Sealts #384]
MD: 229, 440e, 578, 623

New York American: see 360.

New-York Daily Tribune: see 310c.

New York *Herald*: see 29a, 373a.

New York *Mirror*: see 209, 441.

New York Spirit of the Times: see 713a.

New York *Times*: see 469b, 646.

New York *Tribune*: see 259a, 380, 469b.

*518. Nichols, George Ward, *The Story of The Great March. From the Diary of a Staff Officer. By Brevet Major George Ward Nichols, Aid-de-Camp to General Sherman* (New York: Harper, 1865). [*Sealts #384a]
BP: 377b, 388

*519. Nicol, John, *The Life and Adventures of John Nicol, Mariner* (Edinburgh: W. Blackwood, 1822). [*429; *490]
WJ: 212, 419, 429!, 490, 491!

520. Niebuhr, Barthold Georg, *History of Rome* (1827–28), translated into English by J. C. Hare and Bishop Thirlwall in 1828–42.
C: 315; Unspec: 146, 283, 303

521. Niebuhr, Carsten, *Travels through Arabia and Other Countries in the East* (Edinburgh, 1792). [*532]
MD: 532

522. Nietzsche, Friedrich Wilhelm.
Unspec: 182, 303

Nolte, Vincent: see 496.

North, Christopher: see John Wilson.

North American Review: see 256a, 681.

523. *North Western Gazette and Galena Advertiser* (17 July 1840). [*213]
Unspec: 213?

524. Norton, Andrews, *The Evidences of the Genuineness of the Gospels* (1837, 1844).
M: 436; WJ: 436; MD: 436, 440b, 534d; C: 436; TIM: 436, 512b; Unspec: 534d

Nott, J. C.: see 388.

O

Oberon: see 758.

525. O'Brien, Fitz-James, "Our Young Authors—Melville," *Putnam's Monthly Magazine*, 1 (Feb. 1853), 155–64. [Sealts #413]
BT: 603?

*525a. O'Connor, Evangeline Maria (Johnson), *An Analytical Index to the Works of Nathaniel Hawthorne, with a Sketch of His Life* (Boston: Houghton, Mifflin, 1882). [*Sealts #387]
WW: 440f!

*525b. Oken, Lorenz, *Elements of Physiophilosophy* (London: Printed for the Ray Society, 1847). [*Seals #387a]
MD: 481d

526. Olafsson, Eggert, and Bjarni Palsson, *Travels in Iceland*, in *A Collection of Modern and Contemporary Voyages and Travels* (London, 1805), vol. 2. [*148]
MD: 148?

527. *Old Wine in New Bottles or Spare Hours of A Student in Paris*. [*565]
WJ: 565?

528. Olmsted, Francis Allen, *Incidents of a Whaling Voyage. To Which Are Added Observations on the Scenery, Manners and Customs, and Missionary Stations of the Sandwich and Society Islands* (New York, 1841). [*201]
T: 133; O: 480; M: 576d; MD: 147, 182, 201, 229, 487

Omar Khayyam: see 269.

"The Origin of the Arabian Nights' Entertainments Considered": see 598.

529. "The Original Confidence Man in Town.—A Short Chapter on Misplaced Confidence," Albany *Evening Journal* (28 April 1855); reprinted by Springfield *Daily Republican* (5 May 1855). [*484]
CM: 254, 479a!, 484!, 487a, 504b, 544, 686a, 705

530. Osgood, Frances Sargent Locke, *The Poetry of Flowers and the Flowers of Poetry* (1841).
M: 142!, 198, 226, 345a, 488

Ossian: see 467.

531. O'Sullivan, John, "The Great Nation of Futurity," *United States Magazine, and Democratic Review*, 6 (Nov. 1839), 430. [Seals #531; *518]
WJ: 419, 518

"Our Young Authors—Melville": see 525.

532. Ovid, trans. Dryden, Pope, Congreve, Addison, and Others, in *Classical Library* (New York: Harper, [18—]), vols. 20–21. [*Seals #147]
MD: 229, 334; CM: 254, 440c; TIM: 222

533. Owen, Richard, "Observations on the Basilosaurus of Dr. Harlan (Zeuglodon cetoides) Read January 9, 1839" in *Transactions of the Geological Society of London*, 2d series, 6 (1842), 69–79. [*201]
MD: 201, 588

533a. Oxenford, John, "Iconoclasm in German Philosophy," *Westminster Review and Foreign Quarterly Review*, 60 (1 April 1853), 388–407. [*534a]
B: 534a?, 619a?

P

534. Paine, Thomas, *The Age of Reason* (1794–95).
C: 315

535. Paine, Thomas, *The Rights of Man* (1791–92).
C: 369, 503; BB: 369, 503, 559

Palestine: see 511, 538, 667a, 668, 769.

536. Paley, William, *The Evidences of Christianity* (1794).
BC: 342, 365a

537. Paley, William, *Natural Theology; or Evidences of the Existence and Attributes of the Deity* (1802).
MD: 201, 229, 481d, 623; P: 481d; PMP: 481d; PB: 481d

537a. Paley, William, *Reasons for Contentment* (1792).
PMP: 481d; PB: 481d; CM: 481d

*538. Palmer, Edward Henry, *The Desert of the Exodus; Journeys on Foot in the Wilderness of the Forty Years' Wanderings; Undertaken in Connection with the Ordnance Survey of Sinai and the Palestine Exploration Fund ... With Maps and Numerous Illustrations from Photographs and Drawings Taken on the Spot by the Sinai Survey Expedition and C. F. Tyrwhitt Drake* (New York: Harper, 1872). [*Sealts #396]
C: 213, 333!

538a. Palmer, William Pitt, ode, Pittsfield *Sun* (6 Nov. 1834). [*461c]
M: 461c?; JM: 461c?

539. Park, Mungo, *Travels in the Interior of Africa* (1799).
BC: 173!, 557a; Unspec: 198, 228

*540. Parkman, Francis, *The California and Oregon Trail: Being Sketches of Prairie and Rocky Mountain Life* (New York: Putnam, 1849). [*Sealts #397]
RP: 123, 129, 146, 200, 254, 394, 712; R: 394; MD: 394, 712; CM: 394

541. Parkman, Francis, *History of the Conspiracy of Pontiac* (1851).
CM: 254, 394

542. Pascal, Blaise, *Pensees* (1670).
R: 212; MD: 181, 330, 441; P: 181, 330, 441

543. Pascal, Blaise, *Provincial Letters* (1656–57).
P: 181

543a. Payne, John Howard, *Clari; or, The Maid of Milan* (1823).
C: 461b?, 512b?

Peabody, Elizabeth Palmer: see 710.

543b. Peacock, Thomas Love, *Headlong Hall* (1816).
C: 512b; MG: 512b?

*544. *The Penny Cyclopaedia of the Society for the Diffusion of Useful Knowledge* (London: Charles Knight, 1833–43). [*MKB]
R: 481; WJ: 490! [r 491], 491, 662a!, 715!; MD: 628!, 693a; IP: 685; Unspec: 148

545. *Penny Magazine of the Society for the Diffusion of Useful Knowledge* (1832, 1833, 1834).
R: 212, 481
See also 599.

546. Petronius, Gaius, *Petronii arbitri satyricon* (printed in Latin, 1499; in English, 1694).
P: 181?

*547. *The Picture of Liverpool; or Stranger's Guide*, A New Edition, Considerably Enlarged (Liverpool: printed by Jones and Wright, 1808). [*132]
R: 132!, 212, 213, 481, 504c; Unspec: 212

Pigeon, Edward, *The Fossil Remains of the Animal Kingdom*: see 186, vol. 11.

548. Pinkerton, J., *Voyages and Travels* (London, 1808), vol. 2. [*181]
P: 181?

Pinto, Ferdinand Mendez: see 77b.

Pittsfield *Sun*: see 380b, 538a, 731, 737a.

Plato.
M: 178, 488, 686b; MD: 178, 181; P: 178, 181, 318; CM: 72, 178, 254; Unspec: 686b

548.1. Plato, *Apology* (published in English, 1775).
M: 686b; Unspec: 686b

548a. Plato, *Meno* (published separately in English, 1869).
CM: 365a, 686b

‹549. Plato, *Phaedon; or, A Dialogue on the Immortality of the Soul*, trans. Dacier (New York: William Gowan, 1833). [*143]
M: 143, 146, 686b; R: 143; WJ: 143, 416, 686b; MD: 117, 143, 178, 229, 416, 675, 686b; P: 143, 181, 675; CDD: 143, 470, 686b; C: 143; BB: 143; MP: 143; Unspec: 143!, 146, 212, 675

550. Plato, *Phaedrus* (published in English, 1792).
M: 143, 534c, 686b; MD: 143, 229, 686b; P: 143, 181, 511d, 686b

551. Plato, *Republic* (published in English, 1763).
M: 143, 146, 686b; R: 143, 146, 686b; WJ: 143, 686b; MD: 143, 229, 686b; P: 143, 686b, 693b; TP: 686b; UP: 686b; Unspec: 91

552. Plato, *Symposium* [no separate ed. in Melville's lifetime; see 555].
M: 229a; P: 143, 178, 181, 511d, 686b; TIM: 441b; Unspec: 143

553. Plato, *Timaeus* (published in English, 1820).
M: 143, 318, 686b; MD: 318

554. Plato, Taylor-Sydenham version (1804). [*143]
M: 143, 233; Unspec: 686b

‹555. Plato, *Works*, trans. Henry Cary, Henry Davis, and George Burges, 6 vols. (Bohn, 1848–54). [*143]
M: 143; R: 143; MD: 143, 686b; CM: 686b; BB: 143!, 345; Unspec: 143!, 686b

556. Pliny the Elder, Gaius Plinius Secundus.
MD: 148?

557. Plotinus, *Select Works of Plotinus*, trans. Thomas Taylor (London, 1817). [*143]
M: 686b; P: 143, 318; Unspec: 143

558. Plutarch, "On Isis and Osiris" (printed in Greek and English, 1774).
MD: 655

558a. Plutarch, *Parallel Lives*, trans. Sir Thomas North (1579).
Unspec: 440a

559. Plutarch, *The Philosophy Commonly Called the Morals*, trans. Philemon Holland, 2d ed. (London, 1657). [*181; *301]
M: 301, 686b; MD: 143, 165, 229, 301, 365a, 377c, 686b; P: 143, 181; IMC: 143; C: 143; Unspec: 534d

560. Plutarch, *Plutarch's Lives*, trans. John and William Langhorne (1770).
R: 143, 146; WJ: 143, 146; B: 621; TF: 621; JM: 512b; TIM: 146, 166, 229a, 326, 377b, 454!, 488a, 512b, 525, 686b; BB: 454!

‹*561. Poe, Edgar Allan, *The Works of the Late Edgar Allan Poe, with a Memoir by Rufus Wilmot Griswold and Notices of His Life and Genius by N. P. Willis and J. R. Lowell* (New York: Blakeman & Mason, 1859). [*Sealts #404a]
P: 58, 462b, 504d, 551a, 576b; B: 60, 70; LRM: 62; BT: 62, 68, 70; BC: 66; ATT: 90
  "The Assignation": F2: 337; R: 337
  "A Descent into the Maelstrom": R: 229; MD: 229, 291b
  Eureka: CM: 313
  "The Fall of the House of Usher": MD: 353, 516; P: 181?, 551a; BC: 537
  "How to Write a Blackwood Article": WJ: 491?; MD: 491?; BT: 549
  "Ligeia": P: 551a
  "MS. Found in a Bottle": MD: 469a
  The Narrative of Arthur Gordon Pym of Nantucket (1837–38): T: 231, 481c; O: 291a; M: 638; R: 198, 626; MD: 229, 231, 291b, 440e, 643; IP: 685; CM: 481a?; BP: 377b; JM: 626; Unspec: 481a
  "A Predicament: The Scythe of Time": BT: 549
  "The Premature Burial": P: 181?
  "The Raven": B: 265
  "The System of Doctor Tarr and Professor Fether": BC: 537

"Thou Art the Man": CM: 440c
"William Wilson": B: 352?

Poe, Edgar Allan: see also 310c.

‹*562. Pope, Alexander, *The Poetical Works ... with a Life, by Rev. Alexander Dyce* (Boston: Little, Brown, 1856). [*Sealts #405]
O: 480; MD: 229; P: 492; TIM: 222; WW: 489?; Unspec: 265

563. Porter, David, *Journal of a Cruise Made to the Pacific Ocean, by Captain David Porter, in the United States Frigate Essex, In the Years 1812, 1813, and 1814* (1815).
T: 1, 6!, 133!, 133c, 178, 213, 228, 273b, 460, 512c, 721; O: 480; M: 228; E: 109!, 134!, 166, 173, 178, 180a, 213, 379, 387, 421, 428, 535, 604, 621, 648a, 721

*564. Porter, Jane, *Thaddeus of Warsaw* (Flatbush: Riley, 1809). [*Sealts #406]
Unspec: 380

Potter, Israel: see 721.

564a. Prescott, William Hickling, *History of the Conquest of Peru* (1847).
WJ: 662a

565. Prescott, William Hickling, *History of the Reign of Ferdinand and Isabella the Catholic* (1838).
MD: 266; BC: 266; Unspec: 236, 266

566. Priestley [or Priestly], Joseph, *The Doctrine of Philosophical Necessity Illustrated* (1777).
M: 481d, 607; B: 328, 483, 534a, 619a

567. Prior, Matthew, "Alma or the Progress of the Mind" (written in 1718).
O: 14; M: 226 [r 424]

568. Proclus, *The Six Books of Proclus . . . on the Theology of Plato*, trans. Thomas Taylor (London, 1816). [*143; *226]
M: 143!, 213, 226, 233!, 488, 686b; CM: 143, 233; Unspec: 686b

569. "Psalm 18. First Part. L. M./ Deliverance from despair" in *The Psalms and Hymns . . . of the Reformed Protestant Dutch Church in North America*, compiled by Dr. John H. Livingston in 1789, expanded in 1830 and 1846, and approved by the General Synod in 1846. [*272]
MD: 272!, 441b

570. Purchas, Samuel, *Hakluytus Posthumus, or Purchas his Pilgrimes, contayning a History of the World in Sea Voyages and Land Travell by Englishmen and others* (1625).
MD: 182, 201, 229

571. Purchas, Samuel, *Purchas his Pilgrimage, or Relations of the World and the Religions observed in all Ages* (1613).
M: 333

572. *Putnam's Magazine. Original Papers on Literature, Science, Art, and National Interests* (New York, 1853–70). [*Sealts #413]
CM: 625
See also 129, 156, 237, 256, 388, 496, 525, 581, 709, 740.

Q

Quarterly Review: see 596.

573. Quicksand, Timothy, "Dead Letters, Opened and Burned by the Postmaster-General, Revived and Published by Timothy Quicksand," *New-England Magazine*, 1 (1831), 505–11. [*522]
MD: 522?; B: 522

R

574. Rabelais, Francois, *The Works . . . Translated from the French. With Explanatory Notes by Duchat, Ozell, and Others* ([London: Smith, Miller, 1844?]). [*Sealts #417]
M: 26, 31, 32, 101, 116, 129, 133, 163a, 178, 181a, 198, 204, 213, 226!, 265!, 274a, 301, 345a, 441, 481c, 488, 557, 585, 638; WJ: 178; MD: 89!, 95, 178, 229, 265, 291a, 301!, 341, 377c, 441, 481c; P: 115; IP: 265; CM: 73, 178, 254, 441; Unspec: 67, 123, 146, 226, 274a

Radcliffe, Ann.
T: 187a; R: 187a; P: 187a; BC: 187a; ATT: 187a, 380; BB: 187a; Unspec: 187a, 380

574a. Radcliffe, Ann, *The Italian* (1797).
BC: 187a; BB: 187a

574b. Radcliffe, Ann, *The Mysteries of Udolpho* (1794).
T: 187a; C: 187a

575. Radcliffe, Ann, *The Romance of the Forest* (1791).
P: 181, 187a; BC: 187a?

*576. *The Rebellion Record: A Diary of American Events, with Docu-*

ments, Narratives, Illustrative Incidents, Poetry, Etc., ed. Frank
Moore (New York, 1861–69). [*129]
BP: 129!, 166!, 181a, 213, 304, 377b,
393, 441b, 512b, 556

Review of *Bleak House*, by Charles
Dickens: see 129.

577. Review of *Etudes sur les gla-
ciers*, by Louis Agassiz, *Edinburgh
Review* (April 1842), 27–57. [Sealts
#200; *571]
MD: 571?

Review of *Fifty Years in both
Hemispheres*, by Vincent Nolte:
see 496.

577a. Review of *God in Disease; or
the Manifestation of Design in
Morbid Phenomena*, by James F.
Duncan, M.D., *Littell's Living Age*
(4 Sept. 1852). [*504b]
CM: 504b?

*578. Review of *The Life of Maxi-
milien Robespierre*, by G. H. Lewes, *Literary World*, 5 (7 July 1849),
6. [*Sealts #326]
LRM: 576

*579. Review of *Nature, Addresses
and Lectures*, by R. W. Emerson,
"Emerson's Addresses," *Literary
World*, 5 (3 Nov. 1849), 374–76.
[*Sealts #326]
Unspec: 357

*579a. Review of *Nature in Dis-
ease*, by Jacob Bigelow, M.D.,
Harper's New Monthly Magazine,
10 (Jan. 1855), 282. [*Sealts #240]
CM: 487a

Review of *Poems*, by R. W. Emerson: see 253.

Review of *A Selection from the
Public and Private Correspondence of Vice-Admiral Lord Collingwood*: see 397.

*580. Review of *Travels in Peru,
during the years 1838–1842*, by Dr.
J. J. Von Tschudi, *Literary World*,
1 (27 Feb. 1847), 80–83. [*Sealts
#326]
P: 181?

Review of *Types of Mankind*, by J.
C. Nott and George R. Gliddon:
see 388.

*580a. Review of *Xenophon's
Memorabilia of Socrates*, ed.
Charles Anthon, *Literary World*, 3
(14 Oct. 1848), 726. [*Sealts #326]
M: 686b

581. Review of *Walden; or, Life in
the Woods*, by Henry D. Thoreau,
"A Yankee Diogenes," *Putnam's
Monthly Magazine*, 4 (Oct. 1854),
443–48. [Sealts #413]
Unspec: 499

582. Reynolds, Jeremiah N.,
"Mocha Dick: or the White Whale
of the Pacific: A Leaf from a Manuscript Journal," *The Knickerbocker, or New-York Monthly Magazine*, 13 (May 1839), 377–92.
MD: 52!, 54, 88, 96, 104 [r 114,
347a], 133, 147, 162, 165, 182, 198,
228, 229, 274a, 334, 345a, 440e, 596;
Unspec: 104 [r 212], 163a, 212, 213

*583. Reynolds, Jeremiah N., *Voy-
age of the United States Frigate
Potomac, under the Command of
Commodore John Downes, during
the Circumnavigation of the
Globe, in the Years 1831, 1832,*

1833, and 1834 (New York: Harper, 1835). [*Sealts #422]
JM: 166; Unspec: 162, 226, 274a

Reynolds, Jeremiah N.: see also 143.

*584. Reynolds, Sir Joshua, *The Literary Works ... To Which Is Prefixed a Memoir of the Author; with Remarks on His Professional Character, Illustrative of His Principles and Practice. By Henry William Beechy ... New and Improved Edition* (London: Bohn, 1855). [*Sealts #423]
Unspec: 527

584a. Rhys, John, *Lectures on the Origin and Growth of Religion as Illustrated by Celtic Heathendom: Hibbert Lectures, 1886* (London, 1888). [*365a]
BB: 365a?

Ribs and Trucks: see 752b.

585. Richardson, Charles, *A New Dictionary of the English Language* (1836, 1837).
MD: 201, 229

Richter, Johann Paul Friedrich [Jean-Paul].
M: 30; MD: 50, 79; P: 59

*586. Richter, Johann Paul Friedrich, *Flower, Fruit and Thorn Pieces: or, The Married Life, Death, and Wedding of the Advocate of the Poor, Firmian Stanislaus Sibenkas ... Translated from the German by Edward Henry Noel* (London: Smith, 1845). [*Sealts #424]
P: 146; Unspec: 146, 303

587. Richter, Johann Paul Friedrich, *Titan: A Romance*, trans.

Charles T. Brooks (Boston: Ticknor & Fields, 1862, 1863, or 1864). [*Sealts #425]
Unspec: 303

Ringbolt, Captain: see 146.

588. Roberts, George, *The Four Years Voyages of Capt. George Roberts ... With a ... Description and Draught of the Cape de Verd Islands* [attributed to Daniel Defoe] (London, 1726). [*599]
TG: 599?

*589. Robinson, Henry Crabb, *Diary, Reminiscences, and Correspondence ... Selected and Edited by Thomas Sadler* (Boston: Fields, Osgood, 1869). [*Sealts #428]
WW: 440f; Unspec: 146, 183, 303, 442a

‹590. Rousseau, Jean-Jacques, *Confessions* (1781, 1788). [Sealts #429]
T: 133, 146, 229a; O: 146; MD: 229; P: 181; CM: 229a; Unspec: 100, 133, 211, 213

591. Rousseau, Jean-Jacques, *Discourse on the Influence of Learning and Art* (1750).
O: 133

591a. Rowe, Nicholas, *The Fair Penitent* (1703).
R: 504c

592. Rowson, Susanna Haswell, *Charlotte Temple: a Tale of Truth* (pub. in England, 1791; in America, 1794).
P: 159

Rubaiyat of Omar Khayyam: see 269.

"The Ruins of Carthage": see 209.

593. Ruschenberger, William S. W., *A Voyage round the World* (Philadelphia, 1838). [*133]
O: 16, 133, 480; MD: 532

*593a. Ruskin, John, *Modern Painters* (London: Smith, Elder, 1846–60). [*Sealts #430; see also Sealts #431]
BT: 317

594. Russell, Michael, *Polynesia: or, an Historical Account of the Principal Islands in the South Sea*, in *Harper's Family Library* (New York: Harper, 1843). [Sealts #211; *461]
O: 16, 17, 133, 148, 461, 480!; Unspec: 571

595. Russell, William Clark, *The Wreck of the Grosvenor* (1877).
JM: 166, 213, 441b

S

596. "Sacred Geography," London *Quarterly Review*, 94 (March 1854), 357–[387?]. [*315; *333]
C: 315, 333

Sacy, Antoine-Isaac Silvestre de: see 206.

‹*597. Sa'di, *The Gulistan, or Rose-Garden; by Musle-Huddeen Shaik Sady, of Sheeraz. Translated from the Original, by Francis Gladwin, Esq. A New Edition* (London: Kingsbury, Parbury, & Allen, 1822). [*Sealts #434]
MD: 333; C: 315, 333; Unspec: 175, 333!

"Safety of Pacific Principles": see 12b.

*598. Sahal-ben-Haroun [E. G. Langdon], "The Origin of the Arabian Nights' Entertainments Considered," *Literary World*, 3 (12 Feb. 1848), 26–28; (26 Feb. 1848), 63–65; (18 March 1848), 123–25; (25 March 1848), 144–46; (13 May 1848), 284–86. [*Sealts #326]
M: 333

Sailors' Magazine: see 267, 417a, 626.

Saint Augustine: see 31.

599. "Saint Elmo's Fire," *Penny Magazine*, 14 (22 March 1845), 106–7. [*322]
MD: 322?

600. Saint-Evremond, Charles de Marguetel de Saint-Denis de, Letter to the Mareschal de Crequi (1671).
Unspec: 146

601. Sale, Lady Florentina, *Journal of the Disasters in Affghanistan, 1841–1842* (London: Murray, 1843). [*636]
MD: 636?

Salmagundi: see 384.

*602. Salt, Henry Stephens, *The Life of James Thomson ("B. V.") with a Selection from His Letters and a Study of His Writings* (London: Reeves & Turner, 1889). [*Sealts #435; see also Sealts #435a]
Unspec: 143

*603. Saltus, Edgar Evertson, *Balzac* (Boston: Houghton Mifflin, 1884). [*Sealts #436]
Unspec: 274

*604. Sands, Robert Charles, *Life and Correspondence of John Paul Jones, including his Narrative of the Campaign of the Liman* (New York, 1830). [*685]
IP: 108, 346, 469, 685!

*605. Sandys, George, *A Relation of a Journey Begun An. Dom.: 1610*, [5th ed.] (London: Sweeting, 1652). [*Sealts #436a]
C: 259, 315; Unspec: 125a

Satyricon: see 546.

Scenes in "Old Ironsides" During Her Cruise in the Pacific: see 498.

"The Sceptical Genius": see 722.

605a. Schiller, Johann Christoph Friedrich von, *The Ghost-Seer! From the German of Schiller* ([London: Bentley, 1849?]). [Sealts #438a]
MD: 303; Unspec: 125a, 187a

*606. Schiller, Johann Christoph Friedrich von, *The Poems and Ballads . . . Translated by Sir Edward Bulwer Lytton, Bart. With a Brief Sketch of the Author's Life* (Leipzig: Tauchnitz, 1844). [*Sealts #439]
WJ: 440e, 490, 491!, 494; MD: 165, 182, 229, 303, 377c; CM: 254, 303; C: 315, 637a; JM: 213; TIM: 326, 377b, 488a; Unspec: 123, 213, 260, 283, 303, 440e, 580, 637, 637a, 688

607. Schleiermacher, *Reden* [*On Religion: Speeches to its Cultured Despisers*] (1799; first translated into English, 1893). [*701]
Unspec: 701?

608. Schoolcraft, Henry Rowe, *The Indian in His Wigwam* (1848).
MD: 229?

Schopenhauer, Arthur.
BB: 229a, 247, 344, 345, 356; Unspec: 80a, 84, 129, 146, 265, 303, 335, 686b

*609. Schopenhauer, Arthur, *Counsels and Maxims; Being the Second Part of . . . Aphorismen zur Lebensweisheit . . . Translated by T. Bailey Saunders, M.A.* (London: Sonnenschein, 1890). [*Sealts #443; see also Sealts #444]
TIM: 488a; BB: 172a, 247, 324a, 345; Unspec: 274, 324a

*610. Schopenhauer, Arthur, *Religion: A Dialogue, and Other Essays . . . Selected and Translated by T. B. Saunders, M.A.* (London: Sonnenschein, 1890). [*Sealts #445]
BB: 172a, 247, 324a; Unspec: 139, 143, 274, 324a

*611. Schopenhauer, Arthur, *Studies in Pessimism, a Series of Essays . . . Selected and Translated by T. Bailey Saunders, M.A.*, 2d ed. (London: Sonnenschein, 1891). [*Sealts #446]
BB: 247, 324a; Unspec: 139, 183, 274, 324a

*612. Schopenhauer, Arthur, *The Wisdom of Life; Being the First Part of . . . Aphorismen zur Lebensweisheit . . . Translated with a Preface by T. Bailey Saunders, M.A.*, 2d ed. (London: Sonnenschein, 1891). [*Sealts #447]
BB: 324a, 345; Unspec: 183, 247, 274, 324a, 686b

‹*613. Schopenhauer, Arthur, *The World as Will and Idea . . . Translated from the German by R. B. Haldane, M.A., and J. Kemp, M.A.*,

2d ed. (London: Trubner, 1888).
[*Sealts #448]
P: 557?; TIM: 512b; BB: 172a, 274!,
324a, 344, 479; Unspec: 91, 146,
158, 247, 283, 315, 324a

614. Schouten, William Cornelius,
*The Relation of a Wonderful
Voiage Made by William Cornelius
Schouten of Horn* (London, 1619).
[*201]
MD: 201

*614a. Scogan, John, *Scoggin's
Jests; Full of Witty Mirth, and
Pleasant Shifts* (London: Thacker-
ay & Deacon, 1796). [*Sealts #449]
Unspec: 330a

*615. Scoresby, William, *An Ac-
count of the Arctic Regions, with a
History and Description of the
Northern Whale Fishery* (Edinburgh: Constable, 1820). [*Sealts
#450]
MD: 84, 147!, 148, 165, 177, 182!,
199, 201!, 213, 229, 278, 377c, 487,
693a

*616. Scoresby, William, *Journal of
a Voyage to the Northern Whale
Fishery; Including Researches and
Discoveries on the Eastern Coast
of West Greenland . . . in . . . 1822*
(Edinburgh: Constable,   1823).
[*Sealts #451]
MD: 177!, 182, 198, 199, 213, 229

Scott, Sir Walter.
F: 100

617. Scott, Sir Walter, *The Abbot*
(1820).
P: 181

618. Scott, Sir Walter, *The Bride of
Lammermoor* (1819).
P: 181?, 511c, 576b

619. Scott, Sir Walter, *Ivanhoe*
(1819).
F1: 212; P: 181?, 511c

‹*620. Scott, Sir Walter, *The Lay of
the Last Minstrel* (Edinburgh:
Black, 1855). [*Sealts #451a]
MD: 507

621. Scott, Sir Walter, *Letters on
Demonology   and   Witchcraft*
(1830).
MD: 486, 507

622. Scott, Sir Walter, *The Monas-
tery* (1820).
WJ: 416, 511a, 662a; P: 181, 198,
511c, 634

622a. Scott, Sir Walter, "Romance"
[essay], first published in *Encyclopedia Britannica* (1824) and reprinted in *Miscellaneous Prose*
(1827). [*397a]
Unspec: 397a

*623. Scott, Sir Walter, *Tales of a
Grand-Father, First Series, Being
Stories Taken from Scottish His-
tory* (Exeter, N.H.: Williams, 1833).
[*Sealts #454]
Unspec: 212

624. Scott, Sir Walter, *The Talis-
man* (1825).
C: 315

625. Scott, Sir Walter, *Waverley
Novels* (1829–33).
T: 488c; Unspec: 251

626. "The   Seaman's   Retreat,"
Sailors' Magazine (Nov. 1837).
[*481]
R: 481

627. Sedgwick, Catharine Maria, *Hope Leslie, or Early Times in the Massachusetts* (1827).
MD: 229?

628. Sedgwick, Catharine Maria, *The Poor Rich Man, and the Rich Poor Man* (1836).
PMP: 576, 622

629. *Self Teacher* (1834). [*Sealts #456a]
Unspec: 212

*630. Seneca, Lucius Annaeus, *Seneca's Morals by Way of Abstract. To Which Is Added, a Discourse under the Title of An After-Thought. By Sir Roger L'Estrange*, 15th ed. (London: Strahan [etc.], 1746). [*Sealts #458]
M: 136!, 143, 146, 226, 345a, 488, 623, 686b; R: 136; WJ: 136; MD: 136; CM: 136, 254; Unspec: 136!, 213, 229, 557b

*631. Seneca, Lucius Annaeus, *The Workes ... Both Morall and Naturall ... Translated by Tho. Lodge* [The Life of L. A. Seneca Described by J. Lipsius] (London: Stansby, 1614). [*Sealts #457]
CM: 254; Unspec: 229, 440a, 440e, 557b

*632. Sevigne, Marie (de Rabutin-Chantal), Marquise de, *The Letters of Madame de Sevigne to Her Daughter and Friends. Edited by Mrs. Hale* (Boston: Roberts, 1869). [*Sealts #459]
TIM: 377b, 512b?

633. Shaftesbury, Anthony Ashley Cooper, Third Earl of, *Character-istics of Men, Manners, Opinions, Times* (1711; revised ed. 1713).
M: 534c; MD: 534c; P: 146?, 534c; CM: 254, 435, 504b, 534c; C: 534c; BB: 534c; Unspec: 534c

Shakers: see 680.

‹*634. Shakespeare, William, *The Dramatic Works of William Shakspeare; with a Life of the Poet, and Notes, Original and Selected* (Boston: Hilliard, Gray, & Co., 1837). [*Sealts #460; see also Sealts #460a–65]
All Works: 347!, 396; F: 100; M: 265a, 481e; R: 481e, 504c, 534b; HHM: 172b, 644; MD: 53, 137, 139!, 148a, 164!, 172b, 213, 255 [r 281], 265a, 281, 291a, 377c, 440a, 481e, 487, 500, 558, 601; P: 172b, 440a; CM: 440a, 440c, 481e, 487a, 504b, 641; BP: 378; Unspec: 100, 123, 172b, 178, 211, 213, 378, 399, 440a, 440e, 499b, 630, 686b
Tempest: MD: 644; E: 173, 387, 619, 621; BT: 431; TP: 376; BP: 94; C: 315; JM: 377b, 512b; WW: 440f; MP: 193; Unspec: 442a
Merry Wives of Windsor: MD: 229
Twelfth Night: M: 265; P: 181; CM: 254, 686a; Unspec: 265
Measure for Measure: WJ: 440e; MD: 229, 644; TP: 173, 475; WW: 440f; UP: 305
Much Ado about Nothing: MD: 229; Unspec: 442a
Midsummer-Night's Dream: TP: 475, 621; CM: 213, 254, 440d, 705; TIM: 512b; WW: 440f
Love's Labor's Lost: MD: 229; P: 181?; WW: 440f
Merchant of Venice: M: 265; MD: 229, 265; CM: 254; BB: 345

As You Like It: M: 265; MD: 229, 265; E: 387, 619; CM: 213, 254, 686a, 705
All's Well That Ends Well: CM: 254
Taming of the Shrew: MD: 229
Winter's Tale: P: 181; CM: 213, 254, 479a, 686a, 705; C: 488a; BB: 198a, 264, 345; WW: 488a
Macbeth: MD: 112, 131a, 182, 183, 229, 265, 286, 298, 503, 611, 639, 644; P: 172b, 181, 486a, 504, 511c, 551a, 576b; TP: 173, 475; BP: 441b, 512b; JM: 512b
King Richard the Second: MD: 131a, 229, 644; P: 181
King Henry the Fourth, Part First: O: 480; M: 513; R: 568; WJ: 166, 481e, 568; HHM: 513; MD: 229; MP: 166, 513
King Henry the Fourth, Part Second: O: 480; M: 513; WJ: 166; MD: 265; CM: 705; MP: 166, 265, 513
King Henry the Fifth: MD: 229
King Henry the Sixth, Part Second: CM: 213, 254
King Richard the Third: O: 480; MD: 229, 649
King Henry the Eighth: O: 480; MD: 229
Troilus and Cressida: WW: 440f
Timon of Athens: MD: 644; P: 504, 511c; JR: 481e, 533; CM: 254, 639, 705; Unspec: 198, 533
Coriolanus: MD: 644; P: 511c
Julius Caesar: O: 480; MD: 112, 229, 503, 644
Antony and Cleopatra: MD: 112, 164, 229, 265, 578, 644; P: 181, 511c; IP: 503; WW: 440f; Unspec: 131a

Cymbeline: P: 181; TP: 173, 180a, 213, 331, 475, 621; CM: 173, 213, 254, 705
Pericles, Prince of Tyre: TP: 621?; CM: 254
King Lear: O: 480; M: 557; HHM: 131a, 229a; MD: 112, 131a!, 133a, 139, 164!, 165, 168, 184, 213, 229, 265, 298, 330, 440e, 463a, 473, 481e, 500, 578, 639, 644, 686b; P: 172b, 181, 504, 511c; IP: 346; CM: 157, 213, 254, 705; Unspec: 131a!, 198
Romeo and Juliet: MD: 112, 229, 503; P: 181, 258!, 481e, 503, 504, 511c, 551a, 576b; JM: 377b
Hamlet, Prince of Denmark: F: 213; O: 480; M: 481e; WJ: 491; MD: 92b, 112, 139, 168, 213, 229, 252, 291b, 481e, 596, 601, 644; P: 56, 101, 104a, 104b, 148a, 172b, 181!, 188, 213, 258, 265, 291b, 367, 441, 481e, 504, 511c!, 551a, 576b, 639, 686b, 717; IP: 265, 503; TP: 173; CM: 213, 254, 686a, 705, 717; C: 315, 441b; BB: 345; MP: 193; Unspec: 198
Othello, The Moor of Venice: R: 234; MD: 112, 229, 644; P: 181, 503, 504, 511c; BC: 234, 497a; TIM: 489; BB: 234, 345

*634a. Shakespeare, William, *The Poetical Works . . . With the Life of the Author. Cooke's Edition* (London: Cooke, [17—]). *The Poetical Works of William Collins. With the Life of the Author. Cooke's Edition* (London: Cooke, [17—]) [2 vols. in 1]. [*Sealts #464; see also Sealts # 460a]
M: 226; WW: 440f; Unspec: 213, 226

Shakespeare, William: see also 522a.

*635. Shelley, Jane Gibson, Lady, ed., *Shelley Memorials: From Authentic Sources ... To Which Is Added, an Essay on Christianity, by Percy Bysshe Shelley: Now First Printed* (Boston: Ticknor & Fields, 1859). [*Sealts #466]
TIM: 488a; WW: 440f; Unspec: 146, 200, 212, 442a

*636. Shelley, Mary Wollstonecraft Godwin, *Frankenstein: or, The Modern Prometheus. By the Author of "The Last Man" ... Revised, Corrected, and Illustrated with a New Introduction, by the Author* (London: Bentley, 1849). [*Sealts #467]
MD: 229, 363, 481e, 590; P: 181, 511c; BT: 65, 480a, 481e, 534, 547; Unspec: 187a, 380

637. Shelley, Percy Bysshe, *The Cenci* (1819).
WJ: 330; P: 181, 330, 693b!; Unspec: 330

‹*638. Shelley, Percy Bysshe, *Essays, Letters from Abroad, Translations and Fragments*, New Edition, ed. Mrs. Shelley (London: Moxon, 1852). [*Sealts #468]
M: 226, 488; MD: 129; P: 693b; TIM: 686b; JG: 686b; MG: 686b; Unspec: 139, 146, 200, 226, 229, 580, 621

‹*639. Shelley, Percy Bysshe, *The Poetical Works ... Edited by Mrs. Shelley. With a Memoir by James Russell Lowell* (Boston: Little Brown, 1857). [*Sealts #469]
P: 335; C: 652; TIM: 693b; Unspec: 100, 302

"Adonais": M: 150, 226, 265, 488; P: 273b; TIM: 326
"Alastor": F2: 488c; M: 213, 226, 345a, 440, 488
"Prometheus Unbound": MD: 195, 505!; P: 181, 291b; BP: 304; C: 319; Unspec: 229a
"Queen Mab": MD: 229, 229a, 347a; P: 181; Unspec: 229a

640. Sherburne, John Henry, *The Life and Character of John Paul Jones* (Washington, 1825, and New York, 1851). [*685]
IP: 108 [r 685], 346 [r 685], 469

‹*641. Sheridan, Richard Brinsley, *The Rivals* (1775) in *The Plays With an Introduction by Henry Morley*, 8th ed. (London: Routledge, 1887). [*Sealts #471]
F1: 212; F2: 212

Ship of Fools: see 74a.

641a. *The Shipwreck of the Alceste, an English frigate in the Straits of Gaspar, also the Shipwreck of the Medusa, French frigate on the coast of Africa with observations and reflections thereon* [pamphlet] (1846). [*416]
WJ: 416, 662a

642. Sibbald, Sir Robert, *A History, Ancient and Modern, of the Sheriffdoms of Fife and Kinross* (Cupar-Fife, 1803). [*165]
MD: 165, 182, 201, 229

643. Simms, William Gilmore, *Beauchampe: or, The Kentucky Tragedy* (1842).
P: 159

643a. Simms, William Gilmore, *Border Beagles* (1840).
CM: 705?

644. Simms, William Gilmore, *Guy Rivers* (1834).
P: 159

644a. Simms, William Gilmore, *Richard Hurdis* (1838).
CM: 705?

"Sir Patrick Spens": see 139.

645. Skelton, John, "Philip Sparrow" in *The Poetical Works of John Skelton: with notes and some account of the author and his writing by A. Dyce* (London: T. Rodd, 1843). [*425]
M: 425!

646. "Slaughter of the Innocents" [editorial], *New York Times* (22 July 1861), 4. [*698]
BP: 698

647. Sleeper, John Sherburne [Hawser Martingale, pseud.], "Impressment of Seamen" [sketch], *Tales of the Ocean, and Essays for the Forecastle* (1841). [*490]
WJ: 213, 214, 490, 491!, 684

648. Smith, Adam, *Inquiry into the Nature and Causes of the Wealth of Nations* (1776).
R: 156, 212, 373, 481!; CM: 254

649. Smith, Lieutenant H. D., "The Mutiny on the Somers," *American Magazine*, 8 (June 1888), 109–14. [*138]
BB: 138, 174, 181a, 213, 441b, 458

*650. Smith, Joseph Edward Adams, *Taghconic; or Letters and Legends about Our Summer Home. By Godfrey Greylock* [pseud.] (Boston: Redding, 1852). [*Sealts #478]
IP: 685; CM: 504b, 705

651. Smith, Sydney, *The Works* in *The Modern British Essayists* ([Philadelphia: Carey & Hart, 1847–49?]), vol. 3 (1848). [*Sealts #359]
R: 673; CM: 673; BB: 673

651a. Smith, Sir William, *Dictionary of Greek and Roman Antiquities* (1842).
WJ: 416?

Smollett, Tobias George.
O: 100?, 181a, 481c; R: 42; WJ: 139, 163a, 345a, 416, 568; MD: 49; Unspec: 122

652. Smollett, Tobias George, *The Adventures of Ferdinand Count Fathom* (1753).
O: 494a, 511a; WJ: 511a

653. Smollett, Tobias George, *The Adventures of Peregrine Pickle* (1751).
WJ: 213a, 282, 491

654. Smollett, Tobias George, *The Adventures of Roderick Random*, 10th ed. (London: Gardner [etc.], 1778; or London: Cochrane, 1831). [*Sealts #480]
O: 481c; WJ: 96, 107, 121, 129, 133, 178, 213, 345a, 416, 481c, 481e, 491, 575; MD: 301; Unspec: 123

654a. Smollett, Tobias George, *The Expedition of Humphry Clinker* (1771).
M: 282

"Socrates in Camden": see 88.

Somers Mutiny: see 181a, 320, 649.

655. Sophocles, trans. Thomas Francklin, in *Classical Library*

(New York: Harper, [18—]), vol. 14. [*Sealts #147]
MD: 286, 595; BB: 198a

Sotheby, William: see 758.

Southern Literary Messenger: see 701.

656. Southey, Robert, *Commonplace Book*, 2d ed. (1850). [*140]
MD: 140; Unspec: 593?

657. Southey, Robert, *The Doctor* (1834–47).
MD: 50, 229

*658. Southey, Robert, *The Life of Nelson* (New York: Harper, 1855). [*Sealts #481]
BP: 377b; BB: 172a, 213, 217, 274, 345!, 559

*658a. Southey, Robert, *Oliver Newman: A New-England Tale (Unfinished): With Other Poetical Remains* (London: Longman [etc.], 1845). [*Sealts #482]
Unspec: 686b

659. Southey, Robert, *Thalaba the Destroyer* (1801).
M: 22, 226, 345a, 488; MD: 229

660. "Spanish Ladies" [sea song].
WJ: 545; JM: 382

661. Sparks, Jared, *Life of John Ledyard* (1828).
MD: 229

Sparks, Jared: see also 280.

662. *Spectator* (1711–12, 1714).
R: 200; Unspec: 200
See also 3a.
   Spectator, no. 578 (9 Aug. 1714):
   MD: 229 [r 273], 478

*663. Spenser, Edmund, in Robert Anderson, ed., *Poets of Great Britain* (London and Edinburgh, 1792–93), vol. 2. [*692; see also Sealts #483]
F2: 637b; T: 637b; M: 213, 226 [r 424], 229a, 237!, 426, 462a, 488, 576d, 637b!; WJ: 146; MD: 146, 397a, 526, 595, 637b; P: 229a, 526, 622a, 634, 637b; E: 106, 109, 134, 173, 180a, 213, 379, 387!, 428, 451, 462a, 477, 526, 619, 637b!, 692, 693; IP: 213; BT: 173, 439a, 547, 576, 594, 637b!; BC: 349; PT: 146; TP: 331, 620, 637b; CM: 440c, 462a, 637b, 650; C: 315, 637b; JM: 351, 377b, 512b; TIM: 229a; BB: 146, 345; Unspec: 440a

664. Spinoza, Benedict (Baruch) de.
M: 31; MD: 165, 260; P: 181, 260; C: 260; Unspec: 260, 318

Springfield *Daily Republican*: see 263a, 529.

665. Squier, E. G., "Ancient Peru—its People and its Monuments," *Harper's New Monthly Magazine*, 7 (June 1853), 7–[38?]. [Sealts #240]
CM: 435?

St. Augustine: see 31.

Stael-Holstein, Anne-Louise-Germaine Necker, Baronne de [Madame de Stael].
Unspec: 622

‹666. Stael-Holstein, Anne-Louise-Germaine Necker, Baronne de, *Corinne; or, Italy . . . Translated by Isabel Hill; with Metrical Versions of the Odes by L. E. Landon; and a Memoir of the Authoress* (Lon-

don: Bentley, 1833 or later edition). [*Sealts #486]
R: 704; MD: 229?, 341, 377c, 704; P: 213, 303, 504, 511c, 651b; Unspec: 229, 704

*667. Stael-Holstein, Anne-Louise-Germaine Necker, Baronne de, *Germany . . . With Notes and Appendices, by O. W. Wight* (New York: Derby & Jackson, 1859). [*Sealts #487]
MP: 377b; Unspec: 133c, 139, 143, 146, 303, 315, 442a, 504a, 580, 665, 704, 705a

667a. Stanley, Arthur Penrhyn, newspaper accounts of his travels in Palestine during the winter of 1852 and the spring of 1853.
B: 707?

*668. Stanley, Arthur Penrhyn, *Sinai and Palestine in Connection with Their History . . . New Edition, with Maps and Plans* (New York: Widdleton, 1863). [*Sealts #488]
C: 170!, 183, 213, 315!, 333!, 441b, 540, 687; Unspec: 183, 442a

Stanley, Arthur Penrhyn: see also 596.

Starbuck, Hezediah: see 77a.

*669. Stedman, Edmund Clarence, *Poets of America* (Boston and New York: Houghton, Mifflin, 1885). [*Sealts #488a]
Unspec: 647, 691

669a. Stephens, John Lloyd, *Incidents of Travel in Central America* (1841) and *Incidents of Travel in Yucatan* (1843).
Unspec: 163a

Sterne, Laurence.
M: 30; MD: 229a; BB: 229a

670. Sterne, Laurence, *The Life and Opinions of Tristram Shandy, Gent.* (1760, 1761–62, 1765, 1767). [Sealts #490]
MD: 95, 229, 265, 301, 561a, 600b, 624; P: 265; CDD: 176, 600b, 621; TF: 600b; CM: 265!, 561a, 570, 600b; Unspec: 123, 341

671. Stewart, Charles S., *Journal of a Residence in the Sandwich Islands* (New York and London, 1828). [*287]
M: 287

*672. Stewart, Charles S., *A Visit to the South Seas, In the U. S. Ship Vincennes, During the Years 1829 and 1830* (New York, 1831). [*125]
T: 125, 129, 133!, 133c, 178, 213, 228, 273b, 460, 480, 512c; O: 133, 228, 461, 480!; WJ: 662a; Unspec: 198

673. Stirling, William, *Cloister Life of the Emperor Charles the Fifth* (1851, 1852).
BT: 621; BC: 342 [r 523, 528!], 365a [r 528!], 662b

674. Stone, William Leete, *Life of Joseph Brant—Thayendenegea: Including the Border Wars of the American Revolution* ([New York: Dearborn, 1838?]). [*Sealts #491a]
MD: 229

675. Stow, John, *The Chronicles of England* [later *The Annales of England*] (1580).
MD: 201

676. "A Strange Scene at a Theatre," Montreal *Pilot* (11 Dec. 1857). [*608]
BB: 608

677. Strauss, David Friedrich, *The Life of Jesus* (1835). [*303]
C: 283, 315; Unspec: 146, 283, 303

677a. Suckling, Sir John (1609–42), songs.
TIM: 512b?

Sue, Eugene.
P: 55

678. Sue, Eugene, *The Mysteries of Paris* (1842–43; first pub. in English, 1844).
WJ: 543

679. Sue, Eugene, *The Wandering Jew* (1844–45).
C: 652?

*680. *A Summary View of the Millennial Church, or United Society of Believers, Commonly Called Shakers. Comprising the Rise, Progress and Practical Order of the Society,* 2d ed., rev. (Albany: Van Benthysen, 1848). [*Sealts #459a]
MD: 197, 229, 440e, 487; Unspec: 146, 197

681. Sumner, Charles, "The Mutiny of the *Somers,*" *North American Review,* 57 (July 1843). [*459]
BB: 459

Swamy, Mutu Coomara: see 21.

682. Swedenborg, Emanuel, *A New Dictionary of Correspondences* (1794).
MD: 103?

Swift, Jonathan.
P: 519; Unspec: 67

683. Swift, Jonathan, *Gulliver's Travels* (1726).
T: 389?, 512c; M: 19, 21, 23, 29, 32, 111, 198, 204, 226, 377a, 638; P: 265

684. Swift, Jonathan, *A Tale of a Tub* (1704).
M: 226; WJ: 229a; CM: 394?, 471?, 570, 641

684a. Swinburne, Algernon Charles, *Poems and Ballads* (1866).
WW: 512b?

T

Taghconic: see 650.

685. *The Tales of the Genii.*
M: 29

*686. Talfourd, Sir Thomas Noon, *Final Memorials of Charles Lamb; Consisting Chiefly of His Letters Not Before Published, with Sketches of Some of His Companions* (London: Moxon, 1848). [*Sealts #317]
MD: 213, 229?; B: 463; Unspec: 213, 463

687. Taylor, Bayard, *Cyclopaedia of Modern Travel* (1856).
CM: 625

*688. Taylor, Bayard, *Views A-Foot; or, Europe Seen with Knapsack and Staff* (New York: Wiley & Putnam, 1846). [*Sealts #495]
R: 212; MD: 229?

Taylor, Bayard: see also 237.

‹689. Taylor, Jeremy, *The Rule and Exercise of Holy Dying* (Boston:

Little, Brown, [1864?]). [*Sealts #495a]

P: 181?; CM: 254; Unspec: 686b

690. Taylor, John, *The Scripture Doctrine of Original Sin Proposed to Free and Candid Examination* (London: [?], 1701). [*Sealts #496] MD: 485, 623; Unspec: 146

691. Taylor, John Orville, *The District School* (1834). [Sealts #497] Unspec: 212

692. Taylor, Thomas. MD: 675; P: 675; Unspec: 378, 675 See also 554, 557, 568.

Taylor, Tom: see 343.

693. Tegner, Esais, *Frithiof's Saga, or The Legend of Frithiof. By Esais Tegner. Translated from the Swedish* (London: Baily, 1835); or *Frithiof, a Norwegian Story, from the Swedish of Esais Tegner. By R. G. Latham* (London: Hookham, 1838). [*Sealts #500] M: 123, 133, 226, 345a; MD: 229; Unspec: 123, 226

694. Teniers, David. T: 7

695. Tennemann, Wilhelm Gottlieb, *A Manual of the History of Philosophy*, trans. Arthur Johnson (Oxford, 1832), or, trans. J. R. Morrell (London: Bohn, 1852). [*143] Unspec: 143

*696. Tennyson, Alfred Tennyson, Baron, *In Memoriam* (London: Moxon, 1850). [*Sealts #504; see also Sealts #505] C: 319; Unspec: 146

*697. Tennyson, Alfred Tennyson, Baron, *Poems* (Boston: Ticknor,

1842). [*Sealts #507b; see also Sealts #507a, 508] M: 139, 226, 440e, 557; TP: 62, 173, 316a, 475; C: 499a; JM: 377b, 512b; TIM: 693b; BB: 345; WW: 440f; Unspec: 440e

698. Tertullianus, Quintus Septimus Florens, *De praescriptionibus haereticorum* (printed in Latin, 1544; in English, 1722). WJ: 146?

Thackeray, William Makepeace. P: 504, 511c

698a. Thackeray, William Makepeace, *Catherine* (1839–40). P: 511c

699. Thackeray, William Makepeace, *The History of Henry Esmond, Esquire* (1852). IP: 559

700. Thackeray, William Makepeace, *The History of Pendennis* (1848–50). P: 181, 511c

701. Thackeray, William Makepeace, "Sorrows of Werther" [comic ballad], first appeared in the *Southern Literary Messenger* in 1853 and was reprinted in the *Literary World*, 13 (10 Dec. 1853), 313–14; later reprinted in "Thackeray as a Poet," *Putnam's Monthly Magazine*, 6 (Dec. 1855), 626. [*487; Sealts #413] CM: 254, 440c, 487a

*701a. Thackeray, William Makepeace, *Vanity Fair. A Novel without a Hero* (New York: Harper, 1848). [*Sealts #512] P: 511c

Thirty Years from Home: see 440.

Thomas a Kempis: see 417.

702. Thomas, Isaiah, *Massachusetts, Connecticut, Rhode-Island, New-Hampshire and Vermont Almanack* (1779–1820).
MD: 165

703. Thomas, R., *Interesting and Authentic Narratives of the most Remarkable Shipwrecks, Fires, Famines, Calamities, Providential Deliverances, and Lamentable Disasters on the Seas, in most Parts of the World* (entered for copyright in Hartford, Conn., in 1835).
[*156]
R: 156

703a. Thomson, James, *The Castle of Indolence* (1748).
JM: 377b

*704. Thomson, James, *The City of Dreadful Night, and Other Poems* (London: Reeves & Turner, 1880). [*Sealts #517]
Unspec: 95, 100, 139, 146, 163a, 247!, 291b, 297, 393

‹*705. Thomson, James, *Essays and Phantasies* (London: Reeves & Turner, 1881). [*Sealts #518]
C: 580; BB: 247; Unspec: 146, 247!, 303

*706. Thomson, James, *Satires and Profanities* [With a Preface by G. W. Foote] (London: Progressive Publishing Co., 1884). [*Sealts #519]
BB: 247

*707. Thomson, James, *A Voice from the Nile, and Other Poems With a Memoir of the Author by Bertram Dobell* (London: Reeves & Turner, 1884). [*Sealts #522]
Unspec: 131, 247

Thomson, James: see also 17.

*708. Thomson, William McClure, *The Land and the Book; or, Biblical Illustrations Drawn from the Manners and Customs, the Scenes and Scenery of the Holy Land* (New York: Harper, 1859). [*Sealts #523]
C: 315, 333!

709. Thoreau, Henry David, "An Excursion to Canada," *Putnam's Monthly Magazine*, 1 (Jan. 1853), 54–59, (Feb. 1853), 179–84, (March 1853), 321–29. [Sealts #413]
Unspec: 155? [r 499]

710. Thoreau, Henry David, "Resistance to Civil Government" in Elizabeth Palmer Peabody, ed., *Aesthetic Papers* (1849).
B: 155 [r 187, 499]; BB: 641a?

711. Thoreau, Henry David, *Walden, or Life in the Woods* (1854).
MD: 407; CDD: 503; PMP: 488b, 503; ATT: 257, 503, 508b, 512, 635; CM: 265, 440c, 504b; TIM: 166, 512b; BB: 710; MG: 512b

712. Thoreau, Henry David, "Walking" [essay] (1862).
CDD: 309?? [r 470], 317??, 440?, 503??

*713. Thoreau, Henry David, *A Week on the Concord and Merrimack Rivers* (Boston: Munroe, 1849). [*Sealts #524]
CDD: 176 [r 499], 503; ATT: 503?; CM: 133b, 161, 440c, 504b, 635; Unspec: 146, 155 [r 499], 257, 499b

Thoreau, Henry David: see also 581.

713a. Thorpe, Thomas Bangs, "The Big Bear of Arkansas," *New York Spirit of the Times* (21 March 1841) [first printing; later reprinted in *The Hive of "The Bee-Hunter"* (1854) and contemporary periodicals]. [*504b]
CM: 504b

*714. Thorpe, Thomas Bangs, "Remembrances of the Mississippi," *Harper's New Monthly Magazine*, 12 (Dec. 1855), 25–41. [*Sealts #240]
CM: 254, 334, 487a

Tocqueville, Alexis de: see de Tocqueville, Alexis-Charles-Henri Clerel.

715. Todd, Robert B., ed., "Cetacea" in *The Cyclopaedia of Anatomy and Physiology* (London, 1835, 1836), vol. 1. [*201]
MD: 182, 201

The Token: see 394.

Tooke, William: see 458a.

Tormes, Lazarillo de: see 438.

717. Tourneur, Cyril, *The Revenger's Tragedy* (1607).
P: 181?

718. Trimmer, Sarah Kirby, *An Easy Introduction to the Knowledge of Nature* (1780).
Unspec: 571

719. Trollope, Anthony, *North America* (1862).
CDD: 276; PMP: 276

719a. Trollope, Frances (Fanny) Milton, *Domestic Manners of the Americans* (1832).
WJ: 662a

720. Troyes, Chretien de, *Yvain and Lancelot* (c. 1170).
PB: 377?; IMC: 377?

*721. Trumbull, Henry, *Life and Remarkable Adventures of Israel R. Potter* (Providence: Printed by Henry Trumbull, 1824). [Sealts #407; *686]
R: 442a?; IP: 61, 74, 76, 80a, 97!, 100, 108!, 181a, 183, 198, 213, 317, 346, 361a, 440d, 442, 442a [r 686], 448, 481e, 498a, 507a, 559, 685!, 686

*721a. Tucker, Abraham, *An Abridgement* [by William Hazlitt] *of The Light of Nature Pursued . . . Originally Published . . . under the Name of Edward Search, Esq.* (London: Johnson, 1807). [*Sealts #529]
P: 481d; Unspec: 481d

722. Tucker, Henry F., "The Sceptical Genius" [essay on Leopardi] (1853?). [*641]
CM: 641?

723. Turnbull, John, *A Voyage round the World . . . 1800–1804* (Philadelphia, 1810). [*133]
O: 16, 133, 480

723a. Twain, Mark, *The Innocents Abroad* (1869).
C: 512b

*723b. "Two Hundred and Fifty Years Ago: From A Waste Paper Bag of T. Carlyle" [anonymous parody of Thomas Carlyle], *Leigh Hunt's Journal: a Miscellany for the Cultivation of the Memorable,*

the Progressive, and the Beautiful, 1 (London, 7 Dec. 1850) [first installment; second and third installments were published 21 Dec. 1850 and 11 Jan. 1851]. [*Sealts #325; *576a]
MD: 576a

724. Tyerman, Daniel, and George Bennet, *Journal of Voyages and Travels* (Boston: Crocker & Brewster; New York: Leavitt, 1832). [*226]
O: 111; M: 111 [r 226], 127, 133, 226, 488; MD: 111, 176a, 229; Unspec: 176a

U

725. Ulloa, Antonio de, *A Voyage to South America* (1758).
MD: 201?

726. *Uncle Philip's Conversations with Young People about the Whale Fishery, and Polar Regions* (London, 1837). [*229]
MD: 229

Undine: see 432.

United States Magazine, and Democratic Review: see 452, 531.

United States Magazine of Science, Art, Manufactures, Agriculture, Commerce and Trade: see 43a.

727. Urquhart, David, *The Spirit of the East* (1838).
C: 333

728. Urquhart, Sir Thomas [translation of first three books of Rabelais published 1653, 1693].
M: 129; MD: 95

V

*729. Valery, Antoine Claude Pasquin, known as, *Historical, Literary, and Artistical Travels in Italy, a Complete and Methodical Guide for Travellers and Artists . . . Translated with the Special Approbation of the Author, from the Second Corrected and Improved Edition by C. E. Clifton. With a Copious Index and a Road-Map of Italy* (Paris: Baudry, 1852). [*Sealts #533]
C: 315

730. Vancouver, George.
T: 7; O: 16

730a. Van Trump, P., *Cromwell and His Times; Lecture delivered before the American Union Academy of Literature, Art and Science, at Washington City, on Monday Evening, March 18, 1870* (Washington, D.C., 1871). [*172a]
BB: 172a?

731. "Various Items," Pittsfield *Sun* (17 Feb. 1853). [*553]
B: 553

*732. Vasari, Giorgio, *Lives of the Most Eminent Painters, Sculptors, and Architects: Translated from the Italian . . . With Notes and Illustrations Chiefly Selected from Various Commentators. By Mrs. Jonathan Foster* (London: Bohn, 1850–52). [*Sealts #534]
MG: 489

Vathek: see 54.

733. Vigny, Alfred-Victor, Comte de, *Servitude et grandeur militaires* (1835).
BB: 332, 354, 385

734. Virgil, The Eclogues translated by Wrangham, the Georgics by Sotheby, and the Aeneid by Dryden, in *Classical Library* (New York: Harper, [18—]), vols. 11–12. [*Sealts #147]
M: 480; CM: 254, 440c, 487a; C: 315

"The Vision of Sudden Death": see 205.

735. Volney, Constantin Francois de, *Travels Through Syria and Egypt in 1783, 1784, and 1785* (1787).
C: 315, 333

736. Voltaire, Francois-Marie Arouet de, *Candide* (1759).
P: 576b; MG: 489

736a. Voltaire, Francois-Marie Arouet de, *Memnon. Histoire Orientale* (1747).
P: 576b?

736b. Voltaire, Francois-Marie Arouet de, *Semiramis* (1749; first English translation, 1760).
P: 576b?

Von Chamisso, Adelbert: see 125.

737. Von Hardenberg, Friedrich Leopold, *Heinrich von Ofterdingen* (published in German, 1802; in English, 1842).
M: 226

Von Tschudi, J. J.: see 580.

W

737a. W., J., "Incense of the Heart" [poem], Pittsfield *Sun* (3 Dec. 1835). [*461c]
Unspec: 461c?

738. Wafer, Lionel, *A New Voyage and Description of the Isthmus of America, Giving an Account of the Author's Abode There* (London, 1699). [*165]
MD: 165?

*739. Walker, H. H., *The Comedie Humaine and Its Author, with Translations from the French of Balzac* (London: Chatto & Windus, 1879). [*Sealts #543]
Unspec: 183

740. Wallys, Philip, "About Niggers," *Putnam's Monthly Magazine*, 6 (Dec. 1855), 608–12. [Sealts #413]
BC: 299, 414

*741. Walpole, Horace, Earl of Orford, *Anecdotes of Painting in England*, Reprint of the Edition of 1786 (London: Alexander Murray, 1871). [*Sealts #543a]
Unspec: 527

742. Walpole, Horace, Earl of Orford, *The Castle of Otranto: A Gothic Story* (1764). [Sealts #544; see also Sealts #54]
P: 187a, 576b; BT: 439a; Unspec: 100, 187a, 380, 439a

*743. Walpole, Horace, Earl of Orford, *Letter Addressed to the Countess of Ossory, from the Year 1769 to 1797 . . . Now First Printed from Original Mss. Edited, with Notes, by the Rt. Hon. R. Vernor Smith* (London: Bentley, 1848). [*Sealts #545]
Unspec: 100?

744. Walpole, Horace, Earl of Orford, *The Mysterious Mother* (1768).
WJ: 411; P: 181, 187a, 411

745. Walton, Izaak, *Life of George Herbert* (1670).
Unspec: 378

Wandering Jew: see 362, 639, 679.

746. Warburton, Bartholomew Elliott George [known as Eliot Warburton], *Travels in Egypt and the Holy Land; or, The Crescent and the Cross* (Philadelphia, 1859). [*315]
C: 315

747. Ward, Edward [Ned], *The Wooden World Dissected in the Characters of: 1. A Ship of War* [etc.] (1707).
WJ: 543?

747.1. Warton, Thomas, *History of English Poetry* (1774–81).
Unspec: 686b

Washington National Intelligencer: see 195.

747a. Waters, John [pseud. for Henry Cary], "Discursive Thoughts on Chowder," *Knickerbocker* (July 1840), 26–28. [*274a]
MD: 274a
See also 747b.

747b. Waters, John [pseud. for Henry Cary], "Rambler [dated London, July 25]," *American* (21 Aug. 1840); reprinted in *Knickerbocker* (Nov. 1840). [*274a]
MD: 274a

Waters, John: see also 77a.

748. Watts, Isaac, *Hymns and Spiritual Songs* (1707).
MD: 165; CM: 504b?

749. Webber, Charles Wilkins [Charles Winterfield, pseud.], "The Metaphysics of Bear Hunt-ing; An Adventure in the San Saba Hills," *American Review* [later renamed *American Whig Review*], 2 (Aug. 1845), 171–88. [*678]
CM: 467, 678

‹750. Webster, John, *The White Divel* [or *Vittoria Corombona*] (1612) in *The Mermaid Series. The Best Plays of the Old Dramatists* (London: Vizetelly or Unwin, 1887–19[—?]), vol. 12, or in Robert Bell, ed., *Songs from the Dramatists* (London: Parker, 1854). [*Sealts #358 or Sealts #56]
BP: 372, 440f; WW: 351, 372, 377b, 440f, 689

751. Webster, Noah, *An American Dictionary of the English Language* (New York: Harper, 1846 or later edition). [*Sealts #550; see also Sealts #551–52]
MD: 201, 229, 478, 690

752. Weed, Thurlow, *Life of Thurlow Weed including his autobiography and a memoir* (1883–84).
CM: 504b?; BB: 213

Weekly Mirror: see 77b.

752a. Weld, Horatio Hastings, "A Chapter on Whaling," *New-England Magazine* (1835) [first printing; reprinted in *Military and Naval Magazine* (1835) and as the first chapter of H. H. Weld's *Ribs and Trucks* (1842)]. [*334a]
MD: 334a

752b. Weld, Horatio Hastings, *Ribs and Trucks, From Davy's Locker; being Magazine Matter Broke Loose, and Fragments of Sundry Things In-Edited* (Boston, 1842). [*229; *334a]
MD: 147!, 182, 229, 334a

See also 752a.

The Western Souvenir: see 516.

Westminster Review and Foreign Quarterly Review: see 533a.

753. "The Whale, and Whale Catching," *American Magazine of Useful and Entertaining Knowledge*, 2 (Sept. 1835), 5–7. [*229]
MD: 229?

*754. "What is Talked About" [article on the Confidence Man possibly written by Evert A. Duyckinck], *Literary World*, 5 (18 Aug. 1849), 132–34. [*Sealts #326]
CM: 357, 441a, 479a, 504b, 686a, 705

*755. Wheeler, Daniel, *Memoirs of the Life and Gospel Labours of the Late Daniel Wheeler* (London, 1842). [*480]
O: 16, 17, 133, 480

Whig Review: see 749.

Whitman, Walt.
Unspec: 686b

756. Whitman, Walt, *Drum-Taps* (1865).
BP: 647?

757. Whitman, Walt, editorial critiques of Grace Church in *Brooklyn Daily Eagle* (9 and 30 March 1846). [*657]
TT: 657?

Whitman, Walt: see also 88, 669.

758. Wieland, Christoph Martin, *Oberon* (1780); William Sotheby, *Oberon, a Poem from the German of Wieland* (London: Cadell & Davies, 1798). [*226]
M: 226, 345a, 488

759. Wilkes, Charles, *United States Exploring Expedition. During the Years 1838, 1839, 1840, 1841, 1842. Under the Command of Charles Wilkes, U.S.N.* (Philadelphia: Printed for the Congress of the United States by Sherman, 1844), vols. 1–5; (Philadelphia: Sherman, 1846), vol. 6. [*Sealts #532]
T: 228; O: 16, 133, 162, 215, 228, 461, 480!; M: 127!, 133, 162, 226, 228, 488; WJ: 662a; MD: 147, 162, 182, 199, 229, 290 [r 306], 323?, 600a?; CM: 254

760. Willis, Nathaniel Parker, "Hagar in the Wilderness" [poem] (1827).
M: 229?; MD: 420?

761. Willis, Nathaniel Parker, "Necessity for a Promenade Drive." Unspec: 238

761a. Wilson, Horace H., *Two Lectures on the Religious Practices and Opinions of the Hindus* (1840).
MD: 273b?

762. Wilson, James, *A Missionary Voyage . . . in the Ship Duff* (London, 1799). [*480]
O: 16, 480!; Unspec: 571

762a. Wilson, John [real name of Christopher North], essays on *Macbeth* and *Othello* [part of a series entitled "Dies Boreales" or "Christopher under Canvass"], *Blackwood's Edinburgh Magazine* (Nov. 1849, April 1850, May 1850). [*622a]
P: 622a

762b. Wilson, John, *The Foresters* (1825).
P: 366a?

763. Wilson, Thomas, *A Christian Dictionarie* (1612).
BB: 183? [r 345]

Winterfield, Charles: see 749.

764. Wither, George, *Hymnes and Songs of the Church* (1623).
MD: 229?

764a. Wolfe, Charles, "The Burial of Sir John Moore" (1817).
WJ: 511a

765. "Wondrous Tale of Alroy."
M: 18

‹*766. Wordsworth, William, *The Complete Poetical Works. Together With a Description of the Country of the Lakes in the North of England*, ed. Henry Reed (Philadelphia: James Kay, Jun. & Brother; Boston: James Munroe & Co.; Pittsburgh: C. H. Kay & Co., 1839). [*Sealts #563a]
WJ: 637; P: 547a, 551a, 561b, 637; CDD: 641?; E: 273b, 637, 716; CM: 254, 440c, 504b; C: 637; Unspec: 637!
   "Resolution and Independence": CDD: 179, 180a, 213, 350, 470, 637, 641

*767. *The Works of Eminent Masters, in Painting, Sculpture, Architecture, and Decorative Art* (London: Cassell, 1854). [*Sealts #564]
Unspec: 527

*768. Wortley, Lady Emmeline Stuart, *Travels in the United States* (1851), quoted in the *Literary World* (12 July 1851). [Sealts #326; *181]
P: 181?

769. Wright, Thomas, ed., *Early Travels in Palestine* (London: Bohn, 1848). [*315]
C: 315!

Y

770. "The Yankee Boy," *Democratic Press, and Lansingburgh Advertiser* (30 March 1839). [*212]
WJ: 212, 429

"A Yankee Diogenes": see 581.

771. *Yankee Doodle* (New York, 1846–47). [*Sealts #566]
TT: 657?

Yeoman's Gazette: see 259.

772. Young, Alexander, ed., *Chronicles of the First Planters of the Colony of Massachusetts Bay from 1623 to 1636* (1846).
MD: 229?

773. Young, Edward.
R: 212; MD: 212

774. *The Young Man's Own Book: A Manual of Politeness, Intellectual Improvement and Moral Deportment, Calculated to Form the Character on a Solid Basis and to Insure Respectability and Success in Life* (1832).
T: 178, 455

Z

*775. Zschokke, Heinrich, *The Bravo of Venice*, trans. M. G. Lewis, in *Vathek: An Arabian Tale . . . With Notes, Critical and Expository. The Castle of Otranto. By Horace Walpole. The Bravo of Venice [by Heinrich Zschokke]*

Translated by M. G. Lewis
(London: Bentley, 1849), Standard
Novels, no. 41. [*Sealts #54]
Unspec: 303

III

LIST OF
SCHOLARSHIP

SAMPLE ENTRY

Reference number

821. Scholar, Dubious P., "Rogers's *Flowers of Bermuda* and *Mardi*," *Peregrinations: A Journal of Voyage Literature*, 16 (1990), 13–26. 589a

Source number

General Reference Works

Coffler, Gail H., *Melville's Classical Allusions: A Comprehensive Index and Glossary* (Westport, Conn.: Greenwood Press, 1985).

Cowen, Wilson Walker, "Melville's Marginalia" (Ph.D. dissertation, Harvard University, 1965), 11 vols.

Little, Thomas Alexander, "Literary Allusions in the Writings of Herman Melville" (Ph.D. dissertation, University of Nebraska, 1948).

Maeno, Shigeru, *The Sources of Melville's Quotations* (Tokyo: Kaibunsha Ltd., 1981).

Small, Julianne, "Classical Allusions in the Fiction of Herman Melville" (Ph.D. dissertation, University of Tennessee, 1974).

1846
Reviews

1. Review of *Narrative of a Four Months' Residence* (Part I), *Athenaeum* (London), 19 (21 Feb. 1846), 189–91. Reprinted in *Littell's Living Age* (Boston), 9 (April, May, June 1846), 84–89.
563

2. Review of *Narrative of a Four Months' Residence*, "Herman Melville's Residence in the Marquesas," *Spectator* (London), 19 (28 Feb. 1846), 209–10. Reprinted in *Littell's Living Age* (Boston), 9 (April, May, June 1846), 82–84.
196

3. Review of *Narrative of a Four Months' Residence*, *Examiner* (London), (7 March 1846), 147–48.
189

4. Review of *Narrative of a Four Months' Residence*, *John Bull* (London), 26 (7 March 1846), 156.
196

5. Review of *Narrative of a Four Months' Residence* (Part III), *Critic* (London), n.s. 3 (28 March 1846), 315–20.
159

6. Review of *Typee*, "Recent Publications" [signed "B."], *National Anti-Slavery Standard* (New York), 6 (2 April 1846), 175.
563

7. Review of *Four Months' Residence in the Marquesas*, *Times* (London), (6 April 1846), 3.
89, 108, 120, 159, 186, 401, 425, 694, 730

8. Review of "The Story of Toby," *Guardian* (London), 28 (4 Nov. 1846), 445–47.
107

1847
Reviews

9. Review of *Omoo*, "Literary Notices," *Britannia* (London), (10 April 1847), 229–30.
Cooper

10. Review of *Omoo*, *Douglas Jerrold's Weekly Newspaper* (London), (1 May 1847), 533–34.
170, 425

11. Review of *Omoo*, "Notices of New Books," *Boston Daily Bee* (5 May 1847).
189

12. Review of *Omoo*, "Notices of Books," *Parthenon* (Schenectady, N.Y.), n.s. 1 (15 May 1847), 31.
Irving

13. Review of *Omoo*, "Adventures in the South Seas," *National Era* (Washington), 1 (27 May 1847), 2–3.
196

14. Review of *Omoo*, "Notes on New Books," *National Intelligencer* (Washington), (28 May 1847).
567

15. Review of *Omoo*, "Pacific Rovings," *Blackwood's Edinburgh Magazine*, 61 (June 1847), 754–67. Reprinted in *Eclectic Magazine* (New York), 11 (July 1847), 408–19.
159, 196

1848
Reviews

16. Review of *Typee* and *Omoo*, "Protestantism in the Society Islands," *United States Catholic Magazine and Monthly Review* (Baltimore), 7 (Jan. 1848), 1–10.
55, 425, 593, 594, 723, 730, 755, 759, 762

17. Review of *Typee* and *Omoo*, "Typee and Omoo," *Polynesian* (Honolulu), 4 (18 March 1848), 174.
55, 245, 425, 594, 755

1849
Reviews

18. [Chorley, Henry F.], review of *Mardi*, *Athenaeum* (London), no. 1117 (24 March 1849), 296–98. First paragraph reprinted in *Eclectic Magazine* (New York), 17 (May 1849), 144.
Carlyle, 165, Emerson, 765

19. Review of *Mardi*, *Atlas* (London), (24 March 1849), 185–86.
196, 683

20. Review of *Mardi*, "New Novels," *Literary Gazette* (London), 1679 (24 March 1849), 202–3.
150

21. Review of *Mardi*, under "The Literary Examiner," *Examiner* (London), 2148 (31 March 1849), 195–96.
83, 196, 683

22. Review of *Mardi*, "Literature," *New Monthly Magazine and Hu-*

morist (London), 85 (April 1849), 510–12.
490, 659

23. Review of *Mardi*, "Fiction," *Critic* (London), n.s. 8 (1 April 1849), 156–58.
683

24. Review of *Mardi*, *Home News III*, 55 (7 April 1849), 212.
Gray

25. Review of *Mardi*, "New Publications," *Daily Evening Transcript* (Boston), 20 (16 April 1849).
196

26. [Greene, Charles Gordon], review of *Mardi*, "Literary Notices," *Boston Post*, 34 (18 April 1849), [1].
574

27. Review of *Mardi*, "Notices of New Works," *Albion* (New York), n.s. 8 (21 April 1849), 189.
Carlyle

28. [?Duyckinck, Evert A.], review of *Mardi* (Part II), "Second Paper," *Literary World* (New York), 4 (21 April 1849), 351–53.
100, 119

29. Review of *Mardi*, *Spectator* (London), 22 (21 April 1849), 374–75.
18, 159, 683, 685

30. R[ipley, George], review of *Mardi*, *New-York Daily Tribune*, 9 (10 May 1849), [1].
Carlyle, 467, Richter, Sterne

31. Chasles, Philarete, "Voyages reels et fantastiques d'Hermann Melville," *Revue des deux mondes* (Paris), 2 (15 May 1849), 541–42, 561–70. Translated and printed

under "Parisian Critical Sketches" as M. Philarete Chasles, "The Actual and Fantastic Voyages of Herman Melville," *Literary World* (New York), 5 (4 Aug. 1849), 89–90, and (11 Aug. 1849), 101–3.
207, 348, 574, 664

32. Review of *Mardi*, *Morning Chronicle* (London), (19 May 1849), 6. Two paragraphs reprinted in the *Literary World* (New York), 4 (30 June 1849), 556.
159, Disraeli, 322, 462, 467, 504, 574, 683

33. Review of *Mardi*, *Sun* (London), 17,683 (29 May 1849), 3.
63, 371

34. Review of *Redburn*, *Spectator* (London), 22 (27 Oct. 1849), 1020–21. Reprinted in *Littell's Living Age* (Boston), 23 (29 Dec. 1849), 580–83.
481

35. Review of *Redburn*, "Literature," *Daily News* (London) (29 Oct. 1849), 2.
132, 189, 196

36. Review of *Redburn*, "Literature: Books Recently Published," *Morning Herald* (London) (30 Oct. 1849).
Marryat

37. [Hardman, Frederick], review of *Redburn*, "Across the Atlantic," *Blackwood's Edinburgh Magazine*, 66 (Nov. 1849), 567– 80.
Marryat, 481

38. Review of *Redburn*, *Athenaeum* (London), 1150 (10 Nov. 1849), 1131–33.
481

39. Review of *Redburn*, "Passages from New Books," *Literary World* (New York), 5 (10 Nov. 1849), 395–97.
196

40. Review of *Redburn*, "Reviews," *Literary World* (New York), 5 (17 Nov. 1849), 418–20.
196

41. Review of *Redburn*, "Literary Notices," *Boston Post*, 35 (20 Nov. 1849), [1].
196

42. [?Poe, Edgar Allan], review of *Redburn*, "Notices of New Works," *Southern Literary Messenger* (Richmond), 15 (Dec. 1849), 760–62.
Smollett

1850
Reviews

43. Review of *Redburn*, "Review of New Books," *Graham's Magazine* (Philadelphia), 36 (Jan. 1850), 94–95.
196

44. Review of *Redburn*, *Southern Quarterly Review* (Charleston, S.C.), n.s. 1 (April 1850), 259–60.
196, Marryat

45. R[ipley, George], review of *White-Jacket*, "Reviews of New Books," *New York Daily Tribune* (5 April 1850). Reprinted in *Littell's Living Age* (Boston), 25 (4 May 1850), 230–32.
Carlyle

46. Review of *White-Jacket*, *Christian Register* (Boston) (6 April 1850), 55.
189

47. Review of *White–Jacket*, "Literary Notices," *Knickerbocker Magazine* (New York), 35 (May 1850), 448.
189

1851
Reviews

48. Review of *The Whale*, *Morning Advertiser* (London) (24 Oct. 1851).
83, 100, Carlyle, 431

49. [?Duyckinck, Evert A.], review of *Moby-Dick* (Part I), "Literature," *Literary World* (New York), 9 (15 Nov. 1851), [381]–[383]. Partially reprinted in the *Boston Daily Bee*, 20 (19 Nov. 1851), 4. Reprinted (with Part II) in *Holden's Dollar Magazine*, 8 (Dec. 1851), 267–71.
100, Carlyle, 400, Smollett

50. [?Duyckinck, Evert A.], review of *Moby–Dick* (Part II), "Second Notice," *Literary World* (New York), 9 (22 Nov. 1851), 403–4. Reprinted (with Part I) in *Holden's Dollar Magazine*, 8 (Dec. 1851), 271–72.
Carlyle, Emerson, 299, Richter, 657

51. Review of *Moby-Dick*, "Notices of Books," *New-York Commercial Advertiser* (28 Nov. 1851).
Carlyle, 431, Marryat

52. Review of *The Whale*, *International Magazine* (New York), 4 (1 Dec. 1851), 602–4.
582

53. Review of *Moby-Dick*, *National Intelligencer* (Washington), 52 (16 Dec. 1851).
150, 196, 634

1852
Reviews

54. Review of *Moby-Dick*, "Literary Record," *Knickerbocker* (New York), 39 (Jan. 1852), 109.
582

55. Review of *Pierre*, "Notices of New Works," *Albion* (New York), n.s. 11 (21 Aug. 1852), 405.
Sue

56. Review of *Pierre* in "The Editor's Shanty," *Anglo-American Magazine* (Toronto), 1 (Sept. 1852), 273.
302, 634

57. Review of *Pierre*, "Literary Notices," *Herald* (New York) (18 Sept. 1852).
Carlyle

58. Review of *Pierre*, "Review of New Books," *Graham's Magazine* (Philadelphia), 41 (Oct. 1852), 445.
Hawthorne, 561

59. Review of *Pierre*, *American Whig Review* (New York), 16 [n.s. 10] (Nov. 1852), 446–54.
110, Richter

1853
Review

60. Review of "Bartleby," "Literature, Books of the Week, Etc.," *Literary World* (New York), 13 (3 Dec. 1853), 295.
561

1855
Review

61. Review of *Israel Potter*, "Editorial Notes—Literature," *Putnam's Monthly* (New York), 5 (May 1855), 548.
721

1856
Reviews

62. Review of *The Piazza Tales*, *Daily News* (New York) (26 May 1856).
561, 697

63. Review of *The Piazza Tales*, "New Publications," *Daily Evening Traveller* (Boston) (3 June 1856).
Dickens

64. Review of *The Piazza Tales*, "New Publications," *Daily Mercury* (New Bedford) (4 June 1856), 2.
C. B. Brown

65. Review of *The Piazza Tales*, *Churchman* (New York) (5 June 1856).
636

66. Review of *The Piazza Tales*, *Dispatch* (New York) (8 June 1856).
196, 561

67. Review of *The Piazza Tales*, *Daily Advertiser* (Newark) (18 June 1856).
574, Swift

68. Review of *The Piazza Tales*, *Gazette* (Salem) (24 June 1856).
561

69. Review of *The Piazza Tales*, *Republican* (Springfield), 13 (9 July 1856).
Hawthorne

70. Review of *The Piazza Tales*, *United States Democratic Review* (New York), 38 [n.s. 7] (Sept. 1856), 172.
561

1857
Reviews

71. Review of *The Confidence-Man*, *Athenaeum* (London), 1537 (11 April 1857), 462–63.
150

72. Review of *The Confidence-Man*, *Literary Gazette* (London), 2099 (11 April 1857), 348–49.
Plato

73. Review of *The Confidence-Man*, "Books of the Week," *Supplement to the Daily Times* (New York) (11 April 1857).
574

1861
Article

74. "Melville, Herman," in *The New American Cyclopaedia: A Popular Dictionary of General Knowledge*, ed. George Ripley and Charles A. Dana (New York: D. Appleton & Co., 1861), 11, 370–71.
721

1866
Review

75. Review of *Battle-Pieces*, "New Publications," *Albion* (New York), 44 (15 Sept. 1866), 441.
Emerson

1871
Article

76. "Melville, Herman," in *A Critical Dictionary of English Literature and British and American Authors*, by S. Austin Allibone (Philadelphia: J. B. Lippincott & Co., 1871), 2, 1264–65.
721

1876
Reviews

77. [Stedman, Edmund Clarence], review of *Clarel*, "New Publications," *Daily Tribune* (New York) (16 June 1876).
66, 312

78. Review of *Clarel*, "Recent Verse," *Academy* (London), 10 (19 Aug. 1876), 185.
145

1891
Articles

79. "The Literary Wayside," *Springfield Sunday Republican* (4 Oct. 1891), 6.
Richter

80. Stedman, Arthur, "Melville of Marquesas," *Review of Reviews*, 4 (Nov. 1891), 428–30.
189

1892
Book

80a. Stedman, Arthur, "Biographical and Critical Introduction," *Typee: A Real Romance of the South Sea* (Boston: Dana Estes, 1892), pp. xv–xxxvi.
83, 189, 498a, Schopenhauer, 721

Article

81. [Stedman, Arthur], "Melville, Herman," in *Appletons' Annual Cyclopaedia and Register of Important Events of the Year 1891* (New York: D. Appleton & Co., 1892), vol. 31 (n.s. 16), pp. 503–5.
189

1900
Review

82. Review of *Moby-Dick* in the six-title series "Famous Novels of the Sea" (London: Sampson Low, Marston, 1900), "Novels of the Sea," *Literature* (London), 7 (17 Nov. 1900), 386–87.
4

1904
Book

82a. Russell, W. Clark, "Editor's Preface," *Typee: A Real Romance of the South Seas* (London and New York: John Lane, 1904), pp. v–x.
430

1919
Article

83. Craven, H. T., "Tahiti from Melville to Maugham," *Bookman*, 50 (Nov.-Dec. 1919), 262–67.
245

1921
Book

84. Weaver, Raymond M., *Herman Melville: Mariner and Mystic* (New York: George H. Doran Co., 1921). 14, 54, 60, 82, 100, 130, 189, 469, 504, Schopenhauer, 615

Article

85. Tomlinson, H. M., "A Clue to 'Moby Dick,' " in "The Literary Review" of the *New York Evening Post* (5 Nov. 1921), 141–42.
83

1922
Book

86. Handy, Willowdean Chatterson, *Tattooing in the Marquesas* (Honolulu: Bernice P. Bishop Museum, 1922).
433

Articles

87. Colum, Padraic, "Moby Dick as an Epic: A Note," *Measure*, 2 (March 1922), 16–18.
467

88. [Van Doren, Carl], "Mocha Dick," *Nation*, 115 (19 July 1922), 60.
582

1923
Articles

89. Wells, Whitney Hastings, "Moby Dick and Rabelais," *Modern Language Notes*, 38 (Feb. 1923), 123.
574

90. "More Herman Melville," review of *The Apple-Tree Table and Other Sketches* and *John Marr and Other Poems*, *Saturday Review* (London), 135 (7 April 1923).
561

91. [Brooks, Van Wyck], "A Reviewer's Notebook," *Freeman*, 7 (23 May 1923), 262–63.
551, 613

92. Strachey, J. St. Loe, review of Constable edition of *The Works of Herman Melville* and Princeton edition of *John Marr*, "The Complete Works of Herman Melville," *Spectator* (26 May 1923), 887–88.
Balzac, 71, 83, 100, Carlyle, 431

92a. Woolf, Leonard, "The World of Books: Herman Melville," *The Nation & The Athenaeum*, 33 (1 Sept. 1923), 688.
Dickens

1924
Book

92b. Rosenbach, A. S. W., *An Introduction to Herman Melville's Moby-Dick: or The Whale [1851]* (New York: Mitchell Kennerley, 1924).
63, 214, 634

Articles

93. Van Doren, Carl, "Mr. Melville's 'Moby Dick,' " *Bookman*, 59 (April 1924), 154–57.
Carlyle

94. [Murry, John Middleton], "Herman Melville's Silence," *Times Literary Supplement*, 1,173 (10 July 1924), 433–39. Revised and reprinted as John Middleton Murry, "Herman Melville, Who Could Not Surpass Himself," *New York Times Book Review* (10 Aug. 1924).
634

1926
Book

95. Freeman, John, *Herman Melville* (New York: Macmillan, 1926).
53, 54, 83, 102, 190, 203, 212, 405, 477, 574, 670, 704, 728

1928
Book

96. Starr, Nathan Comfort, "The Sea in the English Novel from Defoe to Melville" (Ph.D. dissertation, Harvard University, 1928), pp. 315–62.
35, 130, 325, 582, 654

Articles

97. McCutcheon, Roger P., "The Technique of Melville's Israel Potter," *South Atlantic Quarterly*, 27 (April 1928), 161–74.
721

98. Scudder, Harold H., "Melville's *Benito Cereno* and Captain Delano's Voyages," *Publications of the Modern Language Association of America*, 43 (June 1928), 502–32.
200

99. Mumford, Lewis, "The Writing of 'Moby-Dick,' " *American Mercury*, 15 (Dec. 1928), 482–90.
330

1929
Book

100. Mumford, Lewis, *Herman Melville* (New York: Harcourt, Brace & Co., 1929).
54, 83, 102, 107, 111, 122, 138, Coleridge, Cooper, 189, 196, 200, 203, 296, 330, 372, 385, 405, 424,

431, 477, 499, 506, 590, Scott, 634, 639, Smollett, 704, 721, 742, 743

Articles

101. Damon, S. Foster, "Pierre the Ambiguous," *Hound & Horn*, 2 (Jan.-March 1929), 107–18.
331, 407, 574, 634

102. Stewart, Randall, " 'Ethan Brand,' " *Saturday Review of Literature*, 5 (27 April 1929), 967.
330

103. Gleim, William S., "A Theory of *Moby Dick*," *New England Quarterly*, 2 (July 1929), 402–19.
Goethe, 682

104. Garnett, R. S., "Moby-Dick and Mocha-Dick: A Literary Find," *Blackwood's Magazine*, 226 (Dec. 1929), 841–58.
582

1930
Book

104a. Forsythe, Robert S., "Introduction," *Pierre or the Ambiguities* (New York: Alfred A. Knopf, 1930), pp. xix–xxxviii.
115, 119, 203, 455, 456, 634

Article

104b. Eby, E. H., review of *"Pierre; or, the Ambiguities* ... Edited by Robert S. Forsythe. New York: Alfred A. Knopf. 1930," *American Literature*, 2 (Nov. 1930), 319–21.
455, 634

1931
Articles

105. Brown, E. K., "Hawthorne, Melville, and 'Ethan Brand,' " *American Literature*, 3 (March 1931), 72–75.
330

106. Howard, Leon, "Melville and Spenser—A Note on Criticism," *Modern Language Notes*, 46 (May 1931), 291–92.
663

107. Mordell, Albert, "Melville and 'White Jacket,' " *Saturday Review of Literature*, 7 (4 July 1931), 946.
654

1932
Book

108. Holden, W. Sprague, "Some Sources for Herman Melville's *Israel Potter*" (M.A. thesis, Columbia University, 1932).
9, 163, 280, 604, 640, 721

Articles

109. Thomas, Russell, "Melville's Use of Some Sources in *The Encantadas*," *American Literature*, 3 (Jan. 1932), 432–56.
97, 132, 153, 154, 175, 176, 563, 663

110. Birss, John Howard, "A Book Review by Herman Melville," *New England Quarterly*, 5 (April 1932), 346–48.
167, 170, 171

111. Birss, John Howard, "A Note on Melville's 'Mardi,' " *Notes and Queries*, 162 (4 June 1932), 404.
683, 724

112. Hughes, Raymond G., "Melville and Shakespeare," *Shakespeare Association Bulletin*, 7 (July 1932), 103–12.
634

113. Homans, George C., "The Dark Angel: The Tragedy of Herman Melville," *New England Quarterly*, 5 (Oct. 1932), 699–730.
190

114. Dulles, Foster Rhea, "Sea Adventure," *Saturday Review of Literature*, 9 (19 Nov. 1932), 257.
582

1933
Book

115. Bennett, Arnold, *The Journal of Arnold Bennett: 1896–1928* (New York: The Viking Press, 1933), esp. pp. 862, 877, 882.
574

Articles

116. B[rooks]., V[an]. W[yck]., "Melville, Herman," in *Dictionary of American Biography* (New York: Charles Scribner's Sons, 1933), pp. 522–26.
504, 574

117. Couch, H. N., "*Moby Dick* and the *Phaedo*," *Classical Journal*, 28 (Feb. 1933), 367–68.
549

1934
Articles

118. Howard, Leon, "A Predecessor of Moby-Dick," *Modern Language Notes*, 49 (May 1934), 310–11.
325

119. Birss, John H., "Herman Melville and Blake," *Notes and Queries*, 166 (5 May 1934), 311.
290

1935
Book

120. Gibbings, Robert, "Introduction" to *Narratives of the Wreck of the Whale-Ship Essex* (London: Golden Cockerel Press, 1935), pp. 5–9.
130

Articles

121. Anderson, Charles R., "A Reply to Herman Melville's *White-Jacket* by Rear-Admiral Thomas O. Selfridge, Sr.," *American Literature*, 7 (May 1935), 123–44.
13, 654

122. Larrabee, Stephen A., "Melville against the World," *South Atlantic Quarterly*, 34 (Oct. 1935), 410–18.
83, 100, Smollett

1936
Book

123. Mansfield, Luther Stearns, "Herman Melville: Author and New Yorker, 1844–1851" (Ph.D. dissertation, University of Chicago, 1936). "Some Aspects of Melville's Reading" (pp. 189–208) published as a private edition under the original title (Chicago: University of Chicago Libraries, 1938).
46, 50, 83, 100, 136, 170, 171, 203, 214, 283, 326, 333, 407, 540, 574, 606, 634, 654, 670, 693

Articles

124. Braswell, William, "The Satirical Temper of Melville's *Pierre*," *American Literature*, 7 (Jan. 1936), 424–38.
Carlyle, 407

125. Thomas, Russell, "Yarn for Melville's *Typee*," *Philological Quarterly*, 15 (Jan. 1936), 16–29.
672

125a. Forsythe, Robert S., review of "*Journal up the Straits: October 11, 1856—May 5, 1857* . . . Edited with an Introduction by Raymond Weaver. New York: The Colophon. 1935," *American Literature*, 8 (March 1936), 85–96.
605, 605a

1937
Articles

126. Hart, James D., "Melville and Dana," *American Literature*, 9 (March 1937), 49–55.
189

127. Jaffe, David, "Some Sources of Melville's *Mardi*," *American Literature*, 9 (March 1937), 56–69.
60, 245, 724, 759

128. Braswell, William, "Melville as a Critic of Emerson," *American Literature*, 9 (Nov. 1937), 317–34.
247, 249, 250

1938
Books

128a. Gleim, William S., *The Meaning of Moby Dick* (New York: Brick Row Book Shop, 1938).
63, 93, 504

129. Thorp, Willard, *Herman Melville: Representative Selections, with Introduction, Bibliography, and Notes* (New York: American Book Co., 1938), esp. pp. xi–cxxix.
13, 50, 83, 100, Cooper, 171, 200, Emerson, 327, 328, 331, 333, Irving, 540, 574, 576, Schopenhauer, 638, 654, 672, 728

Articles

130. Mansfield, Luther Stearns, "Melville's Comic Articles on Zachary Taylor," *American Literature*, 9 (Jan. 1938), 411–18.
436

131. Birss, John Howard, "Melville and James Thomson ('B.V.')," *Notes and Queries* (5 March 1938), 171–72.
707

131a. Olson, Charles, "Lear and Moby-Dick," *Twice a Year: A Semi-Annual Journal of Literature, The Arts, and Civil Liberties*, 1 (Fall–Winter 1938), 165–89.
299, 477, 634

132. Thorp, Willard, "Redburn's Prosy Old Guidebook," *PMLA: Publications-of-the-Modern-Language-Association-of-America*, 53 (Dec. 1938), 1146–56.
547

1939
Books

133. Anderson, Charles Roberts, *Melville in the South Seas* (New York: Columbia University Press, 1939).
13, 52, 55, 56, 60, 82, 83, 103, 130, 154, 159, 189, 210, 245, 262, 271,

325, 357, 425, 433, 440, 469, 528, 563, 574, 582, 590, 591, 593, 594, 654, 672, 693, 723, 724, 755, 759

133a. Geist, Stanley, *Herman Melville: The Tragic Vision and the Heroic Ideal* (Cambridge: Harvard University Press, 1939).
634

133b. Oliver, Egbert Samuel, "Melville and the Idea of Progress" (Ph.D. dissertation, University of Washington, 1939).
50, 249, 713

133c. Simon, Jean, *Herman Melville: Marin, metaphysicien et poete* (Paris: Boivin, 1939).
189, 245, 249, 250, 262, 425, 563, 667, 672

Article

133d. Forsythe, Robert S., "Emerson and 'Moby-Dick,' " *Notes and Queries*, 177 (23 Dec. 1939), 457–58.
130

1940
Book

134. Von Hagen, Victor Wolfgang, ed., "Introduction, Critical Epilogue & Bibliographical Notes," *The Encantadas Or, Enchanted Isles* (Burlingame, Calif.: William P. Wreden, 1940), pp. v–xxiii and 101–19.
132, 153, 154, 176, 200, 563, 663

Articles

135. Sackman, Douglas, "The Original of Melville's Apple-Tree Table," *American Literature*, 11 (Jan. 1940), 448–51.
232, 266, 485

136. Braswell, William, "Melville's Use of Seneca," *American Literature*, 12 (March 1940), 98–104.
630

136a. Wright, Nathalia, "Biblical Allusion in Melville's Prose," *American Literature*, 12 (May 1940), 185–99.
63

137. Howard, Leon, "Melville's Struggle with the Angel," *Modern Language Quarterly*, 1 (June 1940), 195–206.
91, 149, 634

138. Anderson, Charles Roberts, "The Genesis of *Billy Budd*," *American Literature*, 12 (Nov. 1940), 329–46.
169, 320, 484, 649

1941
Book

139. Matthiessen, F. O., *American Renaissance: Art and Expression in the Age of Emerson and Whitman* (London: Oxford University Press, 1941), esp. pp. 369–514.
8, 13, 25, 27, 28, 50, 63, 66, 83, 88, 100, Carlyle, 119, 125, Dickens, 230, Emerson, 250, 299, 328, 330, 331, 332, 333, 338, 367, 368, 369, 407, 477, 499, 610, 611, 634, 638, Smollett, 667, 697, 704

Articles

140. Mabbott, T. O., "A Source for the Conclusion of Melville's 'Moby Dick,' " *Notes and Queries*, 181 (26 July 1941), 47–48. Replies

in *Notes and Queries*, 181 (9 Aug. 1941), 80, and (15 Nov. 1941), 278–79. [see also 141a below]
656

141. Purcell, James Mark, "Melville's Contribution to English," *PMLA*, 56 (Sept. 1941), 797–808.
480

141a. Duffy, Charles, "A Source for the Conclusion of Melville's 'Moby Dick' (clxxxi.47, 80)," *Notes and Queries*, 181 (15 Nov. 1941), 278–79. [see also 140 above]
112c

142. Davis, Merrell R., "The Flower Symbolism in *Mardi*," *Modern Language Quarterly*, 2 (Dec. 1941), 625–38.
530

1942
Book

143. Sealts, Merton M., Jr., "Herman Melville's Reading in Ancient Philosophy" (Ph.D. dissertation, Yale University, 1942).
17, 25, 28, 33, 50, 83, 100, 147, 151, 210, 257, 258, 261, 268, 289, 327, 450, 458a, 475, 503, 513, 514, 549, 550, 551, 552, 553, 554, 555, 557, 559, 560, 568, 602, 610, 630, 667, 695

Articles

144. Mills, Gordon, "The Significance of 'Arcturus' in *Mardi*," *American Literature*, 14 (May 1942), 158–61.
20

145. Thorp, Willard, "Did Melville Review *The Scarlet Letter*?"

American Literature, 14 (Nov. 1942), 302–5.
338

1943
Books

146. Braswell, William, *Melville's Religious Thought: An Essay in Interpretation* (Durham, N.C.: Duke University Press, 1943).
9, 10, 19, Arnold, 25, 26, 27, 50, 63, 83, 100, 101, Carlyle, 119, Coleridge, 171, 190, 235, Emerson, 283, 296, 299, 304, 358, 368, 377, 407, 465, 499, 502, 513, 520, 540, 549, 551, 560, 574, 586, 589, 590, 600, Schopenhauer, 613, 630, 633, 635, 638, 663, 667, 677, 680, 690, 696, 698, 704, 705, 713

147. Scott, Wilbur S., Jr., "Melville's Originality: A Study of Some of the Sources of *Moby-Dick*" (Ph.D. dissertation, Princeton University, 1943).
52, 60, 82, 130, 136, 154, 157, 181, 292, 319a, 325, 437, 469, 528, 582, 615, 752b, 759

1944
Books

148. Hillway, Tyrus, "Melville and Nineteenth-Century Science" (Ph.D. dissertation, Yale University, 1944).
52, 60, 124, 185, 186, 191, 278, 307, 308, 428, 436, 446, 510, 526, 544, 556, 594, 615

148a. Sedgwick, William Ellery, *Herman Melville: The Tragedy of Mind* (Cambridge: Harvard University Press, 1944).
4, 63, 133, 190, 477, 634

Articles

148b. Kimpel, Sgt. Ben D., "Two Notes on Herman Melville," *American Literature*, 16 (March 1944), 29–32.
458b

149. Walcutt, Charles Child, "The Fire Symbolism in *Moby Dick*," *Modern Language Notes*, 59 (May 1944), 304–10.
83

150. Hillway, Tyrus, "Taji's Abdication in Herman Melville's *Mardi*," *American Literature*, 16 (Nov. 1944), 204–7.
639

151. Freeman, F. Barron, "The Enigma of Melville's 'Daniel Orme,' " *American Literature*, 16 (Nov. 1944), 208–11.
63

1945
Book

152. Hayford, Harrison, "Melville and Hawthorne: A Biographical and Critical Study" (Ph.D. dissertation, Yale University, 1945).
331, 333, 341

Articles

153. Foster, Elizabeth S., "Melville and Geology," *American Literature*, 17 (March 1945), 50–65.
459

154. Huntress, Keith, "Melville's Use of a Source for *White-Jacket*," *American Literature*, 17 (March 1945), 66–74.
498

155. Oliver, Egbert S., "A Second Look at 'Bartleby,' " *College English*, 6 (May 1945), 431–39.
709, 710, 713

156. Huntress, Keith, "A Note on Melville's *Redburn*," *New England Quarterly*, 18 (June 1945), 259–60.
65, 648, 703

157. Oliver, Egbert S., "Melville's Goneril and Fanny Kemble," *New England Quarterly*, 18 (Dec. 1945), 489–500.
634

158. Watters, R. E., "Melville's 'Isolatoes,' " *PMLA*, 9 (Dec. 1945), 1138–48.
226, 333, 613

1946
Book

159. Yaggy, Elinor, "*Pierre*: Key to the Melville Enigma" (Ph.D. dissertation, University of Washington, 1946).
325, 407, 592, 643, 644

Articles

160. Warren, Robert Penn, "Melville the Poet," *Kenyon Review*, 8 (Spring 1946), 208–23.
405

161. Oliver, Egbert S., "Melville's Picture of Emerson and Thoreau in 'The Confidence-Man,' " *College English*, 8 (Nov. 1946), 61–72.
249, 250, 251, 458, 713

162. Hayford, Harrison, "Hawthorne, Melville, and the Sea," *New England Quarterly*, 19 (Dec. 1946), 435–52.
341, 476, 582, 583, 759

163. Mabbott, T. O., "Possible Melville MS," *Melville Society Newsletter*, 2 (14 Dec. 1946), [1].
453

1947
Books

163a. Brooks, Van Wyck, *The Times of Melville and Whitman* (New York: E. P. Dutton, 1947).
40, 82, 83, 100, 102, Hawthorne, 574, Smollett, 582, 669a, 704

164. Olson, Charles, *Call Me Ishmael* (New York: Reynal & Hitchcock, 1947).
122, 130, 634

165. Thorp, Willard, ed., *Moby-Dick or The Whale* (New York: Oxford University Press, 1947).
52, 60, 63, 82, 83, 107, 115, 130, 154, 186, 201, 216, 246, 282, 323, 421, 444, 469, 512, 559, 582, 606, 615, 634, 642, 664, 702, 738, 748

166. Vincent, Howard P., ed., "Explanatory Notes," *Collected Poems of Herman Melville* (Chicago: Packard & Co., Hendricks House, 1947), pp. 445–89.
50, 63, 111, 112, 289, 502, 505, 560, 563, 576, 583, 595, 634, 711

Articles

167. Levin, Harry, " 'Don Quixote' and 'Moby Dick,' " in *Cervantes across the Centuries*, ed. Angel Flores and M. J. Benardete (New York: Dryden Press, 1947), pp. 217–26.
53, 122

168. Belgion, Montgomery, "Heterodoxy on *Moby Dick?*" *Sewanee Review*, 55 (Winter 1947), 108–25.
63, 83, 634

169. Pommer, Henry F., "Melville's 'The Gesture' and the Schoolbook Verses," *American Notes & Queries*, 6 (Jan. 1947), 150–51.
453

170. Wright, Nathalia, "A Source for Melville's *Clarel*: Dean Stanley's *Sinai and Palestine*," *Modern Language Notes*, 62 (Feb. 1947), 110–16.
668

171. Arms, George, " 'Moby-Dick' and 'The Village Blacksmith,' " *Notes and Queries*, 192 (3 May 1947), 187–88.
457

172. Feltenstein, Rosalie, "Melville's 'Benito Cereno,' " *American Literature*, 19 (Nov. 1947), 245–55.
200

1948
Books

172a. Freeman, F. Barron, ed., *Melville's Billy Budd* (Cambridge: Harvard University Press, 1948), esp. "Introduction," pp. 1–126.
52a, 63, 112a, 169, 181a, 320, 332, 333, 392, 465, 499, 609, 610, 613, 658, 730a

172b. Haave, Ethel-Mae, "Herman Melville's *Pierre*: A Critical Study" (Ph.D. dissertation, Yale University, 1948).
Carlyle, 115, 119, 149, 190, 235, Emerson, 249, 296, 634

173. Oliver, Egbert S., ed., "Explanatory Notes," *The Piazza Tales* (New York: Hendricks House, 1948), pp. 225–50.
63, 97, 100, 132, 153, 154, 200, 330, 439, 539, 563, 634, 663, 697

Articles

174. Arvin, Newton, "A Note on the Background of *Billy Budd*," *American Literature*, 20 (March 1948), 51–55.
649

175. Vietor, Alexander O., "Five Inches of Books," *Yale University Library Gazette*, 22 (April 1948), 124–28.
286, 346, 427, 453, 597

176. Oliver, Egbert S., " 'Cock-A-Doodle-Doo!' and Transcendental Hocus-Pocus," *New England Quarterly*, 21 (June 1948), 204–16.
670, 713

176a. Pommer, Henry F., "Herman Melville and the Wake of the *Essex*," *American Literature*, 20 (Nov. 1948), 290–304.
60, 130, 469, 724

177. Heflin, Wilson L., "The Source of Ahab's Lordship over the Level Loadstone," *American Literature*, 20 (Nov. 1948), 323–27.
615, 616

1949
Books

178. Barrett, Laurence, "Fiery Hunt: A Study of Melville's Theories of the Artist" (Ph.D. dissertation, Princeton University, 1949).
63, 82, 83, 100, 235, 245, Goethe, 296, 299, 304, 357, 502, Plato, 549, 552, 563, 574, 634, 654, 672, 774

179. Chase, Richard, *Herman Melville: A Critical Study* (New York: Macmillan, 1949).
8, 25, 28, 63, 190, 247, 317, 469, 766

180. Conner, Frederick William, *Cosmic Optimism: A Study of the Interpretation of Evolution by American Poets from Emerson to Robinson* (Gainesville: University of Florida Press, 1949), esp. chapter 6.
460

180a. Leyda, Jay, ed., *The Complete Stories of Herman Melville* (New York: Random House, 1949).
63, 97, 200, 225a, 266, 343, 485, 563, 634, 663, 766

181. Murray, Henry A., ed., "Introduction" and "Explanatory Notes," *Pierre Or, The Ambiguities* (New York: Hendricks House, 1949), pp. xiii–ciii and 429–504.
32, 33, 50, 53, 63, 71, 83, 93, 100, 106, 107, Carlyle, 117, 119, 162, 168, 190, 202, 203, 212, Disraeli, 217, 218, 219, 220, 221, 239, Emerson, 247, 277, 284, 295, Goethe, 296, 298, 309, 327, 328, 333, 375, 391, 410, 411, 413, 414, 456, 499, 542, 543, 546, 548, Plato, 549, 550, 552, 559, 561, 575, 580, 590, 617, 618, 619, 622, 634, 636, 639, 664, 689, 700, 717, 744, 768

181a. Stone, Geoffrey, *Melville* (New York: Sheed & Ward, 1949).
63, 83, 102, Carlyle, 190, 333, 372, 574, 576, 649, Smollett, 721

182. Vincent, Howard P., *The Trying-Out of Moby-Dick* (Boston: Houghton Mifflin Co., 1949).
13, 35, 50, 52, 60, 63, 82, 100, 111, 130, 136, 150, 154, 185, 186, 188a, 189, 235, 260, 296, 313, 319, 321, 323, 325, 330, 333, 421, 425a, 433, 436, 444, 469, 476, 492, 493, 498, 512, 522, 528, 570, 582, 606, 615, 616, 634, 642, 715, 752b, 759

183. Wright, Nathalia, *Melville's Use of the Bible* (Durham, N.C.: Duke University Press, 1949).
8, 25, 63, 222, 223, 245, 249, 268, 589, 611, 612, 634, 668, 721, 739, 763

Articles

184. Lash, Kenneth, "Captain Ahab and King Lear," *New Mexico Quarterly Review*, 19 (Winter 1949), 438–45.
634

185. Hillway, Tyrus, "Melville and the Spirit of Science," *South Atlantic Quarterly*, 48 (Jan. 1949), 77–88.
472

186. Sealts, Merton M., Jr., "Melville's 'Friend Atahalpa,' " *Notes and Queries*, 194 (22 Jan. 1949), 37–38.
83

187. Kazin, Alfred, "Ishmael in His Academic Heaven," *New Yorker*, 24 (12 Feb. 1949), 84–89.
710

187a. Arvin, Newton, "Melville and the Gothic Novel," *New England Quarterly*, 22 (March 1949), 33–48.
54, 116, 295, 445, 489a, 508, Radcliffe, 574a, 574b, 575, 605a, 636, 742, 744

188. Giovannini, G., "Melville's *Pierre* and Dante's *Inferno*," *PMLA*, 64 (March 1949), 70–78.
68, 190, 272, 272a, 634

189. Hillway, Tyrus, "Melville's Use of Two Pseudo-Sciences," *Modern Language Notes*, 64 (March 1949), 145–50.
136, 436

190. Hillway, Tyrus, "Melville's Geological Knowledge," *American Literature*, 21 (May 1949), 232–37.
124, 278, 307, 308

191. Paul, Sherman, "Morgan Neville, Melville and the Folk-Hero," *Notes and Queries*, 194 (25 June 1949), 278.
516

192. Stevens, Harry R., "Melville's Music," *Musicology*, 2 (July 1949), 405–21.
208, 225

193. Arvin, Newton, "Melville's Shorter Poems," *Partisan Review*, 16 (Oct. 1949), 1034-46.
63, 405, 634

194. Weber, Walter, "Some Characteristic Symbols in Herman Melville's Works," *English Studies*, 30 (Oct. 1949), 217–24.
63

195. Mabbott, T. O., "Melville's *Moby Dick*," *Explicator*, 8 (Nov. 1949), Item 15.
639

196. Mathews, J. Chesley, "Melville and Dante," *PMLA*, 64 (Dec. 1949), 1238.
190

197. Sealts, Merton M., Jr., "Melville and the Shakers," *Studies in Bibliography*, 2 (1949–1950), 105–14.
680

1950
Books

198. Arvin, Newton, *Herman Melville* (New York: William Sloane Associates, 1950).
8, 13, 25, 40, 52, 63, 82, 111, 130, 136, 189, 200, 245, 366, 445, 499, 530, 539, 561, 574, 582, 616, 622, 634, 672, 683, 721

198a. Chase, Richard, ed., "Introduction," *Selected Tales and Poems by Herman Melville* (New York: Rinehart & Co., 1950), pp. v–xix.
634, 655

199. Hillway, Tyrus, *Melville and the Whale* (Stonington, Conn.: Stonington Publishing Co., 1950).
52, 60, 83, 136, 307, 615, 616, 759

200. Pommer, Henry F., *Milton and Melville* (Pittsburgh: University of Pittsburgh Press, 1950).
25, 27, 84, 98, 127, 128, 132, 136, 222, 279, 367, 453, 467, 498c, 499, 499a, 513, 540, 635, 638, 662

201. Scott, Sumner W. D., "The Whale in *Moby Dick*" (Ph.D. dissertation, University of Chicago, 1950).
52, 60, 82, 83, 130, 136, 154, 159, 176, 186, 188a, 191, 283, 307, 313, 323, 325, 433, 446, 493, 528, 533, 537, 570, 585, 614, 615, 642, 675, 725, 751

Articles

202. Mills, Gordon H., "The Castaway in *Moby-Dick*," *University of Texas Studies in English*, 29 (1950), 231–48.
103, 177

203. Dauner, Louise, "The 'Case' of Tobias Pearson: Hawthorne and the Ambiguities," *American Literature*, 21 (Jan. 1950), 464–72.
341

204. Arvin, Newton, "Melville's *Mardi*," *American Quarterly*, 2 (Spring 1950), 71–81. [Included in his *Herman Melville* (198).]
574, 683

205. Giovannini, G., "Melville and Dante," *PMLA*, 65 (March 1950), 329.
190

206. Lewis, R. W. B., "Melville on Homer," *American Literature*, 22 (May 1950), 166–76.
367, 368, 369

207. Procter, Page S., Jr., "A Source for the Flogging Incident in *White-Jacket*," *American Literature*, 22 (May 1950), 176–77.
441

208. [Mabbott, T. O.], "Notes," *Melville Society Newsletter*, 6 (June 1950), [3].
372

209. Leyda, Jay, ed., "An Albany Journal by Gansevoort Melville," *Boston Public Library Quarterly*, 2 (Oct. 1950), 327–47.
104, 451

210. Hamilton, Charles, "More about the Pequod," *Melville Society Newsletter*, 6 (Dec. 1950), [2].
182

1951
Books

211. Canfield, Rev. Francis X., "Herman Melville's Vision of Conflict" (Ph.D. dissertation, University of Ottawa, 1951).
28, 117, 119, 203, 348, 409, 590, 634

212. Gilman, William H., *Melville's Early Life and Redburn* (New York: New York University Press and London: Oxford University Press, 1951).
13, 18, 46, 50, 51, 63, 82, 83, 96, 100, 104, 105, 107, 113, 137, 138, 146, 152, Cooper, 170, 189, 236, 243, 244, 275, 326, 389, 403, 431, 440, 447, 453, 467, 481, 497, 498, 504, 509, 519, 542, 545, 547, 549, 582, 619, 623, 629, 635, 641, 648, 688, 691, 770, 773

213. Howard, Leon, *Herman Melville: A Biography* (Berkeley and Los Angeles: University of California Press, 1951).
1, 9, 13, 15, 25, 41, 47, 48, 49, 50, 52, 60, 61, 63, 72, 73, 82, 83, 91, 97, 100, 107, 112, 119, 122, 123, 130, 132, 147, 149, 153, 154, 156, 161, 170, 176, 189, 190, 197, 200, 203, 214, 245, 252, 262, 263, 266, 296, 320, 327, 328, 331, 332, 333, 351, 353, 356, 357, 367, 368, Irving, 392, 399, 405, 410, 422, 427, 430, 431, 432, 433, 453, 463, 466, 467, 469, 477, Marryat, 485, 498, 499, 502, 513, 523, 538, 547, 563, 568, 574, 576, 582, 590, 595, 606, 615, 616, 630, 634, 634a, 639, 647, 649, 654, 658, 663, 666, 668, 672, 686, 721, 752, 766

213a. Mason, Ronald, *The Spirit above the Dust: A Study of Herman Melville* (London: John Lehmann, 1951).
133, 212, 333, 499, 653

Articles

214. Heflin, Wilson L., "Melville and Nantucket," in *Proceedings of the Nantucket Historical Association, 1951*, pp. 22–30. Reprinted in *Moby-Dick Centennial Essays*, ed. Tyrus Hillway and Luther S. Mansfield (Dallas: Southern Methodist University Press, 1953), pp. 165–79.
130, 469, 647

215. Foster, Elizabeth S., "Another Note on Melville and Geology," *American Literature*, 22 (Jan. 1951), 479–87.
124, 278, 307, 308, 759

216. Heflin, Wilson L., "A Man-of-War Button Divides Two Cousins," *Boston Public Library Quarterly*, 3 (Jan. 1951), 51–60.
169

217. Pearson, Norman Holmes, "Billy Budd: 'The King's Yarn,'" *American Quarterly*, 3 (Summer 1951), 99–114.
63, 499, 658

218. Hillway, Tyrus, "Melville as Amateur Zoologist," *Modern Language Quarterly*, 12 (June 1951), 159–64.
60, 191, 307

219. Shroeder, John W., "Sources and Symbols for Melville's *Confi-*

dence-Man," PMLA, 66 (June 1951), 363–80.
63, 93, 212, 333

220. Paul, Sherman, "Hawthorne's Ahab," *Notes and Queries*, 196 (9 June 1951), 255–57.
330

221. Hayford, Harrison, "The Sailor Poet of *White-Jacket*," *Boston Public Library Quarterly*, 3 (July 1951), 221–28.
356, 498

222. Sutton, Walter, "Melville's 'Pleasure Party' and the Art of Concealment," *Philological Quarterly*, 30 (July 1951), 316–27.
499, 532, 562

223. Bell, Millicent, "Pierre Bayle and *Moby Dick*," *PMLA*, 66 (Sept. 1951), 626–48.
50, 123, 421

224. Haber, Tom Burns, "A Note on Melville's 'Benito Cereno,'" *Nineteenth-Century Fiction*, 6 (Sept. 1951), 146–47.
200

225. Murray, Henry A., "In Nomine Diaboli," *New England Quarterly*, 24 (Dec. 1951), 435–52. Reprinted in *Moby-Dick Centennial Essays*, ed. Tyrus Hillway and Luther S. Mansfield (Dallas: Southern Methodist University Press, 1953), pp. 3–21.
499

1952
Books

226. Davis, Merrell R., *Melville's Mardi: A Chartless Voyage* (New Haven: Yale University Press, 1952).
15, 16, 46, 57, 60, 73, 82, 83, 100, 105, 107, 119, 123, 124, 147, 161, 190, 191, 215, 245, Emerson, 297, 323, 326, 327, 382, 389, 410, 411, 432, 450, 467, 472, 494, 499, 502, 504, 509, 510, 530, 567, 568, 574, 583, 630, 634a, 638, 639, 659, 663, 683, 684, 693, 697, 724, 737, 758, 759

227. Griffith, Frank Clark, "Melville and the Quest for God" (Ph.D. dissertation, State University of Iowa, 1952).
50, 83, 100, 502

228. Key, Howard Cresap, "The Influence of Travel Literature upon Melville's Fictional Technique" (Ph.D. dissertation, Stanford University, 1952).
60, 73, 82, 87, 159, 191, 245, 316, 418, 433, 434, 470, 498, 539, 563, 582, 672, 759

229. Mansfield, Luther S., and Howard P. Vincent, eds., "Introduction" and "Explanatory Notes," *Moby-Dick Or, The Whale* (New York: Hendricks House, 1952), pp. ix–xxxiii and 569–832.
2, 13, 28, 31, 50, 52, 60, 63, 72, 82, 83, 93, 107, 111, 115, 117, 119, 122, 130, 136, 150, 154, 155, 160, 167, 168, 176, 177, 178, 186, 187, 189, 190, 191, 192, 201, 203, 205, 216, 226, 232, 235, Emerson, 249, 254, 260, 264, 283, 292, 296, 299, 306, 307, 319a, 323, 325, 326, 330, 333, 338, 341, 352, 358, 360, 372, 421, 422, 426, 431, 436, 437, 444, 469, 476, 477, 495, 499, 502, 507, 517, 528, 532, 537, 549, 550, 551, 559, 561, 562, 570, 574, 582, 585, 590,

606, 608, 615, 616, 627, 630, 631, 634, 636, 638, 639, 642, 657, 659, 661, 662, 666, 670, 674, 680, 686, 688, 693, 724, 726, 751, 752b, 753, 759, 760, 764, 772

229a. Thompson, Lawrance, *Melville's Quarrel with God* (Princeton, N.J.: Princeton University Press, 1952).
10, 50, 63, 83, 93, 106, 107, 111, 115, 117, 119, 181a, 190, 299, 358, 392, 499, 502, 552, 560, 590, Schopenhauer, 634, 639, 663, Sterne, 684

Articles

230. Fogle, Richard Harter, "The Monk and the Bachelor: Melville's *Benito Cereno*," *Tulane Studies in English*, 3 (1952), 155–78.
333

231. Quinn, Patrick F., "Poe's Imaginary Voyage," *Hudson Review*, 4 (Winter 1952), 562–85.
561

232. Canfield, Francis X., "Moby Dick and the Book of Job," *Catholic World*, 174 (Jan. 1952), 254–60.
63

233. Sealts, Merton M., Jr., "Melville's 'Neoplatonical Originals'," *Modern Language Notes*, 67 (Feb. 1952), 80–86.
554, 568

234. Vogelback, Arthur L., "Shakespeare and Melville's *Benito Cereno*," *Modern Language Notes*, 67 (Feb. 1952), 113–16.
634

235. Bell, Millicent, "Melville and Hawthorne at the Grave of St. John (A Debt to Pierre Bayle)," *Modern Language Notes*, 67 (Feb. 1952), 116–18.
50

236. Williams, Stanley T., "Spanish Influences in American Fiction: Melville and Others," *New Mexico Quarterly*, 22 (Spring 1952), 5–14.
6, 109, 122, 438, 565

236a. Bell, Millicent, "Hawthorne's 'Fire Worship': Interpretation and Source," *American Literature*, 24 (March 1952), 31–39.
333

237. Wright, Nathalia, "A Note on Melville's Use of Spenser: Hautia and the Bower of Bliss," *American Literature*, 24 (March 1952), 83–85.
663

238. Fiess, Edward, "Melville as a Reader and Student of Byron," *American Literature*, 24 (May 1952), 186–94.
107, 761

239. Kaplan, Sidney, "Herman Melville and the Whaling Enderbys," *American Literature*, 24 (May 1952), 224–30.
60

240. Pafford, Ward, and Floyd C. Watkins, " 'Benito Cereno': A Note in Rebuttal," *Nineteenth-Century Fiction*, 7 (June 1952), 68– 71.
200

241. Wright, Nathalia, "*Mosses from an Old Manse* and *Moby-Dick*: The Shock of Discovery," *Modern Language Notes*, 67 (June 1952), 387–92.
299, 330, 331, 333, 338, 341

242. Stewart, Randall, "Melville and Hawthorne," *South Atlantic Quarterly*, 51 (July 1952), 436–46. Reprinted in *Moby-Dick Centennial Essays*, ed. Tyrus Hillway and Luther S. Mansfield (Dallas: Southern Methodist University Press, 1953), pp. 153–64.
330, 333

243. Thompson, Francis J., "Mangan in America, 1850–1860: Mitchel, Maryland and Melville," *Dublin Magazine*, n.s. 27 (July-Sept. 1952), 30–41.
475

244. Wright, Nathalia, "The Confidence Men of Melville and Cooper: An American Indictment," *American Quarterly*, 4 (Fall 1952), 266–68.
164

245. Pearce, Roy Harvey, "Melville's Indian-Hater: A Note on a Meaning of *The Confidence-Man*," *PMLA*, 67 (Dec. 1952), 942–48.
317

1953
Books

246. Stackpole, Edouard A., *The Sea-Hunters: The New England Whalemen During Two Centuries 1635–1835* (Philadelphia: J. B. Lippincott Co., 1953), esp. pp. 335–37.
130

247. Stavig, Richard Thorson, "Melville's *Billy Budd*: A New Approach to the Problem of Inter-

pretation" (Ph.D. dissertation, Princeton University, 1953).
Balzac, 38, 41, 144, Schopenhauer, 609, 610, 611, 612, 613, 704, 705, 706, 707

Articles

248. Leisy, Ernest E., "Fatalism in Moby-Dick," in *Moby-Dick Centennial Essays*, ed. Tyrus Hillway and Luther S. Mansfield (Dallas: Southern Methodist University Press, 1953), pp. 76–88.
50, 421

249. Howard, Leon, review of Mansfield-Vincent Hendricks House edition of *Moby-Dick*, "Moby-Dick," *Nineteenth-Century Fiction*, 7 (March 1953), 303–4.
149, Cooper

249a. Nunez, Estuardo, "Herman Melville en la America Latina," *Cuadernos Americanos*, Ano 12, vol. 68 (March-April 1953), 209–21.
200

250. Bond, William H., "Melville and *Two Years Before the Mast*," *Harvard Library Bulletin*, 7 (Autumn 1953), 362–65.
189, 189a

251. Miller, Perry, "Melville and Transcendentalism," *Virginia Quarterly Review*, 29 (Autumn 1953), 556–75.
Carlyle, Cooper, Emerson, 247, 249, 625

252. Stone, Edward, "Melville's Pip and Coleridge's Servant Girl," *American Literature*, 25 (Nov. 1953), 358–60.
147, 634

1954
Books

253. Betts, William W., Jr., "The Fortunes of Faust in American Literature" (Ph.D. dissertation, Pennsylvania State University, 1954), pp. 117–30.
296, 299, 477

254. Foster, Elizabeth S., ed., "Introduction" and "Explanatory Notes," *The Confidence-Man: His Masquerade* (New York: Hendricks House, 1954), pp. xiii–xcv and 287–365.
5, 8, 14, 23, 31, 33, 43, 46a, 50, 62, 63, 64, 72, 93, 100, 117, 122, 133, Cooper, 183, 216, 231, Emerson, 249, 250, 257, 289, 302, 314, 315, 317, 333, 368, 369, 373, 377, 378, 435, 448, 458, 462, 485, 499, 513, 529, 532, 540, 541, Plato, 574, 606, 630, 631, 633, 634, 648, 689, 701, 714, 734, 759, 766

254a. Whipple, A. B. C., *Yankee Whalers in the South Seas* (Garden City, N.Y.: Doubleday, 1954), pp. 40–54.
130

Articles

255. Stewart, George R., "The Two Moby-Dicks," *American Literature*, 25 (Jan. 1954), 417–48.
634

256. Geiger, Don, "Melville's Black God: Contrary Evidence in 'The Town-Ho's Story,'" *American Literature*, 25 (Jan. 1954), 464–71.
63

257. Davidson, Frank, "Melville, Thoreau, and 'The Apple-Tree Table,'" *American Literature*, 25 (Jan. 1954), 479–88.
266, 711, 713

257a. Connolly, Thomas E., "A Note on Name-Symbolism in Melville," *American Literature*, 25 (Jan. 1954), 489–90.
200

258. Yaggy, Elinor, "Shakespeare and Melville's *Pierre*," *Boston Public Library Quarterly*, 6 (Jan. 1954), 43–51.
634

259. Bezanson, Walter E., "Melville's *Clarel*: The Complex Passion," *ELH: A Journal of English Literary History*, 21 (June 1954), 146–59.
Goethe, 605

260. Bezanson, Walter E., "Melville's Reading of Arnold's Poetry," *PMLA*, 69 (June 1954), 365–91.
Arnold, 28, 29, 606, 664

261. Rockwell, Frederick S., "DeQuincey and the Ending of 'Moby-Dick,'" *Nineteenth-Century Fiction*, 9 (Dec. 1954), 161–68.
203, 204, 205

1955
Books

262. Gross, John J., "Herman Melville and the Search for Community" (Ph.D. dissertation, State University of Iowa, 1955).
293

263. Lewis, R. W. B., *The American Adam: Innocence, Tragedy and Tradition in the Nineteenth Cen-*

tury (Chicago: University of Chicago Press, 1955).
367, 368, 369, 499

264. Marshall, Thomas F., *Three Voices of the American Tradition: Edgar Allan Poe, Herman Melville, Ernest Hemingway* (Athens, 1955).
634

265. Rosenberry, Edward H., *Melville and the Comic Spirit* (Cambridge: Harvard University Press, 1955).
36, 84, 119, Dickens, 223, Emerson, 249, 251, 333, 382, 407, 427, 438, 458, 561, 562, 574, Schopenhauer, 634, 639, 670, 683, 711

265a. Untermeyer, Louis, "Herman Melville," in his *Makers of the Modern World: The Lives of Ninety-two Writers, Artists, Scientists, Statesmen, Inventors, Philosophers, Composers, and Other Creators Who Formed the Pattern of Our Century* (New York: Simon & Schuster, 1955), pp. 47–59.
634

266. Williams, Stanley T., *The Spanish Background of American Literature* (New Haven: Yale University Press, 1955), esp. pp. 224–27.
109, 122, 565

Articles

266a. Blackmur, R. P., "The Craft of Herman Melville: A Putative Statement," in his *The Lion and the Honeycomb* (New York: Harcourt, Brace & World, 1955). Reprinted in *Twentieth Century Views: Melville: A Collection of*

Critical Essays, ed. Richard Chase (Englewood Cliffs, N.J.: Prentice-Hall, 1962), pp. 75–90.
477

267. Stockton, Eric W., "A Commentary on Melville's 'The Lightning-Rod Man,'" *Papers of the Michigan Academy of Science, Arts, and Letters*, 40 (1955), 321–28.
242, 373

268. Sherbo, Arthur, "Melville's 'Portuguese Catholic Priest,'" *American Literature*, 26 (Jan. 1955), 563–64.
449

269. Miller, James E., Jr., "Hawthorne and Melville: The Unpardonable Sin," *PMLA*, 70 (March 1955), 91–114.
330, 333, 338

270. McElderry, B. R., Jr., "Three Earlier Treatments of the *Billy Budd* Theme," *American Literature*, 27 (May 1955), 251–57.
398, 399, 479

271. Stein, William Bysshe, "The Moral Axis of 'Benito Cereno,'" *Accent*, 15 (Summer 1955), 221–33.
63

272. Battenfeld, David H., "The Source for the Hymn in *Moby-Dick*," *American Literature*, 27 (Nov. 1955), 393–96.
569

273. Grdseloff, Dorothee, "A Note on the Origin of Fedallah in *Moby-Dick*," *American Literature*, 27 (Nov. 1955), 396–403.
206, 662

273a. Cook, Charles H., Jr., "Ahab's 'Intolerable Allegory,'" *Boston University Studies in English*, 1 (1955–56), 45–52. Reprinted in *Discussions of Moby-Dick*, ed. Milton R. Stern (Boston: D. C. Heath, 1960), pp. 60–65.
63, 499

1956
Books

273b. Baird, James, *Ishmael* (Baltimore: Johns Hopkins Press, 1956).
63, 124b, 190, 223a, 276a, 418, 424, 492, 498b, 563, 639, 672, 761a, 766

274. Fite, Olive LaRue, "The Interpretation of Melville's *Billy Budd*" (Ph.D. dissertation, Northwestern University, 1956).
36, 37, 39, 40, 41, 499, 603, 609, 610, 611, 612, 613, 658

274a. Miller, Perry, *The Raven and the Whale: The War of Words and Wits in the Era of Poe and Melville* (New York: Harcourt, Brace, 1956).
77, 77a, 77b, 78a, 325, 326, 469, 487, 495, 574, 582, 583, 747a, 747b

275. Vogel, Dan, "Melville's Shorter Published Poetry: A Critical Study of the Lyrics in *Mardi*, of *Battle-Pieces*, *John Marr* and *Timoleon*" (Ph.D. dissertation, New York University, 1956).
25, 475

Articles

276. Lacy, Patricia, "The Agatha Theme in Melville's Stories," *Studies in English* (University of Texas), 35 (1956), 96–105.
719

277. [Cameron, Kenneth Walter], "*Billy Budd* and 'An Execution at Sea,'" *Emerson Society Quarterly*, 2 (I Quarter 1956), 13–15.
259

278. Dickinson, Leon T., "The 'Speksnyder' in *Moby-Dick*," *Melville Society Newsletter*, 12 (Spring 1956), [2].
615

279. Marx, Leo, "The Machine in the Garden," *New England Quarterly*, 29 (March 1956), 27–42.
330

280. Jeffrey, Lloyd N., "A Concordance to the Biblical Allusions in *Moby Dick*," *Bulletin of Bibliography and Magazine Notes*, 21 (May-Aug. 1956), 223–29.
63

281. Stone, Edward, "*Moby Dick* and Shakespeare: A Remonstrance," *Shakespeare Quarterly*, 7 (Autumn 1956), 445–48.
634

1957
Books

282. Farnsworth, Robert M., "Melville's Use of Point of View in His First Seven Novels" (Ph.D. dissertation, Tulane University, 1957).
653, 654a

283. Pochmann, Henry A., *German Culture in America: Philosophical and Literary Influences: 1600–1900* (Madison: University of Wisconsin Press, 1957), esp. pp. 436–40.
Carlyle, Coleridge, Goethe, 358, 408, 432, 436, 520, 606, 613, 677

Articles

284. Gollin, Richard and Rita, "Justice in an Earlier Treatment of the *Billy Budd* 'Theme,' " *American Literature*, 28 (Jan. 1957), 513–15.
398

285. Kaplan, Sidney, "Herman Melville and the American National Sin: The Meaning of Benito Cereno," *Journal of Negro History*, 42 (Jan. 1957), 11–37.
200, 299

286. Dale, T. R., "Melville and Aristotle: The Conclusion of *Moby-Dick* as a Classical Tragedy," *Boston University Studies in English*, 3 (Spring 1957), 45–50.
22, 634, 655

287. Day, A. Grove, "Hawaiian Echoes in Melville's *Mardi*," *Modern Language Quarterly*, 18 (March 1957), 3–8.
245, 671

288. Yates, Norris, "An Instance of Parallel Imagery in Hawthorne, Melville, and Frost," *Philological Quarterly*, 36 (April 1957), 276–80.
328

289. Dobbyn, Dermot, "The Birthplace of 'Moby Dick,' " *Catholic World* (Sept. 1957), 431–35.
63

290. Jaffe, David, "Some Origins of *Moby-Dick*: New Finds in an Old Source," *American Literature*, 29 (Nov. 1957), 263–77.
759

291. Cawelti, John G., "Some Notes on the Structure of *The Confidence-Man*," *American Literature*, 29 (Nov. 1957), 278–88.
338

1958
Books

291a. Levin, Harry, *The Power of Blackness: Hawthorne, Poe, Melville* (New York: Alfred A. Knopf, 1958).
63, 76a, 130, 318, 332, 333, 561, 574, 634

291b. Mayoux, Jean-Jacques, *Melville par lui-meme* (Paris: Editions du Seuil, 1958). Translated by John Ashbery as *Melville* (New York: Grove Press, 1960).
37, 63, 100, 150, 189, 203, Emerson, 331, 333, 338, 405, 499, 561, 634, 639, 704

Articles

292. Hicks, Granville, "A Re-Reading of *Moby Dick*: Melville, 1851," in *Twelve Original Essays on Great American Novels*, ed. Charles Shapiro (Detroit: Wayne State University Press, 1958), pp. 44–68.
107, 119

293. Philbrick, Thomas L., "Another Source for *White-Jacket*," *American Literature*, 29 (Jan. 1958), 431–39.
497

294. Stone, Harry, "Dickens and Melville Go to Chapel," *Dickensian*, 54 (Jan. 1958), 50–52.
210

295. Sealts, Merton M., Jr., "Melville's Burgundy Club Sketches,"

Harvard Library Bulletin, 12 (Spring 1958), 253–67.
61, 312, 373

296. Stein, William Bysshe, "The Old Man and the Triple Goddess: Melville's 'The Haglets,' " *ELH*, 25 (March 1958), 43–59.
354

297. Holman, C. Hugh, "The Reconciliation of Ishmael: *Moby-Dick* and the Book of Job," *South Atlantic Quarterly*, 57 (Autumn 1958), 477–90.
63, 111, 704

297a. Welsh, Alexander, "A Melville Debt to Carlyle," *Modern Language Notes*, 73 (Nov. 1958), 489–91.
113a

298. Vogel, Dan, "The Dramatic Chapters in *Moby Dick*," *Nineteenth-Century Fiction*, 13 (Dec. 1958), 239–47.
634

298a. Leiter, Louis, "Queequeg's Coffin," *Nineteenth-Century Fiction*, 13 (Dec. 1958), 249–54.
63

1959
Books

299. Kaplan, Sidney, "Herman Melville and the American National Sin" (Ph.D. dissertation, Harvard University, 1959).
200, 283, 299, 345, 388, 740

300. Nault, Clifford A., Jr., "Melville's Two-Stranded Novel: An Interpretation of *Moby-Dick* as an Enactment of Father Mapple's Sermon and the Lesser Prophe-cies, with an Essay on Melville Interpretation" (Ph.D. dissertation, Wayne State University, 1959).
63, 227, 239, Emerson, 484

301. Shulman, Robert Philip, "Toward *Moby-Dick*: Melville and Some Baroque Worthies" (Ph.D. dissertation, Ohio State University, 1959).
83, 100, Coleridge, 196, 283, 327, 489, 502, 559, 574, 654, 670

302. Ward, Joseph Thomas, "Herman Melville: The Forms and Forces of Evil" (Ph.D. dissertation, University of Notre Dame, 1959).
50, 91, 106, Hawthorne, 330, 639

Articles

303. Betts, William W., Jr., "*Moby Dick*: Melville's *Faust*," *Lock Haven Bulletin*, 1 (1959), 31–44.
34, 54, 109, 116, 125, 235, 288, Goethe, 296, 297, 298, 299, 300, 302, 303, 304, 349, 408, 432, 477, 520, 522, 586, 587, 589, 606, Schopenhauer, 666, 667, 677, 705, 775

304. Fogle, Richard Harter, "Melville and the Civil War," *Tulane Studies in English*, 9 (1959), 61–89.
139, 499, 576, 639

305. Tilton, Eleanor M., "Melville's 'Rammon': A Text and Commentary," *Harvard Library Bulletin*, 13 (Winter 1959), 50–91.
63, 634

306. Rosenberry, Edward H., "Queequeg's Coffin-Canoe: Made in Typee," *American Literature*, 30 (Jan. 1959), 529–30.
759

307. Satterfield, John, "Perth: An Organic Digression in *Moby-Dick*," *Modern Language Notes*, 74 (Feb. 1959), 106–7.
369

308. Dahl, Curtis, "Moby Dick's Cousin Behemoth," *American Literature*, 31 (March 1959), 21–29.
487

309. Stein, William Bysshe, "Melville Roasts Thoreau's Cock," *Modern Language Notes*, 74 (March 1959), 218–19.
712

310. Stanton, Robert, "*Typee* and Milton: Paradise Well Lost," *Modern Language Notes*, 74 (May 1959), 407–11.
499

311. Bratcher, James T., "Moby Dick: A Riddle Propounded," *Descant*, 4 (Autumn 1959), 34–39.
63, 477

312. Lucid, Robert F., "The Influence of *Two Years Before the Mast* on Herman Melville," *American Literature*, 31 (Nov. 1959), 243–56.
189, 440

313. Hayford, Harrison, "Poe in *The Confidence-Man*," *Nineteenth-Century Fiction*, 14 (Dec. 1959), 207–18.
78, 561

314. Ridge, George Ross, and Davy S. Ridge, "A Bird and a Motto: Source for 'Benito Cereno,' " *Mississippi Quarterly*, 13 (Winter 1959–60), 22–29.
149, 150

1960
Books

315. Bezanson, Walter E., ed., "Introduction" and "Explanatory Notes," *Clarel: A Poem and Pilgrimage in the Holy Land* (New York: Hendricks House, 1960), pp. ix–cxvii and 550–643.
7, 8, 25, 28, 29, 47, 48, 49, 54, 63, 67, 85, 94, 102, 107, 115, 122, 130, 131, 133, 134, 139, 147, 184, 190, 191, 198, 289, 332, 334, 335, 336, 337, 338, 341, 368, 371, 372, 406, 415, 418, 421, 429, 465, 475, 499, 511, 520, 534, 596, 597, 605, 606, 613, 624, 634, 663, 667, 668, 677, 708, 729, 734, 735, 746, 769

316. Fiedler, Leslie A., *Love and Death in the American Novel* (New York: Criterion Books, 1960).
53, 63, 385

316a. Fogle, Richard Harter, *Melville's Shorter Tales* (Norman: University of Oklahoma Press, 1960).
133, 333, 339, 697

317. Hoyle, Norman Eugene, "Melville as a Magazinist" (Ph.D. dissertation, Duke University, 1960).
9, 263, 266, 431, 466, 593a, 712, 721

318. Plumstead, Arthur William, "Time's Endless Tunnel: A Study of Herman Melville's Concern with Time" (Ph.D. dissertation, University of Rochester, 1960).
63, 83, 119, 327, Plato, 553, 557, 664

Articles

319. Fogle, Richard Harter, "Melville's *Clarel*: Doubt and Belief,"

Tulane Studies in English, 10 (1960), 101–16.
28, 61, 639, 696

320. Weathers, Willie T., "*Moby Dick* and the Nineteenth-Century Scene," *Studies in Literature and Language* (University of Texas), 1 (Winter 1960), 477–501.
Jefferson, 396

321. Schless, Howard H., "Flaxman, Dante, and Melville's *Pierre*," *Bulletin of the New York Public Library*, 64 (Feb. 1960), 65–82.
190, 272a

322. Cameron, Kenneth Walter, "A Note on the Corpusants in *Moby-Dick*," *Emerson Society Quarterly*, 19 (II Quarter 1960), 22–24.
599

323. Jaffe, David, "The Captain Who Sat for the Portrait of Ahab," *Boston University Studies in English*, 4 (Spring 1960), 1–22.
759

324. Wright, Nathalia, "*Pierre*: Herman Melville's *Inferno*," *American Literature*, 32 (May 1960), 167–81.
190

324a. Sutton, Walter, "Melville and the Great God Budd," *Prairie Schooner*, 34 (Summer 1960), 128–33.
609, 610, 611, 612, 613

325. Woodruff, Stuart C., "Melville and His Chimney," *PMLA*, 75 (June 1960), 283–92.
63

326. Abel, Darrel, " 'Laurel Twined With Thorn': The Theme of Melville's *Timoleon*," *Personalist*, 41 (July 1960), 330–40.
289, 411, 560, 606, 639

327. Philbrick, Thomas, "Melville's 'Best Authorities,' " *Nineteenth-Century Fiction*, 15 (Sept. 1960), 171–79.
359, 397, 452

328. Kasegawa, Koh, "Melville's Image of Solitude," *Aoyama Journal of General Education*, 1 (Nov. 1960), 157–99.
239, 566

329. Jackson, Margaret Y., "Melville's Use of a Real Slave Mutiny in 'Benito Cereno,' " *CLA Journal*, 4 (Dec. 1960), 79–93.
200

330. Kasegawa, Koh, "On the Symbolic Meanings of Blackness and Darkness in Melville," *Thought Currents in English Literature*, 33 (Dec. 1960), 75–103.
542, 634, 637

330a. Rosenberry, Edward H., "Melville's Ship of Fools," *PMLA*, 75 (Dec. 1960), 604–8.
74a, 100, 145a, 405, 614a

331. Stein, William Bysshe, "Melville's Comedy of Faith," *ELH*, 27 (Dec. 1960), 315–33.
63, 256, 634, 663

332. Berthoff, Warner, " 'Certain Phenomenal Men': The Example of *Billy Budd*," *ELH*, 27 (Dec. 1960), 334–51.
733

1961
Books

333. Finkelstein, Dorothee Metlitsky, *Melville's Orienda* (New Haven and London: Yale University Press, 1961).
18, 24, 25, 47, 48, 49, 54, 59, 87, 104, 107, 131, 193, 247, 269, 270, 294, 323, 372, 429, 464, 504, 538, 571, 596, 597, 598, 668, 708, 727, 735

334. Hoffman, Daniel G., *Form and Fable in American Fiction* (New York: Oxford University Press, 1961), esp. pp. 219–313.
50, 63, 83, 93, 122, 150, 250, 299, 333, 421, 485, 486, 499, 532, 582, 714

334a. Philbrick, Thomas, *James Fenimore Cooper and the Development of American Sea Fiction* (Cambridge: Harvard University Press, 1961).
63, 78a, 146, 170, 171, 325, 385, 441, 441a, 476a, 498, 752a, 752b

Articles

335. Boies, J. J., "Existential Nihilism and Herman Melville," *Transactions of the Wisconsin Academy of Sciences, Arts, and Letters*, 50 (1961), 307–20.
Schopenhauer, 639

336. Fogle, Richard Harter, "The Themes of Melville's Later Poetry," *Tulane Studies in English*, 11 (1961), 65–86.
147

337. Frank, Von Max, "Melville und Poe: Eine Quellenstudie zu 'Fragments from a Writing Desk No. 2,' 'Redburn,' und 'The Assig-

nation,' " in *Kleine Beitrage zur Amerikanischen Literaturgeschichte*, ed. Hans Galinsky and Hans-Joachim Lang (Heidelberg: Carl Winter-Universitatsverlag, 1961), pp. 19–23.
561

338. Ward, Robert S., "Longfellow and Melville: The Ship and the Whale," *Emerson Society Quarterly*, 22 (I Quarter 1961), 57–63.
454, 455, 456, 457

339. Hoffman, Daniel G., "Moby-Dick: Jonah's Whale or Job's?" *Sewanee Review*, 69 (April–June 1961), 205–24.
50, 63, 299, 421

340. Schless, Howard H., "Moby Dick and Dante: A Critique and Time Scheme," *Bulletin of the New York Public Library*, 65 (May 1961), 289–312.
190, 272a

341. Shulman, Robert, "The Serious Functions of Melville's Phallic Jokes," *American Literature*, 33 (May 1961), 179–94.
574, 666, 670

342. Franklin, H. Bruce, " 'Apparent Symbol of Despotic Command': Melville's *Benito Cereno*," *New England Quarterly*, 34 (Dec. 1961), 462–77. Slightly revised and reprinted as chapter 5, "*Benito Cereno*: The Ascetic's Agony," in H. Bruce Franklin, *The Wake of the Gods: Melville's Mythology* (Stanford: Stanford University Press, 1963), pp. 136–50.
63, 463, 536, 673

1962
Books

343. Bell, Millicent, *Hawthorne's View of the Artist* (Albany: State University of New York, 1962).
331

344. Eckardt, Sister Mary Ellen, I.H.M., "An Interpretive Analysis of the Patterns of Imagery in *Moby-Dick* and *Billy Budd*" (Ph.D. dissertation, University of Notre Dame, 1962).
436, Schopenhauer, 613

345. Hayford, Harrison, and Merton M. Sealts, Jr., eds., "Notes & Commentary," *Billy Budd, Sailor (An Inside Narrative)* (Chicago: University of Chicago Press, 1962), pp. 133–202.
11, Arnold, 25, 63, 72, 111, 112, 115, 170, 172, 173, 189a, 305, 333, 338, 374, 392, 397, 398, 483, 484, 497, 499, 502, 555, Schopenhauer, 609, 612, 634, 658, 663, 697, 763

345a. Humphreys, A. R., *Melville* (Edinburgh and London: Oliver & Boyd, 1962).
13, 16, 60, 82, 83, 101a, 115, 119, 130, 149, 170, 203, Emerson, 296, 325, 333, 410, 432, 440, 467, 485, 530, 574, 582, 630, 639, Smollett, 654, 659, 693, 758

346. Jones, Walter Dickinson, "A Critical Study of Herman Melville's *Israel Potter*" (Ph.D. dissertation, University of Alabama, 1962).
9, 163, 263, 280, 343, 604, 634, 640, 721

347. Rosen, Roma, "Melville's Uses of Shakespeare's Plays" (Ph.D. dis-sertation, Northwestern University, 1962).
634

347a. Stano[v]nik, Janez, *Moby Dick: The Myth and the Symbol: A Study in Folklore and Literature* (Ljubljana, Yugoslavia: Ljubljana University Press, 1962).
63, 333, 372, 499, 582, 639

Articles

348. Kilbourne, W. G., Jr., "Montaigne and Captain Vere," *American Literature*, 33 (Jan. 1962), 514–17.
502

349. Magowan, Robin, "Masque and Symbol in Melville's 'Benito Cereno,'" *College English*, 23 (Feb. 1962), 346–51.
663

350. Stein, William Bysshe, "Mel-ville's Cock and the Bell of Saint Paul," *Emerson Society Quarterly*, 27 (II Quarter 1962), 5–10.
63, 766

351. Stein, William Bysshe, "Mel-ville's Poetry: Two Rising Notes," *Emerson Society Quarterly*, 27 (II Quarter 1962), 10–13.
663, 750

352. Davidson, Frank, " 'Bartleby': A Few Observations," *Emerson Society Quarterly*, 27 (II Quarter 1962), 25–32.
250, 561

353. McAleer, John J., "Poe and Gothic Elements in *Moby-Dick*," *Emerson Society Quarterly*, 27 (II Quarter 1962), 34.
561

354. London, Philip W., "The Military Necessity: *Billy Budd* and Vigny," *Comparative Literature*, 14 (Spring 1962), 174–86.
733

355. Oates, J. C., "Melville and the Manichean Illusion," *Texas Studies in Literature and Language*, 4 (Spring 1962), 117–29. Slightly expanded and reprinted as chapter 3, "Melville and the Tragedy of Nihilism" in Joyce Carol Oates, *The Edge of Impossibility: Tragic Forms in Literature* (New York: Vanguard, 1972), pp. 59–83.
499

356. Ledbetter, Kenneth, "The Ambiguity of *Billy Budd*," *Texas Studies in Literature and Language*, 4 (Spring 1962), 130–34.
Schopenhauer

357. Smith, Paul, "*The Confidence-Man* and the Literary World of New York," *Nineteenth-Century Fiction*, 16 (March 1962), 329–37.
579, 754

358. Putzel, Max, "The Source and the Symbols of Melville's 'Benito Cereno,' " *American Literature*, 34 (May 1962), 191–206.
200

359. Wiley, Elizabeth, "Four Strange Cases," *Dickensian*, 58 (May 1962), 120–25.
81, 478

360. Mansfield, Luther Stearns, "Symbolism and Biblical Allusion in *Moby-Dick*," *Emerson Society Quarterly*, 28 (III Quarter 1962), 20–23.
63

361. Booth, Thornton Y., "*Moby Dick*: Standing up to God," *Nineteenth-Century Fiction*, 17 (June 1962), 33–43.
63

361a. Frederick, John T., "Symbol and Theme in Melville's *Israel Potter*," *Modern Fiction Studies*, 8 (Autumn 1962), 265–75.
721

362. Eby, Cecil D., Jr., "William Starbuck Mayo and Herman Melville," *New England Quarterly*, 35 (Dec. 1962), 515–20.
495

363. Nelson, Lowry, Jr., "Night Thoughts on the Gothic Novel," *Yale Review*, 52 (Dec. 1962), 236–57.
54, 636

364. Shulman, Robert, "Melville's Thomas Fuller: An Outline for Starbuck and an Instance of the Creator as Critic," *Modern Language Quarterly*, 23 (Dec. 1962), 337–52.
283

1963
Books

365. Blansett, Barbara Ruth Nieweg, "Melville and Emersonian Transcendentalism" (Ph.D. dissertation, University of Texas, 1963).
Emerson, 247, 249

365a. Franklin, H. Bruce, *The Wake of the Gods: Melville's My-*

thology (Stanford, Calif.: Stanford University Press, 1963).
27, 50, 63, 215a, 245, 254, 352, 377a, 380a, 431, 463, 491, 492, 536, 548a, 559, 584a, 673

366. Grenberg, Bruce Leonard, "Thomas Carlyle and Herman Melville: Parallels, Obliques, and Perpendiculars" (Ph.D. dissertation, University of North Carolina, 1963).
Carlyle, 114, 115, 118, 119

366a. Hillway, Tyrus, *Herman Melville* (New York: Twayne, 1963).
119, 499, 762b

367. Lucas, Thomas Edward, "Herman Melville as Literary Theorist" (Ph.D. dissertation, University of Denver, 1963).
190, 634

368. Parker, Hershel, "Melville and Politics: A Scrutiny of the Political Milieux of Herman Melville's Life and Works" (Ph.D. dissertation, Northwestern University, 1963).
96, 318

Articles

369. Browne, Ray B., "*Billy Budd*: Gospel of Democracy," *Nineteenth-Century Fiction*, 17 (March 1963), 321–37.
8, 95, 96, 208, 535

370. Seelye, John D., "Timothy Flint's 'Wicked River' and *The Confidence-Man*," *PMLA*, 78 (March 1963), 75–79.
274, 276

371. Hirsch, David H., "The Dilemma of the Liberal Intellectual:

Melville's Ishmael," *Texas Studies in Literature and Language*, 5 (Summer 1963), 169–88.
63, 450

372. Cohen, Hennig, "Melville and Webster's *The White Devil*," *Emerson Society Quarterly*, 33 (IV Quarter 1963), 33.
750

373. Ward, Joseph A., Jr., "Melville and Failure," *Emerson Society Quarterly*, 33 (IV Quarter 1963), 43–46.
648

374. Monteiro, George, "Melville and Keats," *Emerson Society Quarterly*, 33 (IV Quarter 1963), 55.
412

375. Guttmann, Allen, "From *Typee* to *Moby-Dick*: Melville's Allusive Art," *Modern Language Quarterly*, 24 (Sept. 1963), 237–44.
63, 119, 492, 499

375a. Parker, Hershel, "The Metaphysics of Indian-hating," *Nineteenth-Century Fiction*, 18 (Sept. 1963), 165–73.
63, 485

376. Turner, Darwin T., "A View of Melville's 'Piazza,'" *CLA Journal*, 7 (Sept. 1963), 56–62.
634

377. Beringause, A. F., "Melville and Chretien de Troyes," *American Notes & Queries*, 2 (Oct. 1963), 20–21.
720

1964
Books

377a. Bernstein, John, *Pacifism and Rebellion in the Writings of Herman Melville* (The Hague: Mouton, 1964).
63, 133, 377, 683

377b. Cohen, Hennig, ed., *Selected Poems of Herman Melville* (Garden City: Doubleday, 1964).
41, 50, 61, 63, 107, 111, 122, 130, 146, 147, 160a, 203, 208, 258a, 261, 269, 289, 333, 369, 499, 502, 505, 518, 560, 561, 576, 606, 632, 634, 658, 663, 667, 697, 703a, 750

377c. Feidelson, Charles, Jr., ed., *Moby-Dick or, The Whale* (Indianapolis: Bobbs-Merrill, 1964).
50, 52, 63, 82, 83, 93, 119, 130, 190, 282, 307a, 360, 369, 421, 423a, 469, 477, 499, 559, 574, 606, 615, 634, 666

378. Keller, Karl, "The Metaphysical Strain in Nineteenth-Century American Poetry" (Ph.D. dissertation, University of Minnesota, 1964), pp. 154–74.
2, 83, 147, 149, Emerson, 351, 484, 634, 692, 745

379. Newbery, Ilse Sofie Magdalene, "The Unity of Melville's *Piazza Tales*" (Ph.D. dissertation, University of British Columbia, 1964).
132, 153, 175, 190, 191, 200, 563, 663

380. Star, Morris, "Melville's Use of the Visual Arts" (Ph.D. dissertation, Northwestern University, 1964).
54, 107, 190, 272a, 295, 363, 467, 508, 564, Radcliffe, 636, 742

Articles

381. Shulman, Robert, "Montaigne and the Techniques and Tragedy of Melville's *Billy Budd*," *Comparative Literature*, 16 (1964), 322–30.
502

382. Cannon, Agnes Dicken, "Melville's Use of Sea Ballads and Songs," *Western Folklore*, 23 (Jan. 1964), 1–16.
82, 139, 189, 465, 660

383. Gale, Robert L., "Melville's *Moby Dick*, Chapters 91–93," *Explicator*, 22 (Jan. 1964), Item 32.
63

384. Perkins, George, "Death by Spontaneous Combustion in Marryat, Melville, Dickens, Zola, and Others," *Dickensian*, 60 (Jan. 1964), 57–63.
81, 308, 478

385. Sherwood, John C., "Vere as Collingwood: A Key to *Billy Budd*," *American Literature*, 35 (Jan. 1964), 476–84.
733

385a. Mansfield, Luther S., "The Emersonian Idiom and the Romantic Period in American Literature," *Emerson Society Quarterly*, 35 (II Quarter 1964), 23–28.
Emerson

386. Oliver, Egbert S., "To Light the Gay Bridals: One Aspect of *Moby-Dick*," *Emerson Society Quarterly*, 35 (II Quarter 1964), 30–34.
63

387. Jones, Buford, "Spenser and Shakespeare in *The Encantadas*,

Sketch VI," *Emerson Society Quarterly*, 35 (II Quarter 1964), 68–73.
154, 499, 563, 634, 663

388. Day, Frank L., "Melville and Sherman March to the Sea," *American Notes & Queries*, 2 (May 1964), 134–36.
518

389. Fletcher, Richard M., "Melville's Use of Marquesan," *American Speech*, 39 (May 1964), 135–38.
683

390. Nathanson, Leonard, "Melville's *Billy Budd*, Chapter 1," *Explicator*, 22 (May 1964), Item 75.
499

391. Doubleday, Neal F., "Jack Easy and Billy Budd," *English Language Notes*, 2 (Sept. 1964), 39–42.
480

392. Jones, Buford, "Melville's Buccaneers and Crebillon's Sofa," *English Language Notes*, 2 (Dec. 1964), 122–26.
154, 310

1965
Books

393. Donoghue, Denis, *Connoisseurs of Chaos: Ideas of Order in Modern American Poetry* (New York: Macmillan, 1965), esp. pp. 76– 99.
289, 576, 704

394. Fussell, Edwin, *Frontier: American Literature and the American West* (Princeton, N.J.: Princeton University Press, 1965), esp. pp. 232–326 and 375–96.
82, 86, 166, 189, 317, 361, 540, 541, 684

395. Haverstick, Iola, and Betty Shepard, eds., *The Wreck of the Whaleship Essex* (New York: Harcourt, Brace & World, 1965), esp. pp. 117–18.
130

395a. Hoar, Victor Myers, Jr., "The Confidence Man in American Literature" (Ph.D. dissertation, University of Illinois, 1965).
164

396. Long, Raymond Ronald, "The Hidden Sun: A Study of the Influence of Shakespeare on the Creative Imagination of Herman Melville" (Ph.D. dissertation, University of California at Los Angeles, 1965).
634

397. Rosen, Bruce John, "*Typee* and *Omoo*: Melville's Literary Apprenticeship" (Ph.D. dissertation, New York University, 1965).
401

397a. Trimpi, Helen Pinkerton, "Romance Structure and Melville's Use of Demonology and Witchcraft in *Moby-Dick*" (Ph.D. dissertation, Harvard University, 1965).
50, 63, 83, 100, 203, 296, 333, 390, 477, 622a, 663

398. Williams, John Brindley, "The Impact of Transcendentalism on the Novels of Herman Melville" (Ph.D. dissertation, University of Southern California, 1965).
Emerson

Articles

399. Falk, Robert, "Shakespeare in America: A Survey to 1900," in *Shakespeare Survey: An Annual Survey of Shakespearian Study & Production*, ed. Allardyce Nicoll, 18 (Cambridge: University Press, 1965), pp. 102–[118?].
634

400. McAleer, John J., "Biblical Symbols in American Literature: A Utilitarian Design," *English Studies*, 46 (1965), 310–17.
63

401. Kimmey, John L., "Pierre and Robin: Melville's Debt to Hawthorne," *Emerson Society Quarterly*, 38 (I Quarter 1965), 90– 92.
339

402. Austin, Allen, "The Three-Stranded Allegory of *Moby-Dick*," *College English*, 26 (Feb. 1965), 344–49.
249

403. Maxwell, J. C., "Melville and Milton," *Notes & Queries*, n.s. 12 (Feb. 1965), 60.
499

404. Pilkington, William T., "Melville's *Benito Cereno*: Source and Technique," *Studies in Short Fiction*, 2 (Spring 1965), 247– 55.
200

405. Levy, Leo B., "Hawthorne, Melville, and the *Monitor*," *American Literature*, 37 (March 1965), 33–40.
329

406. Hoeltje, Hubert H., "Hawthorne, Melville, and 'Black-ness,' " *American Literature*, 37 (March 1965), 41–51.
119, 333

407. Yu, Beongcheon, "Ishmael's Equal Eye: The Source of Balance in *Moby-Dick*," *ELH*, 32 (March 1965), 110–25.
4, 235, Emerson, 296, Keats, 711

408. Wright, Nathalia, "Moby Dick: Jonah's or Job's Whale?" *American Literature*, 37 (May 1965), 190–95.
63

409. Mogan, Joseph J., Jr., "*Pierre* and *Manfred*: Melville's Study of the Byronic Hero," *Papers on English Language & Literature*, 1 (Summer 1965), 230–40.
107

410. Friedrich, Gerhard, "A Note on Quakerism and *Moby Dick*: Hawthorne's 'The Gentle Boy' as a Possible Source," *Quaker History: The Bulletin of Friends Historical Association*, 54 (Autumn 1965), 94–102.
341

411. Rose, Edward J., " 'The Queenly Personality': Walpole, Melville and Mother," *Literature and Psychology*, 15 (Fall 1965), 216–29.
744

412. Slater, Judith, "The Domestic Adventurer in Melville's Tales," *American Literature*, 37 (Nov. 1965), 267–79.
241

413. Ross, Morton L., "Captain Truck and Captain Boomer,"

American Literature, 37 (Nov. 1965), 316.
164

414. Gross, Seymour L., "Mungo Park and Ledyard in Melville's *Benito Cereno*," *English Language Notes*, 3 (Dec. 1965), 122–23.
740

1966
Books

415. Dew, Marjorie Cannon, "Herman Melville's Existential View of the Universe: Essays in Phenomenological Interpretation" (Ph.D. dissertation, Kent State University, 1966).
200

416. Humphreys, A[rthur]. R., ed., *White-Jacket or The World in a Man-of-War* (London: Oxford University Press, 1966).
13, 54, 82, 111, 115, 171, 189, 341, 405, 497, 498, 499, 549, 622, 641a, 651a, Smollett, 654

417. Hutchinson, William Henry, "Demonology in Melville's Vocabulary of Evil" (Ph.D. dissertation, Northwestern University, 1966).
190

418. Tick, Stanley, "Forms of the Novel in the Nineteenth Century: Studies in Dickens, Melville, and George Eliot" (Ph.D. dissertation, University of California at San Diego, 1966).
213

419. Zirker, Priscilla Allen, "The Major and Minor Themes of Melville's *White-Jacket*" (Ph.D. dissertation, Cornell University, 1966).
111, 208, 326, 357, 440, 497, 498, 515, 519, 531

Articles

420. Asselineau, Roger, "Ishmael—or the Theme of Solitude in American Literature," in *USA in Focus: Recent Re-Interpretations*, ed. Sigmund Skard (Oslo: Universitetsforlaget, 1966), pp. 107–19.
168, 760

421. Ekner, Reidar, "*The Encantadas* and *Benito Cereno*—On Sources and Imagination in Melville," *Moderna Sprak*, 60 (1966), 258–73.
154, 176, 188, 191, 200, 563

421a. Friedman, Maurice, "Bartleby and the Modern Exile," in *Melville Annual 1965/A Symposium: Bartleby the Scrivener*, ed. Howard P. Vincent (Kent, Ohio: Kent State University Press, 1966), pp. 64–81.
63

421b. D'Avanzo, Mario L., "Melville's 'Bartleby' and Carlyle," in *Melville Annual 1965/A Symposium: Bartleby the Scrivener*, ed. Howard P. Vincent (Kent, Ohio: Kent State University Press, 1966), pp. 113–39.
117, 119

422. Mayoux, J. J., "Thomas De Quincey and Herman Melville: A Study in Affinities," *English Studies Today*, 4 (1966), 395–407.
203

423. Rosenfeld, William, "Uncertain Faith: Queequeg's Coffin and

Melville's Use of the Bible," *Texas Studies in Literature and Language*, 7 (Winter 1966), 317–27.
63

424. Rees, Robert A., "Melville's Alma and *The Book of Mormon*," *Emerson Society Quarterly*, 43 (II Quarter 1966), 41–46.
70, 567, 663

425. Davison, Richard Allan, "Melville's *Mardi* and John Skelton," *Emerson Society Quarterly*, 43 (II Quarter 1966), 86–87.
645

426. Travis, Mildred K., "*Mardi*: Melville's Allegory of Love," *Emerson Society Quarterly*, 43 (II Quarter 1966), 88–94.
663

427. Drummond, C. Q., "Nature: Meek Ass or White Whale?," *Sage: A Humanities Review* (University of Wyoming), 11 (Spring 1966), 71–84.
Emerson

428. Newbery, I., " 'The Encantadas': Melville's *Inferno*," *American Literature*, 38 (March 1966), 49–68.
132, 153, 175, 190, 191, 200, 563, 663

429. Seelye, John D., " 'Spontaneous Impress of Truth': Melville's Jack Chase: a Source, an Analogue, a Conjecture," *Nineteenth-Century Fiction*, 20 (March 1966), 367–76.
441, 442, 519, 770

430. Bridgman, Richard, "Melville's Roses," *Texas Studies in Literature and Language*, 8 (Summer 1966), 235–44.
365

431. Fisher, Marvin, "Melville's 'Bell-Tower': A Double Thrust," *American Quarterly*, 18 (Summer 1966), 200–207.
634

432. Schroeder, Fred E. H., "*Enter Ahab, Then All*: Theatrical Elements in Melville's Fiction," *Dalhousie Review*, 46 (Summer 1966), 223–32.
282

432a. Stein, William Bysshe, "Time, History, and Religion: A Glimpse of Melville's Late Poetry," *Arizona Quarterly*, 22 (Summer 1966), 136–45.
353

433. Fiess, Edward, "Byron's Dark Blue Ocean and Melville's Rolling Sea," *English Language Notes*, 3 (June 1966), 274–78.
107

434. Karcher, Carolyn Lury, "The Story of Charlemont: A Dramatization of Melville's Concepts of Fiction in *The Confidence-Man: His Masquerade*," *Nineteenth-Century Fiction*, 21 (June 1966), 73–84.
63

435. Tuveson, Ernest, "The Creed of the Confidence-Man," *ELH*, 33 (June 1966), 247–70.
50, 633, 665

436. Vargish, Thomas, "Gnostic Mythos in *Moby-Dick*," *PMLA*, 81 (June 1966), 272–77.
50, 289, 421, 524

437. Zirker, Priscilla Allen, "Evidence of the Slavery Dilemma in *White-Jacket*," *American Quarterly*, 18 (Fall 1966), 477–92.
13, 440, 441, 498

438. Duerksen, Roland A., "Caleb Williams, Political Justice, *and* Billy Budd," *American Literature*, 38 (Nov. 1966), 372–76.
295

439. Pickering, James H., "Melville's 'Ducking' Duyckinck," *Bulletin of the New York Public Library*, 70 (Nov. 1966), 551–52.
382

1967
Books

439a. Boudreau, Gordon Vincent, "Herman Melville: Master Mason of the Gothic" (Ph.D. dissertation, Indiana University, 1967).
54, 63, 91, 190, 245, 499, 663, 742

440. Braun, Julie Ann, "Melville's Use of Carlyle's *Sartor Resartus*: 1846–1857" (Ph.D. dissertation, University of California at Los Angeles, 1967).
107, 119, 302, 639, 712

440a. Eddy, Darlene Fern Mathis, "A Dark Similitude: Melville and the Elizabethan-Jacobean Perspective" (Ph.D. dissertation, Rutgers University, 1967).
53, 63, 66a, 147, 149, 224a, 258b, 346, 347a, 368, 405, 430, 453, 477, 497a, 502a, 513, 558a, 631, 634, 663

440b. Faigelman, Steven Henry, "The Development of Narrative Consciousness in *Moby-Dick*" (Ph.D. dissertation, Cornell University, 1967).
13, 524

440c. Franklin, H. Bruce, ed., *The Confidence-Man: His Masquerade* (Indianapolis: Bobbs-Merrill, 1967).
3a, 12b, 63, 86, 93, 98, 183, 212, 216a, 231, 249, 254, 283, 302, 317, 378, 431, 444a, 454b, 499, 532, 561, 634, 663, 701, 711, 713, 734, 766

440d. Hoefer, Jacqueline Stanhope, "After *Moby Dick*: A Study of Melville's Later Novels" (Ph.D. dissertation, Washington University, 1967).
9, 63, 263, 466, 499, 634, 721

440e. Noel, Daniel Calhoun, "The Portent Unwound: Religious and Psychological Development in the Imagery of Herman Melville, 1819–1851" (Ph.D. dissertation, Drew University, 1967).
18, 52, 63, 107, 113a, 130, 170, 189, 286, 296, 331, 333, 341, 430, 453, 513, 517, 561, 582, 606, 631, 634, 680, 697

440f. Ryan, Robert Charles, *"Weeds and Wildings Chiefly: With a Rose or Two* by Herman Melville. Reading Text and Genetic Text, edited from the Manuscripts, with Introduction and Notes" (Ph.D. dissertation, Northwestern University, 1967).
63, 87a, 134, 250, 252, 269, 296, 311a, 332, 333, 346, 365, 385, 387, 405, 499, 513, 525a, 589, 634, 634a, 635, 697, 750

441. Stevens, Sister Mary Dominic, O.P., "Melville: Sceptic" (Ph.D. dis-

sertation, Loyola University, 1967).
37, 50, 83, 123, 216, 377, 408, 502, 542, 574, 634

441a. Wadlington, Warwick Paul, "The Theme of the Confidence Game in Certain Major American Writers" (Ph.D. dissertation, Tulane University, 1967).
63, 754

441b. Warren, Robert Penn, ed., "Introduction" and "Notes on the Text," *Selected Poems of Herman Melville: A Reader's Edition* (New York: Random House, 1967), pp. 3–88 and 351-451.
28, 63, 131, 139, 148, 167a, 190, 320, 329, 405, 414a, Kipling, Landor, 432a, 482b, 484, 499, 552, 569, 576, 595, 634, 649, 668

Articles

442. Bach, Bert C., "Melville's Israel Potter: A Revelation of It's Reputation and Meaning," *Cithara*, 7 (1967), 39–50.
721

442a. Cowen, Walker, "Melville's 'Discoveries': A Dialogue of the Mind with Itself," in *The Recognition of Herman Melville*, ed. Hershel Parker (Ann Arbor: University of Michigan Press, 1967), pp. 333–46.
37, 40, 41, 122, 125, 132, 249, 268, 405, 589, 634, 635, 667, 668, 721

443. Lang, Hans–Joachim, "Ein Argerteufel bei Hawthorne und Melville: Quellenuntersuchung zu *The Confidence-Man*," *Jahr-*

buch für Amerikastudien, 12 (1967), 246–51.
341

444. Cowan, S. A., "In Praise of Self-Reliance: The Role of Bulkington in *Moby-Dick*," *American Literature*, 38 (Jan. 1967), 547–56.
249

445. Maxwell, J. C., "Three Notes on 'Moby-Dick,'" *Notes and Queries*, n.s. 14 (Feb. 1967), 53.
2, 142, 150

446. Davison, Richard Allan, "Redburn, Pierre and Robin: Melville's Debt to Hawthorne?" *Emerson Society Quarterly*, 47 (II Quarter 1967), 32–34.
339

447. Levy, Leo B., "Hawthorne and the Idea of 'Bartleby,'" *Emerson Society Quarterly*, 47 (II Quarter 1967), 66–69.
333

448. Hull, Raymona, "London and Melville's *Israel Potter*," *Emerson Society Quarterly*, 47 (II Quarter 1967), 78–81.
422, 721

449. Hirsch, David H., "Melville's Ishmaelite," *American Notes & Queries*, 5 (April 1967), 115–16.
117

450. Cohen, Hennig, "Melville's Copy of Broughton's 'Popular Poetry of the Hindoos,'" *Papers of the Bibliographical Society of America*, 61 (3rd Quarter 1967), 266–67.
80

451. Franklin, H. Bruce, "The Island Worlds of Darwin and Mel-

ville," *Centennial Review*, 11 (Summer 1967), 353–70.
191, 663

452. Eby, Cecil D., Jr., "Another Breaching of 'Mocha Dick,' " *English Language Notes*, 4 (June 1967), 277–79.
143

453. Magaw, Malcolm O., "Apocalyptic Imagery in Melville's 'The Apple-Tree Table,' " *Midwest Quarterly*, 8 (July 1967), 357–69.
63

454. Shulman, Robert, "Melville's 'Timoleon': From Plutarch to the Early Stages of *Billy Budd*," *Comparative Literature*, 19 (Fall 1967), 351–61.
560

455. Hillway, Tyrus, "Two Books in Young Melville's Library," *Bulletin of the New York Public Library*, 71 (Sept. 1967), 474–76.
443, 774

456. Regan, Charles L., "Melville's Horned Woman," *English Language Notes*, 5 (Sept. 1967), 34–39.
482a, 500

457. Bush, C. W., "This Stupendous Fabric: The Metaphysics of Order in Melville's *Pierre* and Nathanael West's *Miss Lonelyhearts*," *Journal of American Studies*, 1 (Oct. 1967), 269–74.
190

458. Warren, Robert Penn, "Melville's Poems," *Southern Review*, n.s. 3 (Oct. 1967), 799–855.
320, 499, 649

459. Kimball, William J., "Charles Sumner's Contribution to Chapter XVIII of Billy Budd," *South Atlantic Bulletin*, 32 (Nov. 1967), 13–14.
681

1968
Books

459a. Corey, James Robert, "Herman Melville and the Theory of Evolution" (Ph.D. dissertation, Washington State University, 1968).
124, 124a, 191, 460a

459b. Devers, James, "Melancholy, Myth, and Symbol in Melville's 'Benito Cereno'; An Interpretive Study" (Ph.D. dissertation, University of California at Los Angeles, 1968).
100

459c. Dryden, Edgar A., *Melville's Thematics of Form: The Great Art of Telling the Truth* (Baltimore: Johns Hopkins Press, 1968).
50, 63, 100, 421

460. Howard, Leon, "Historical Note," in *Typee: A Peep at Polynesian Life*, ed. Harrison Hayford, Hershel Parker, and G. Thomas Tanselle (Evanston and Chicago: Northwestern University Press and The Newberry Library, 1968), pp. 277–302.
245, 357, 433, 563, 672

461. Roper, Gordon, "Historical Note," in *Omoo: A Narrative of Adventures in the South Seas*, ed. Harrison Hayford, Hershel Parker, and G. Thomas Tanselle (Evanston and Chicago: Northwestern

University Press and The Newberry Library, 1968), pp. 319–44.
245, 357, 433, 594, 672, 759

461a. Seelye, John, "Introduction," *The Confidence-Man: His Masquerade* [a facsimile of the first edition] (San Francisco: Chandler, 1968), pp. vii–xl.
46a, 183a, 274, 384

461b. Shurr, William Howard, "The Symbolic Structure of Herman Melville's *Clarel*" (Ph.D. dissertation, University of North Carolina at Chapel Hill, 1968).
28, 63, 190, 206a, 252, 373, 499, 543a

Articles

461c. Howes, Jeanne C., "Melville's Sensitive Years," in *Melville & Hawthorne in the Berkshires: A Symposium/Melville Annual 1966*, ed. Howard P. Vincent (Kent, Ohio: Kent State University Press, 1968), pp. 22–41.
380b, 538a, 737a

461d. Miller, F. DeWolfe, "Another Chapter in the History of the Great White Whale," in *Melville & Hawthorne in the Berkshires: A Symposium/Melville Annual 1966*, ed. Howard P. Vincent (Kent, Ohio: Kent State University Press, 1968), pp. 109–17, 158.
156c, 157, 158a, 437

462. Stevens, Aretta J., "The Edition of Montaigne Read by Melville," *Papers of the Bibliographical Society of America*, 62 (1st Quarter 1968), 130–34.
502

462a. Travis, Mildred K., "Spenserian Analogues in *Mardi* and *The Confidence Man*," *Emerson Society Quarterly*, 50, Supplement (I Quarter 1968), 55–58.
663

462b. Travis, Mildred K., "The Idea of Poe in *Pierre*," *Emerson Society Quarterly*, 50, Supplement (I Quarter 1968), 59–62.
561

462c. D'Avanzo, Mario L., " 'The Cassock' and Carlyle's 'Church-Clothes,' " *Emerson Society Quarterly*, 50, Supplement (I Quarter 1968), 74–76.
119

463. Conarroe, Joel O., "Melville's Bartleby and Charles Lamb," *Studies in Short Fiction*, 5 (Winter 1968), 113–18.
431, 686

463a. Markels, Julian, "*King Lear* and *Moby-Dick*: The Cultural Connection," *Massachusetts Review*, 9 (Winter 1968), 169–76.
634

463b. Gollin, Rita, "*Pierre's* Metamorphosis of Dante's *Inferno*," *American Literature*, 39 (Jan. 1968), 542–45.
190

464. Frederick, John T., "Melville's Early Acquaintance with Bayle," *American Literature*, 39 (Jan. 1968), 545–47.
513

465. Dillingham, William B., "The Narrator of *Moby-Dick*," *English Studies*, 49 (Feb. 1968), 20–29.
150

466. Millgate, Michael, "Melville and Marvell: A Note on Billy Budd," *English Studies*, 49 (Feb. 1968), 47–50.
484

467. Mulqueen, James E., "Foreshadowing of Melville & Faulkner," *American Notes & Queries*, 6 (March 1968), 102.
749

468. Raleigh, John Henry, "The Novel and the City: England and America in the Nineteenth Century," *Victorian Studies*, 11 (March 1968), 291–328.
Dickens

469. Russell, Jack, "*Israel Potter* and 'Song of Myself,' " *American Literature*, 40 (March 1968), 72–77.
604, 640

469a. Scherting, Jack, "The Bottle and the Coffin: Further Speculation on Poe and *Moby-Dick*," *Poe Newsletter*, 1 (April 1968), 22.
561

470. Moss, Sidney P., " 'Cock-A-Doodle-Doo!' and Some Legends in Melville Scholarship," *American Literature*, 40 (May 1968), 192–210.
488, 549, 712, 766

471. Swanson, Donald R., "The Structure of *The Confidence Man*," *CEA Critic*, 30 (May 1968), 6–7.
684

472. Reid, B. L., "Old Melville's Fable," *MR: The Massachusetts Review*, 9 (Summer 1968), 529–46.
499

473. Walcutt, Charles Child, "The Soundings of Moby Dick," *Arizona Quarterly*, 24 (Summer 1968), 101–16.
52, 83, 634

474. Aspiz, Harold, "Phrenologizing the Whale," *Nineteenth-Century Fiction*, 23 (June 1968), 18–27.
436

475. Breinig, Helmbrecht, "The Destruction of Fairyland: Melville's 'Piazza' in the Tradition of the American Imagination," *ELH*, 35 (June 1968), 254–83.
333, 634, 697

475a. Isani, Mukhtar Ali, "Melville and the 'Bloody Battle in Affghanistan,' " *American Quarterly*, 20 (Fall 1968), 645–49.
256a, 322a

475b. Lease, Benjamin, "Two Sides to a Tortoise: Darwin and Melville in the Pacific," *Personalist*, 49 (Autumn 1968), 531–39.
191, 425

476. Narveson, Robert, "The Name 'Claggart' in 'Billy Budd,' " *American Speech*, 43 (Oct. 1968), 229–32.
63, 299, 499

477. Eddy, D. Mathis, "Melville's Response to Beaumont and Fletcher: A New Source for *The Encantadas*," *American Literature*, 40 (Nov. 1968), 374–80.
53, 430, 663

478. Isani, Mukhtar Ali, "The Naming of Fedallah in *Moby-Dick*," *American Literature*, 40 (Nov. 1968), 380–85.
54, 206, 372, 419, 504, 662, 751

479. Fite, Olive L., "Billy Budd, Claggart, and Schopenhauer," *Nineteenth-Century Fiction*, 23 (Dec. 1968), 336–43.
613

1969
Books

479a. Bergmann, Johannes Dietrich, "The Original Confidence Man: The Development of the American Confidence Man in the Sources and Backgrounds of Herman Melville's *The Confidence-Man: His Masquerade*" (Ph.D. dissertation, University of Connecticut, 1969).
29a, 46a, 46b, 266a, 310a, 310b, 373a, 405, 485, 529, 634, 754

479b. Carothers, Robert Lee, "Herman Melville and the Search for the Father: An Interpretation of the Novels" (Ph.D. dissertation, Kent State University, 1969).
483

479c. Frederick, John T., "Herman Melville," in *The Darkened Sky: Nineteenth-Century American Novelists and Religion* (Notre Dame, Ind.: University of Notre Dame Press, 1969), pp. 79–122.
28, 513

480. Hayford, Harrison, and Walter Blair, eds., "Editors' Introduction" and "Explanatory Notes," *Omoo: A Narrative of Adventures in the South Seas* (New York: Hendricks House, 1969), pp. xvii–lii and 341–438.
55, 60, 63, 73, 102, 103, 245, 357, 358, 363, 425, 433, 499, 528, 562, 563, 593, 594, 634, 672, 723, 734, 755, 759, 762

480a. Mandel, Ruth B., "Herman Melville and the Gothic Outlook" (Ph.D. dissertation, University of Connecticut, 1969).
54, 362a, 636

481. Parker, Hershel, "Historical Note," in *Redburn: His First Voyage. Being the Sailor-boy Confessions and Reminiscences of the Son-of-a-Gentleman, in the Merchant Service*, ed. Harrison Hayford, Hershel Parker, and G. Thomas Tanselle (Evanston and Chicago: Northwestern University Press and The Newberry Library, 1969), pp. 315–52.
267, 385, 544, 545, 547, 626, 648

481a. Porte, Joel, *The Romance in America: Studies in Cooper, Poe, Hawthorne, Melville, and James* (Middletown, Conn.: Wesleyan University Press, 1969), pp. 152–92.
561

481b. Reiss, John Peter, Jr., "Problems of the Family Novel: Cooper, Hawthorne, and Melville" (Ph.D. dissertation, University of Wisconsin, 1969), esp. pp. 94–140 and 157–64.
63, 107, 164a, 169, 170, 171, 173a, 250, 328, 331, 338, 341

481c. Schultz, Donald Deidrich, "Herman Melville and the Tradition of the Anatomy: A Study in Genre" (Ph.D. dissertation, Vanderbilt University, 1969).
100, 102, 119, 165, 171, 189, 203, 216, 266a, 401, 421, 432, 458a, 480, 481, 495, 561, 574, Smollett, 654

481d. Turlish, Lewis Afton, "A Study of Teleological Concepts in

the Novels of Herman Melville" (Ph.D. dissertation, University of Michigan, 1969).
50, 83, 123, 307, 308, 377, 502, 525b, 537, 537a, 566, 721a

481e. Watson, Charles Nelles, Jr., "Characters and Characterization in the Works of Herman Melville" (Ph.D. dissertation, Duke University, 1969).
9, 107, 200, 214, 263, 266b, 466, 634, 636, 654, 721

Articles

481f. Vande Kieft, Ruth M., " 'When Big Hearts Strike Together': The Concussion of Melville and Sir Thomas Browne," *Papers on Language & Literature*, 5 (Winter 1969), 39–50.
83

482. Simpson, Eleanor E., "Melville and the Negro: From *Typee* to 'Benito Cereno,' " *American Literature*, 41 (March 1969), 19–38.
126

483. Patrick, Walton R., "Melville's 'Bartleby' and the Doctrine of Necessity," *American Literature*, 41 (March 1969), 39–54.
239, 566

484. Bergmann, Johannes Dietrich, "The Original Confidence Man," *American Quarterly*, 21 (Fall 1969), 560–77.
529

485. Herbert, T. Walter, Jr., "Calvinism and Cosmic Evil in *Moby-Dick*," *PMLA*, 84 (Oct. 1969), 1613–19.
690

486. Trimpi, Helen P., "Melville's Use of Demonology and Witchcraft in *Moby-Dick*," *Journal of the History of Ideas*, 30 (Oct.–Dec. 1969), 543–62.
83, 100, 390, 621

486a. Nelson, Raymond J., "The Art of Herman Melville: The Author of *Pierre*," *Yale Review*, 59 (Dec. 1969), 197–214.
122, 246a, 634

1970
Books

487. Barbour, James Francis, "The Writing of *Moby Dick*" (Ph.D. dissertation, University of California at Los Angeles, 1970).
52, 60, 82, 119, 130, 136, 149, 170, 325, 331, 333, 528, 615, 634, 680

487a. Branch, Watson Gailey, "*The Confidence-Man: His Masquerade*, by Herman Melville. An Edition with an Introduction and Notes" (Ph.D. dissertation, Northwestern University, 1970).
63, 100, 167a, 183, 212, 317, 325, 333, 341, 373a, 431, 499, 529, 579a, 634, 701, 714, 734

487b. Christy, Wallace McVay, "The Shock of Recognition: A Psycho-Literary Study of Hawthorne's Influence on Melville's Short Fiction" (Ph.D. dissertation, Brown University, 1970).
328, 331, 333, 338

488. Foster, Elizabeth S., "Historical Note," in *Mardi: and A Voyage Thither*, ed. Harrison Hayford, Hershel Parker, and G. Thomas Tanselle (Evanston and Chicago: Northwestern University Press

and The Newberry Library, 1970),
pp. 657–81.
18, 59, 60, 100, 107, 245, 410, 432,
504, 530, Plato, 568, 574, 630, 638,
639, 659, 663, 724, 758, 759

488a. Freibert, Sister Lucy Marie,
"Meditative Voice in the Poetry of
Herman Melville" (Ph.D. dissertation, University of Wisconsin,
1970).
5, 23a, 25, 41, 84, R. Browning, 84b,
112, 289, 433a, 453, 475, 484, 513,
560, 606, 609, 634, 635

488b. Pops, Martin Leonard, *The
Melville Archetype* (Kent, Ohio:
Kent State University Press, 1970).
385, 711

488c. Seelye, John, *Melville: The
Ironic Diagram* (Evanston, Ill:
Northwestern University Press,
1970).
18, 122, 625, 639

489. Stein, William Bysshe, *The
Poetry of Melville's Late Years:
Time, History, Myth, and Religion*
(Albany: State University of New
York Press, 1970).
16, 29, 50, 63, 75, 107, 139, 148, 190,
228, 269, 273, 353, 385, 417, 562,
634, 732, 736

490. Thorp, Willard, "Historical
Note," in *White-Jacket: or The
World in a Man–of–War*, ed. Harrison Hayford, Hershel Parker, and
G. Thomas Tanselle (Evanston
and Chicago: Northwestern University Press and The Newberry
Library, 1970), pp. 403–40.
13, 30, 77, 79, 169, 189, 359, 397,
440, 441, 452, 497, 498, 519, 544,
606, 647

491. Vincent, Howard P., *The Tailoring of Melville's White-Jacket*
(Evanston: Northwestern University Press, 1970).
13, 58, 79, 119, 150, 189, 265, 311,
350, 356, 359, 397, 424, 440, 497,
498, 506, 519, 544, 561, 606, 634,
647, 653, 654

Articles

492. Minamizuka, Takao, "Novel-
istic Amorality: A Study of Melvil-
lian World," *Bulletin of Tokyo
Kyoiku University* (1970).
562

493. Kirkham, E. Bruce, "The Iron
Crown of Lombardy in *Moby
Dick*," *ESQ*, 58 (I Quarter 1970),
127–29.
119

493a. Waggoner, Hyatt H., "Hawthorne and Melville Acquaint the
Reader with Their Abodes," *Studies in the Novel*, 2 (Winter 1970),
420–24.
333

494. Noel, Daniel C., "Figures of
Transfiguration: *Moby-Dick* as
Radical Theology," *Cross Currents*, 20 (Spring 1970), 201–20.
331, 606

494a. Dillingham, William B.,
"Melville's Long Ghost and Smollett's Count Fathom," *American
Literature*, 42 ([May] 1970), 232–35.
652

495. Lowance, Mason I., Jr., "Veils
and Illusion in *Benito Cereno*,"
Arizona Quarterly, 26 (Summer
1970), 113–26.
63

496. Seelye, John, "The Contemporary 'Bartleby,'" *American Transcendental Quarterly*, 7 (Summer 1970), 12–18.
255, 384

497. Fiene, Donald M., "Bartleby the Christ," *American Transcendental Quarterly*, 7 (Summer 1970), 18–23.
63

497a. Swanson, Donald R., "The Exercise of Irony in 'Benito Cereno,'" *American Transcendental Quarterly*, 7 (Summer 1970), 23–31.
634

497b. Mengeling, Marvin E., "Through 'The Encantadas': An Experienced Guide and You," *American Transcendental Quarterly*, 7 (Summer 1970), 37–43.
385

498. Rosenberry, Edward H., "Melville and His *Mosses*," *American Transcendental Quarterly*, 7 (Summer 1970), 47–51.
333

498a. Neff, Winifred, "Satirical Use of a 'Silly Reference' in *Israel Potter*," *American Transcendental Quarterly*, 7 (Summer 1970), 51–53.
263, 721

499. Parker, Hershel, "Melville's Satire of Emerson and Thoreau: An Evaluation of the Evidence," *American Transcendental Quarterly*, 7 (Summer 1970), 61–67. "Corrections," *American Transcendental Quarterly*, 9 (1971), 70.
249, 251, 458, 581, 709, 710, 713

499a. Knapp, Joseph G., "Melville's *Clarel*: Dynamic Synthesis," *American Transcendental Quarterly*, 7 (Summer 1970), 67–76.
28, 102, 107, 697

499b. Willett, Maurita, "The Silences of Herman Melville," *American Transcendental Quarterly*, 7 (Summer 1970), 85–92.
Carlyle, 168, 171, 454a, 634, 713

499c. Stout, Janis, "Melville's Use of the Book of Job," *Nineteenth-Century Fiction*, 25 (June 1970), 69–83.
63

500. Rice, Julian C., "*Moby-Dick* and Shakespearean Tragedy," *Centennial Review*, 14 (Fall 1970), 444–68.
634

500a. Tuerk, Richard, "Melville's 'Bartleby' and Isaac D'Israeli's *Curiosities of Literature*, Second Series," *Studies in Short Fiction*, 7 (Fall 1970), 647–49.
222

500b. Rowland, Beryl, "Melville's Waterloo in 'Rich Man's Crumbs,'" *Nineteenth-Century Fiction*, 25 (Sept. 1970), 216–21.
180, 422

500c. Rosenthal, Bernard, "Melville, Marryat, and the Evil-Eyed Villain," *Nineteenth-Century Fiction*, 25 (Sept. 1970), 221–24.
481a

501. Werge, Thomas, "*Moby-Dick*: Scriptural Source of 'Blackness of Darkness,'" *American Notes & Queries*, 9 (Sept. 1970), 6.
63, 119, 240

502. Kroeger, Frederick P., "Longfellow, Melville and Hawthorne: The Passage into the Iron Age," *Illinois Quarterly*, 33 (Dec. 1970), 30–41.
329

1971
Books

503. Browne, Ray B., *Melville's Drive to Humanism* (Lafayette, Ind.: Purdue University Studies, 1971).
96, 150, 208, 232, 330, 333, 338, 341, 471, 535, 634, 711, 712, 713

503a. Bruner, Margaret Reed, "The Gospel According to Herman Melville: A Reading of *The Confidence-Man: His Masquerade*" (Ph.D. dissertation, Vanderbilt University, 1971).
63, 143a, 143b, 421, 421a, 431, 490a

504. Howard, Leon, and Hershel Parker, "Historical Note," in *Pierre; or, The Ambiguities*, ed. Harrison Hayford, Hershel Parker, and G. Thomas Tanselle (Evanston and Chicago: Northwestern University Press and The Newberry Library, 1971), pp. 365–410.
92, Carlyle, 190, Dickens, 407, 634, 666, Thackeray

504a. Knapp, Joseph G., *Tortured Synthesis: The Meaning of Melville's Clarel* (New York: Philosophical Library, 1971).
25, 27, 28, 102, 107, 222, 249, 250, 502b, 667

504b. Parker, Hershel, ed., Notes and "Backgrounds and Sources," *The Confidence-Man: His Mas-*

querade (New York: W. W. Norton, 1971), pp. 1–217 and 227–66.
29a, 46a, 63, 63a, 200, 212, 231, 249, 250, 280, 315a, 317, 333, 341, 378, 410, 463, 499, 529, 577a, 633, 634, 650, 711, 713, 713a, 748, 752, 754, 766

504c. Schaible, Robert Manly, "An Annotated Edition of Herman Melville's *Redburn*" (Ph.D. dissertation, University of Tennessee, 1971).
63, 382, 499, 514a, 547, 591a, 634

504d. Travis, Mildred Klein, "Toward the Explication of *Pierre*: New Perspectives in Technique and Meaning" (Ph.D. dissertation, Arizona State University, 1971).
250a, 250b, 250c, 251, 296, 561

Articles

505. D'Avanzo, Mario L., "Ahab, The Grecian Pantheon and Shelley's *Prometheus Unbound*: The Dynamics of Myth in *Moby Dick*," *Books at Brown*, 24 (1971), 19–44.
119, 639

506. Hirsch, David H., "Verbal Reverberations and the Problem of Reality in *Moby Dick*," *Books at Brown*, 24 (1971), 45–67.
291, 421

507. Trimpi, Helen P., "Conventions of Romance in *Moby-Dick*," *Southern Review*, n.s. 7 (Jan. 1971), 115–29.
130, 620, 621

507a. Banta, Martha, "The Man of History and the Mythy Man in Melville," *American Transcenden-*

tal Quarterly, 10 (Spring 1971), 3–11.
280, 721

508. Karcher, Carolyn L., "The 'Spiritual Lesson' of Melville's 'The Apple-Tree Table,' " *American Quarterly*, 23 (Spring 1971), 101–9.
86

508a. McWilliams, John P., Jr., " 'Drum Taps' and *Battle-Pieces*: The Blossom of War," *American Quarterly*, 23 (May 1971), 181–201.
63, 499

508b. Fisher, Marvin, "Bug and Humbug in Melville's 'Apple-Tree Table,' " *Studies in Short Fiction*, 8 (Summer 1971), 459–66.
385, 711

508c. Rosenthal, Bernard, "Elegy for Jack Chase," *Studies in Romanticism*, 10 (Summer 1971), 213–29.
63, 479, 481a

509. Garrison, Daniel H., "Melville's Doubloon and the Shield of Achilles," *Nineteenth-Century Fiction*, 26 (Sept. 1971), 171–84.
369

510. Huntress, Keith, "Melville, Henry Cheever, and 'The Lee Shore,' " *New England Quarterly*, 44 (Sept. 1971), 468–75.
136

510a. Stone, Edward, "Melville's Late Pale Usher," *English Language Notes*, 9 (Sept. 1971), 51–53.
369a

510b. Reynolds, Michael S., "The Prototype for Melville's Confi-

dence-Man," *PMLA*, 86 (Oct. 1971), 1009–13.
29a, 373a

1972
Books

511. Bird, Christine Murphy, "Melville's Debt to Cooper's Sea Novels" (Ph.D. dissertation, Tulane University, 1972).
162, 169, 170, 171

511a. Dillingham, William B., *An Artist in the Rigging: The Early Work of Herman Melville* (Athens: University of Georgia Press, 1972).
13, 63, 409a, 622, 652, 764a

511b. Evans, Walter Everett, "The Development of the Lyric Short Story in America, Irving to Melville" (Ph.D. dissertation, University of Chicago, 1972), esp. 209–44.
200, 333

511c. Higgins, Brian, "The English Background of Melville's *Pierre*" (Ph.D. dissertation, University of Southern California, 1972).
92, 106, 107, 119, Dickens, 212, 212a, 217, 218, 219, 220, 221, 295, 407, 618, 619, 622, 634, 636, 666, Thackeray, 698a, 700, 701a

511d. Hodgson, John Alfred, "The World's Mysterious Doom: Melville and Shelley on the Failure of the Imagination" (Ph.D. dissertation, Yale University, 1972).
550, 552

512. Kerr, Howard, *Mediums, and Spirit-Rappers, and Roaring Radicals: Spiritualism in American Literature, 1850–1900* (Urbana:

University of Illinois Press, 1972), esp. pp. 42–54 and 66–68.
135, 238, 485, 711

512a. Morgan, Sophia Steriades, "Death of a Myth: A Reading of *Moby Dick* as Quixotic Literature" (Ph.D. dissertation, University of Michigan, 1972).
122

512b. Shurr, William H., *The Mystery of Iniquity: Melville as Poet, 1857–1891* (Lexington: The University Press of Kentucky, 1972).
a, 28, 50, 54, 63, 80, 84a, 95, 100, 150, 190, 190a, 206a, 211, 269, 290, 331, 333, 338, 339, 351, 373, 376a, 421, 446a, 460, 469a, 499, 524, 543a, 543b, 560, 576, 613, 632, 634, 663, 677a, 684a, 697, 711, 723a

512c. Woodcock, George, ed., *Typee: A Peep at Polynesian Life* (Harmondsworth, Middlesex, England: Penguin, 1972).
63, 91a, 196, 245, 563, 672, 683

Articles

513. Eddy, Darlene Mathis, "Bloody Battles and High Tragedies: Melville and the Theatre of the 1840's," *Ball State University Forum*, 13 (Winter 1972), 34–45.
199, 431, 634

514. Fisher, Marvin, " 'Poor Man's Pudding': Melville's Meditation on Grace," *American Transcendental Quarterly*, 13 (Winter 1972), 32–36.
251, 385

515. [Parker, Hershel], "Bartleby's Dead Letter Office," *Extracts/An occasional newsletter*, 10 (Jan. 1972), 5.
195

516. Boudreau, Gordon V., "Of Pale Ushers and Gothic Piles: Melville's Architectural Symbology," *ESQ*, 18 (II Quarter 1972), 67–82.
561

517. Bickley, R. Bruce, Jr., "The Minor Fiction of Hawthorne and Melville," *American Transcendental Quarterly*, 14 (Spring 1972), 149–52.
333, 421, 431

517a. Cameron, Kenneth Walter, "Another Newspaper Anticipation of *Billy Budd*," *American Transcendental Quarterly*, 14 (Spring 1972), 167–68.
259a

518. Gerlach, John, "Messianic Nationalism in the Early Works of Herman Melville: Against Perry Miller," *Arizona Quarterly*, 28 (Spring 1972), 5–26.
42, 531

519. Higgins, Brian, "Plinlimmon and the Pamphlet Again," *Studies in the Novel*, 4 (Spring 1972), 27–38.
32, Swift

520. Shusterman, Alan, "Melville's 'The Lightning–Rod Man': A Reading," *Studies in Short Fiction*, 9 (Spring 1972), 165–74.
63, 134, 242

521. Kelly, Michael J., "Claggart's 'Equivocal Words' and Lamb's 'Popular Fallacies,' " *Studies in*

Short Fiction, 9 (Spring 1972), 183–86.
431

522. Monteiro, George, "Melville, 'Timothy Quicksand,' and the Dead-Letter Office," *Studies in Short Fiction*, 9 (Spring 1972), 198–201.
573

523. Gaillard, Theodore L., Jr., "Melville's Riddle for Our Time: 'Benito Cereno,' " *English Journal*, 61 (April 1972), 479–87.
673

524. Rowland, Beryl, "Sitting Up with a Corpse: Malthus according to Melville in 'Poor Man's Pudding and Rich Man's Crumbs,' " *Journal of American Studies*, 6 (April 1972), 69–83.
423, 472, 473, 474

525. Shurr, William H., "Melville and Emerson," *Extracts/An occasional newsletter*, 11 (May 1972), 2.
255, 560

526. Rees, John O., Jr., "Spenserian Analogues in *Moby-Dick*," *ESQ*, 18 (III Quarter 1972), 174–78.
663

527. Star, Morris, "Melville's Markings in Walpole's *Anecdotes of Painting in England*," *Papers of the Bibliographical Society of America*, 66 (3rd Quarter 1972), 321–27.
395, 468, 584, 741, 767

528. Parker, Hershel, " 'Benito Cereno' and *Cloister-Life*: A Rescrutiny of a 'Source,' " *Studies in*

Short Fiction, 9 (Summer 1972), 221–32.
673

529. Stone, Edward, "Bartleby and Miss Norman," *Studies in Short Fiction*, 9 (Summer 1972), 271–74.
370

530. Isani, Mukhtar A., "Melville's Use of John and Awnsham Churchill's *Collection of Voyages and Travels*," *Studies in the Novel*, 4 (Fall 1972), 390–95.
141, 323, 404, 492, 504

531. Lane, Lauriat, Jr., "Melville and Dickens' *American Notes*," *Extracts/An occasional newsletter*, 12 (Oct. 1972), 3–4.
210

532. Isani, Mukhtar Ali, "Zoroastrianism and the Fire Symbolism in *Moby-Dick*," *American Literature*, 44 (Nov. 1972), 385–97.
50, 141, 281, 289, 333, 372, 421, 504, 521, 593

533. Watson, Charles N., Jr., "Melville and the Theme of Timonism: From *Pierre* to *The Confidence-Man*," *American Literature*, 44 (Nov. 1972), 398–413.
634

534. Morsberger, Robert E., "Melville's 'The Bell-Tower' and Benvenuto Cellini," *American Literature*, 44 (Nov. 1972), 459–62.
121, 636

534a. Stempel, Daniel, and Bruce M. Stillians, "*Bartleby the Scrivener*: A Parable of Pessimism," *Nineteenth-Century Fiction*, 27 (Dec. 1972), 268–82.
237a, 239, 533a, 566

1973
Books

534b. Harris, Duncan S., "Melville and the Allegorical Tradition" (Ph.D. dissertation, Brandeis University, 1973).
63, 333, 634

534c. Wakefield, John, "The Opposing View: A Study of Melville's Style and Thought" (Ph.D. dissertation, State University of New York at Buffalo, 1973).
5, 101, 119, 203, 550, 633

534d. Welsh, [Bernard] Howard, "Herman Melville as Magian: Zoroastrianism and Manicheism in the Major Prose Fiction" (Ph.D. dissertation, Auburn University, 1973).
50, 421, 524, 559

Articles

535. Cohen, Hennig, "A Comic Mode of the Romantic Imagination: Poe, Hawthorne, Melville," in *The Comic Imagination in American Literature*, ed. Louis D. Rubin, Jr. (New Brunswick, N.J.: Rutgers University Press, 1973), pp. 85–99.
563

536. Kenny, Vincent, "Melville's Problem of Detachment and Engagement," *American Transcendental Quarterly*, 19 (1973), 30–37.
8

537. Lang, H. J., "Poe in Melville's 'Benito Cereno,' " *English Studies Today*, 5 (1973), 405–29.
162, 376, 561

538. Porat, Zephyra, "Melville's Praise of Folly: Gnostic Irony, Greek Tragedy, and Innocent Ignorance in *Billy Budd*," *Scripta Hierosolymitana*, 25 (1973), 167–88.
50

539. Stein, Allen F., "Ahab's Turbid Wake and Job's Leviathan," *American Transcendental Quarterly*, 17 (Winter 1973), 13–14.
63

540. Cannon, Agnes, "On Dating the Composition of *Clarel*," *Extracts/An occasional newsletter*, 13 (Jan. 1973), 6.
25, 28, 668

541. Portnoy, Howard N., "Emerson, Melville, and 'The Poet,' " *Junction*, 1 (Spring 1973), 172–75.
Emerson, 250

542. Alexis, Gerhard T., "Two Footnotes on a Faceless Whale," *American Notes & Queries*, 11 (March 1973), [99]–[100].
63, 83, 229

543. Allen, Priscilla, "*White-Jacket*: Melville and the Man-of-War Microcosm," *American Quarterly*, 25 (March 1973), 32–47.
13, 90, 440, 678, 747

544. Branch, Watson G., "The Genesis, Composition, and Structure of *The Confidence-Man*," *Nineteenth-Century Fiction*, 27 (March 1973), 424–48.
63, 325, 341, 529

545. Schwendinger, Robert J., "The Language of the Sea: Relationships between the Language of Herman Melville and Sea Shanties of the 19th Century," *South-*

ern Folklore Quarterly, 37 (March 1973), 53–73.
208, 660

546. Fisher, Marvin, "Melville's 'Brave Officer,' " *Extracts/An occasional newsletter,* 14 (April 1973), 7–8.
392

547. Sweeney, Gerard M., "Melville's Hawthornian Bell-Tower: A Fairy-Tale Source," *American Literature,* 45 (May 1973), 279–85.
50, 340, 636, 663

547a. Moore, Maxine, "Melville's Pierre and Wordsworth: Intimations of Immorality," *New Letters,* 39 (Summer 1973), 89–107.
63, 766

548. Yannella, Donald, "Source for the Diddling of William Cream in *The Confidence-Man?*" *American Transcendental Quarterly,* 17 (Summer 1973), 22–24.
174

549. Travis, Mildred K., "A Note on 'The Bell-Tower': Melville's 'Blackwood Article,' " *Poe Studies,* 6 (June 1973), 28–29.
561

550. Furrow, Sharon, "The Terrible Made Visible: Melville, Salvator Rosa, and Piranesi," *ESQ,* 19 (IV Quarter 1973), 237–53.
54, 203

551. Asquino, Mark L., "Hawthorne's Village Uncle and Melville's Moby Dick," *Studies in Short Fiction,* 10 (Fall 1973), 413–14.
341

551a. Bell, Michael Davitt, "The Glendinning Heritage: Melville's Literary Borrowings in *Pierre,*" *Studies in Romanticism,* 12 (Fall 1973), 741–62.
63, 93, 107, Cooper, 190, 266b, 310c, 561, 634, 766

552. Berkeley, David S., "Figurae Futurarum in Moby-Dick," *Bucknell Review,* 21 (Fall 1973), 108–23.
63, 69, 177, 499

553. Middleton, John, "Source for 'Bartleby,' " *Extracts/An occasional newsletter,* 15 (Sept. 1973), 9.
731

554. Wheelock, C. Webster, "Vere's Allusion to Ananias," *Extracts/An occasional newsletter,* 15 (Sept. 1973), 9–10.
63

555. D'Avanzo, Mario L., "*Pierre* and the Wisdom of Keats's Melancholy," *Extracts/An occasional newsletter,* 16 (Nov. 1973), 6–9.
414, 416

556. Adler, Joyce Sparer, "Melville and the Civil War," *New Letters,* 40 (Dec. 1973), 99–117.
22, 148, 576

1974
Books

556a. Cook, Dayton Grover, "The Apocalyptic Novel: *Moby-Dick* and *Doktor Faustus*" (Ph.D. dissertation, University of Colorado, 1974).
63

557. Flibbert, Joseph, *Melville and the Art of Burlesque* (Amsterdam:

Rodopi N. V., 1974) [*Melville Studies in American Culture*, ed. Robert Brainard Pearsall, vol. 3].
77b, 82, 263, 280, 433, 574, 613, 634, 697

557a. Nnolim, Charles E., *Melville's "Benito Cereno": A Study in Meaning of Name Symbolism* (New York: New Voices Publishing Co., 1974).
63, 200, 539

557b. Small, Julianne, "Classical Allusions in the Fiction of Herman Melville" (Ph.D. dissertation, University of Tennessee, 1974).
216, 513, 630, 631

558. Vogel, Dan, *The Three Masks of American Tragedy* (Baton Rouge: Louisiana State University Press, 1974), esp. "In Nomine Diaboli" in chapter 3, "The Mask of Satan," pp. 151–59.
63, 499, 634

Articles

559. Henderson, Harry B., III, "Melville: Rebellion, Tragedy, and Historical Judgment," in *Versions of the Past: The Historical Imagination in American Fiction* (New York: Oxford University Press, 1974), pp. 127–74 and 318–22.
9, 96, 200, 254, 263, 280, 535, 658, 699, 721

560. Rosenthal, Bernard, "Melville's Island," *Studies in Short Fiction*, 11 (Winter 1974), 1–9.
63, 393

561. Hanson, Elizabeth I., "Melville and the Polynesian-Indian,"

Extracts/An occasional newsletter, 17 (Feb. 1974), 13–14.
74

561a. McCarthy, Paul, "Elements of Anatomy in Melville's Fiction," *Studies in the Novel*, 6 (Spring 1974), 38–61.
670

561b. Wilson, James D., "Incest and American Romantic Fiction," *Studies in the Literary Imagination*, 7 (Spring 1974), 31–50.
147a, 414, 766

562. Quirk, Tom, "Saint Paul's Types of the Faithful and Melville's Confidence Man," *Nineteenth-Century Fiction*, 28 (March 1974), 472–77.
63

563. Sten, Christopher W., "Bartleby the Transcendentalist: Melville's Dead Letter to Emerson," *Modern Language Quarterly*, 35 (March 1974), 30–44.
255

564. Thompson, G. R., "A Visual Analogue for 'The Cassock' Chapter of *Moby-Dick*?" *Extracts/An occasional newsletter*, 18 (May 1974), 1–2.
287

565. Regan, Charles Lionel, "Dilemma of Melville's Horned Woman," *American Notes & Queries*, 12 (May/June 1974), 133–34.
527

566. Fisher, Marvin, "Prospect and Perspective in Melville's 'Piazza,'" *Criticism*, 16 (Summer 1974), 203–16.
253, 333, 385

567. Loving, Jerome M., "Melville's Pardonable Sin," *New England Quarterly*, 47 (June 1974), 262–78.
119, 333

568. Watson, Charles N., Jr., "Melville's Fiction in the Early 1970's," *ESQ,* 20 (IV Quarter 1974), 291–97.
214, 634, Smollett

569. Eberwein, Jane Donahue, "Joel Barlow and *The Confidence-Man*," *American Transcendental Quarterly*, 24 (Fall 1974), 28–29.
44, 45

570. Stein, William Bysshe, "Melville's *The Confidence Man*: Quicksands of the Word," *American Transcendental Quarterly*, 24 (Fall 1974), 38–50.
670, 684

571. Hillway, Tyrus, "Melville's Education in Science," *Texas Studies in Literature and Language*, 16 (Fall 1974), 411–25.
58, 76, 97, 103, 108, 124, 176, 186, 191, 245, 265, 307, 308, 311, 350, 357, 379, 436, 443, 577, 594, 718, 762

572. McElroy, John Harmon, "Cannibalism in Melville's *Benito Cereno*," *Essays in Literature*, 1 (Fall 1974), 206–18.
100, 200

573. Heflin, Wilson L., "New Light on Cruise of Herman Melville in the Charles and Henry," *Historic Nantucket*, 22 (Oct. 1974), 6–27. Reprinted by The Melville Society.
364

574. Moore, Richard S., "The Whiteness and Darkness of the Whale," *Extracts/An occasional newsletter*, 20 (Nov. 1974), 1–2.
233, 234

575. Watson, Charles N., Jr., "Melville's Selvagee: Another Hint from Smollett," *Extracts/An occasional newsletter*, 20 (Nov. 1974), 4–5.
654

1975
Books

576. Bickley, R. Bruce, Jr., *The Method of Melville's Short Fiction* (Durham, N.C.: Duke University Press, 1975).
200, Hawthorne, 331, 333, 341, 381, 384, 385, 386, 387, 422, 431, 578, 628, 663

576a. Brent, Julia Deener, "Thomas Carlyle and the American Renaissance: The Use of Sources and the Nature of Influence" (Ph.D. dissertation, George Washington University, 1975), esp. pp. 107–207.
Carlyle, 113a, 114, 115, 117, 119, 723b

576b. Hauser, Helen Ann, "A Multi-Genre Analysis of Melville's *Pierre*: The Patterns Almost Followed" (Ph.D. dissertation, University of Florida, 1975).
50, 92, 100, 107, 122, 164a, 190, 401, 430, 477, 489a, 561, 618, 634, 736, 736a, 736b, 742

576c. Klopf, Dorothy Cuff, "The Ironic Romance Tradition in America" (Ph.D. dissertation, Cornell University, 1975), esp. pp. 233–83.
63, 248, 249, 255, 330

576d. Moore, Maxine, *That Lonely Game: Melville, Mardi, and the Almanac* (Columbia: University of Missouri Press, 1975).
12a, 63, 100, 159a, 190, 245, 251, 477a, 514b, 528, 663

576e. Pollard, Carole A., "Melville's Hall of Mirrors: Reflective Imagery in *Pierre*" (Ph.D. dissertation, Kent State University, 1975).
190, 333

Articles

577. Gollin, Rita K., "The Forbidden Fruit of Typee," *Modern Language Studies*, 5, ii (1975), 31–34.
499

578. Marovitz, Sanford E., "Old Man Ahab," in *Artful Thunder: Versions of the Romantic Tradition in American Literature in Honor of Howard P. Vincent*, ed. Robert J. DeMott and Sanford E. Marovitz (Kent, Ohio: Kent State University Press, 1975), pp. 139–61.
517, 634

579. Mosher, Bernard, " 'No Trust' and Melville Scholarship," *Leviathan: A Journal of Melville and the Sea*, 6 (1975), 1–16.
776

580. Cannon, Agnes D., "Melville's Concepts of the Poet and Poetry," *Arizona Quarterly*, 31 (Winter 1975), 315–39.
25, 29, 247, 250, 346, 367, 606, 638, 667, 705

581. Fisher, Marvin, "Portrait of the Artist in America: 'Hawthorne and His Mosses,' " *Southern Review*, 11 (Jan. 1975), 156–66.
232, 333

582. Kehler, [Harold], "On Naming White-Jacket," *Extracts/An occasional newsletter*, 21 (Feb. 1975), 4–5.
394

583. Moore, Richard S., "Melville and Lyell's *Second Voyage*," *Extracts/An occasional newsletter*, 21 (Feb. 1975), 6–7.
461

584. Freibert, L. M., "Andrew Marvell and Melville's *Bellipotent*," *Extracts/An occasional newsletter*, 21 (Feb. 1975), 7–8.
484

585. Cook, Richard M., "The Grotesque and Melville's *Mardi*," *ESQ*, 21 (II Quarter 1975), 103–10.
574

586. Billy, Ted, "Eros and Thanatos in 'Bartleby,' " *Arizona Quarterly*, 31 (Spring 1975), 21–32.
63

587. Stein, Allen F., "Hawthorne's Zenobia and Melville's Urania," *American Transcendental Quarterly*, 26 (Spring 1975), 11–14.
328

588. Moore, Richard S., "Owen's and Melville's Fossil Whale," *American Transcendental Quarterly*, 26 (Spring 1975), 24.
533

590. Stelzig, Eugene L., "Romantic Paradoxes of *Moby-Dick*," *American Transcendental Quarterly*, 26 (Spring 1975), 41–44.
4, 150, 636

591. Gollin, Rita K., "The Intelligence Offices of Hawthorne and Melville," *American Transcendental Quarterly*, 26 (Spring 1975), 44–47.
333

592. Williams, David, "Peeping Tommo: *Typee* as Satire," *Canadian Review of American Studies*, 6 (Spring 1975), 36–49.
499

593. Moore, Richard S., "A New Review by Melville," *American Literature*, 47 (May 1975), 265–70.
283, 656

594. Ward, W. H., "Law and Order in Melville's 'The Bell-Tower,'" *Extracts/An occasional newsletter*, 22 (May 1975), 4–5.
63, 663

595. Gilmore, Michael T., "Melville's Apocalypse: American Millennialism and *Moby-Dick*," *ESQ*, 21 (III Quarter 1975), 154–61.
63, 499, 655, 663

596. Hays, Peter L., "Mocha and Moby Dick," *Extracts/An occasional newsletter*, 23 (Sept. 1975), 9–10.
582, 634

597. Heflin, Wilson, "A Biblical Source for 'The Whale-Watch' in *Moby-Dick*," *Extracts/An occasional newsletter*, 23 (Sept. 1975), 13.
63

598. McHaney, Thomas L., "*The Confidence-Man* and Satan's Disguises in *Paradise Lost*," *Nineteenth-Century Fiction*, 30 (Sept. 1975), 200–206.
499

599. Karcher, Carolyn L., "Melville's 'The 'Gees': A Forgotten Satire on Scientific Racism," *American Quarterly*, 27 (Oct. 1975), 421–42.
388, 588

599a. Bergmann, Johannes Dietrich, "'Bartleby' and *The Lawyer's Story*," *American Literature*, 47 (Nov. 1975), 432–36.
469b

1976
Books

600. Brodhead, Richard H., *Hawthorne, Melville, and the Novel* (Chicago and London: University of Chicago Press, 1976).
331, 338

600a. Jaffe, David, *The Stormy Petrel and the Whale: Some Origins of Moby-Dick* (Baltimore: Privately printed, 1976).
759

600b. Pinker, Michael Joseph, "The Sterne Voyage of the Pequod: The Tale of a Tub in American Literature" (Ph.D. dissertation, State University of New York at Binghamton, 1976).
670

600c. Roundy, Nancy Louise, "The Right Whale's Head and the Sperm Whale's Head: A Tension in Herman Melville's Work" (Ph.D. dissertation, University of Iowa, 1976).
95, 147

Articles

601. Hirsch, David H., "*Hamlet, Moby-Dick*, and Passional Thinking," in *Shakespeare: Aspects of Influence*, ed. G. B. Evans (Cambridge: Harvard University Press, 1976), pp. 135–62 [*Harvard English Studies*, 7].
63, 634

602. Howard, Leon, "Melville and the American Tragic Hero," in *Four Makers of the American Mind: Emerson, Thoreau, Whitman, and Melville: A Bicentennial Tribute*, ed. Thomas Edward Crawley (Durham, N.C.: Duke University Press, 1976), pp. 65–82.
52, 82, 119, 149

603. Kime, Wayne R., " 'The Bell-Tower': Melville's Reply to a Review," *ESQ*, 22 (I Quarter 1976), 28–38.
3, 83, 402, 525

604. Franzosa, John, "Darwin and Melville: Why a Tortoise?" *American Imago*, 33 (Winter 1976), 361–79.
63, 191, 563

605. Myerson, Joel, "Comstock's White Whale and *Moby-Dick*," *American Transcendental Quarterly*, 29 (Winter 1976), 8–27.
158

606. Moore, Richard S., "Burke, Melville, and the 'Power of Blackness,' " *American Transcendental Quarterly*, 29 (Winter 1976), 30–33.
95

607. Chaffee, Patricia, "Paradox in *Mardi*," *American Transcendental Quarterly*, 29 (Winter 1976), 80–83.
327, 566

608. Kennedy, Frederick James, "A Strange Scene at a Theatre," *Extracts/An occasional newsletter*, 25 (Feb. 1976), 12–13.
676

609. Glenn, Barbara, "Melville and the Sublime in *Moby-Dick*," *American Literature*, 48 (May 1976), 165–82.
95

610. Cochran, Robert, "Babo's Name in 'Benito Cereno': An Unnecessary Controversy?" *American Literature*, 48 (May 1976), 217–19.
200

611. Jeske, Jeffrey M., "Macbeth, Ahab, and the Unconscious," *American Transcendental Quarterly*, 31 (Summer 1976), 8–12.
634

612. Reynolds, Larry J., "Melville's Use of 'Young Goodman Brown,' " *American Transcendental Quarterly*, 31 (Summer 1976), 12–14.
333

613. Korkowski, Eugene, "Melville and Des Periers: An Analogue for *The Confidence Man*," *American Transcendental Quarterly*, 31 (Summer 1976), 14–19.
50, 100

614. Sattelmeyer, Robert, "The Origin of Harry Bolton in *Redburn*," *American Transcendental Quarterly*, 31 (Summer 1976), 23–25.
82, 146

615. Barbour, James, and Leon Howard, "Carlyle and the Conclusion of *Moby-Dick*," *New England Quarterly*, 49 (June 1976), 214–24.
119

616. Sheldon, Leslie E., " 'That Anaconda of an Old Man' and Milton's Satan," *Extracts/An occasional newsletter*, 26 (June 1976), 11.
499

617. Mathieu, Bertrand, " 'Plain Mechanic Power': Melville's Earliest Poems, *Battle-Pieces and Aspects of the War*," *Essays in Arts and Sciences*, 5 (July 1976), 113–28.
499

618. Shurr, William H., "Melville and Christianity," *Essays in Arts and Sciences*, 5 (July 1976), 129–48.
63, 150, 404, 492

619. Roberts, David A., "Structure and Meaning in Melville's 'The Encantadas,' " *ESQ*, 22 (IV Quarter 1976), 234–44.
190, 634, 663

619a. Emery, Allan Moore, "The Alternatives of Melville's 'Bartleby,' " *Nineteenth-Century Fiction*, 31 (Sept. 1976), 170–87.
60a, 142, 239, 240a, 450, 533a, 566

620. Moses, Carole, "Melville's Use of Spenser in 'The Piazza,' " *CLA Journal*, 20 (Dec. 1976), 222–31.
663

1977
Books

621. Dillingham, William B., *Melville's Short Fiction: 1853–1856* (Athens: University of Georgia Press, 1977).
63, 67, 100, 122, 190, 200, 209, 224, 232, 266, 328, 333, 338, 341, 342, 385, 485, 499, 560, 563, 634, 638, 670, 673

622. Douglas, Ann, *The Feminization of American Culture* (New York: Alfred A. Knopf, 1977).
420, 628, de Stael

622a. Dyer, Susan Athearn, "Plinlimmon's Theme: The Aspirations and Limitations of Man in the Novels of Herman Melville" (Ph.D. dissertation, Duke University, 1977).
122, 255, 333, 341, 663, 762a

623. Herbert, T. Walter, Jr., *Moby-Dick and Calvinism: A World Dismantled* (New Brunswick, N.J.: Rutgers University Press, 1977).
63, 83, 517, 537, 630, 690

Articles

624. Fabricant, Carole, "*Tristram Shandy* and *Moby-Dick*: A Cock and Bull Story and a Tale of a Tub," *Journal of Narrative Technique*, 7 (1977), 57–69.
670

625. Lang, Hans-Joachim, and Benjamin Lease, "Melville's Cosmopolitan: Bayard Taylor in *The Confidence-Man*," *Amerikastudien/American Studies*, 22 (1977), 286–89.
237, 572, 687

626. Eisiminger, Sterling, "Melville's Small Debt to Poe," *American Notes & Queries*, 15 (Jan. 1977), 70–71.
561

627. Heflin, Wilson, "Melville, Celestial Navigation, and Dead Reckoning," *Extracts/An occasional newsletter*, 29 (Jan. 1977), 3.
194

628. Gaines, Kendra H., "A Consideration of an Additional Source for Melville's *Moby-Dick*," *Extracts/An occasional newsletter*, 29 (Jan. 1977), 6–12.
544

629. Sattelmeyer, Robert, and James Barbour, "A Possible Source and Model for 'The Story of China Aster' in Melville's *The Confidence-Man*," *American Literature*, 48 (Jan. 1977), 577–83.
63, 140, 250

630. Markels, Julian, "Melville's Markings in Shakespeare's Plays," *American Literature*, 49 (March 1977), 34–48.
634

631. Hauser, Helen A., "Spinozan Philosophy in *Pierre*," *American Literature*, 49 (March 1977), 49–56.
50, 296

632. Marshall, Margaret Wiley, "A Footnote to *Billy Budd*," *Extracts/An occasional newsletter*, 30 (May 1977), 1–3.
21

633. Duban, James, "The Translation of Pierre Bayle's *An Historical and Critical Dictionary* Owned by Melville," *Papers of the Bibliographical Society of America*, 71 (3rd Quarter 1977), 347–51.
50

633a. Garner, Stanton, "Melville and Thomas Campbell: The 'Deadly Space Between,'" *English Language Notes*, 14 (June 1977), 289–90.
112b

634. Duban, James, "The Spenserian Maze of Melville's *Pierre*," *ESQ*, 23 (IV Quarter 1977), 217–25.
248, 622, 663

635. Breinig, Helmbrecht, "Symbol, Satire, and the Will to Communicate in Melville's 'The Apple-Tree Table,'" *Amerikastudien/American Studies*, 22 (Fall 1977), 269–85.
711, 713

636. McElroy, John Harmon, "The Dating of the Action in *Moby Dick*," *Papers on Language & Literature*, 13 (Fall 1977), 420–23.
601

637. Heffernan, Thomas F., "Melville and Wordsworth," *American Literature*, 49 (Nov. 1977), 338–51.
343, 344, 347, 355, 606, 766

1978
Books

637a. Dettlaff, Shirley M., "Hebraism and Hellenism in Melville's *Clarel*: The Influence of Arnold, Goethe, and Schiller" (Ph.D. dissertation, University of Southern California, 1978).
25, 25a, 25b, Goethe, 296, 606

637b. Moses, Carole Horsburgh, "Like Race to Run: Melville's Use

of Spenser" (Ph.D. dissertation, State University of New York at Binghamton, 1978).
663

637c. Nelson, James Andrew, "Herman Melville's Use of the Bible in *Billy Budd*" (Ph.D. dissertation, University of Iowa, 1978).
63

Articles

638. Brodhead, Richard H., "*Mardi*: Creating the Creative," in *New Perspectives on Melville*, ed. Faith Pullin (Edinburgh: Edinburgh University Press, and Kent, Ohio: Kent State University Press, 1978), pp. 29–53.
561, 574, 683

639. Ziff, Larzer, "Shakespeare and Melville's America," in *New Perspectives on Melville*, ed. Faith Pullin (Edinburgh: Edinburgh University Press, and Kent, Ohio: Kent State University Press, 1978), pp. 54–67.
634

640. Goldman, Arnold, "Melville's England," in *New Perspectives on Melville*, ed. Faith Pullin (Edinburgh: Edinburgh University Press, and Kent, Ohio: Kent State University Press, 1978), pp. 68–85.
385

641. Leavis, Q. D., "Melville: The 1853–6 Phase," in *New Perspectives on Melville*, ed. Faith Pullin (Edinburgh: Edinburgh University Press, and Kent, Ohio: Kent State University Press, 1978), pp. 197–228.
63, 333, 634, 684, 722, 766

641a. Cheikin, Miriam Quen, "Captain Vere: Darkness Made Visible," *Arizona Quarterly*, 34 (Winter 1978), 293–310.
499, 710

642. D'Avanzo, Mario L., " 'A Bower in the Arsacides' and Solomon's Temple," *Arizona Quarterly*, 34 (Winter 1978), 317–26.
63

642a. Zlatic, Thomas D., " 'Benito Cereno': Melville's 'Back-Handed-Well-Knot,' " *Arizona Quarterly*, 34 (Winter 1978), 327–43.
200

643. Lee, Grace Farrell, "*Pym* and *Moby-Dick*: Essential Connections," *American Transcendental Quarterly*, 37 (Winter 1978), 73–86.
561

644. Dean, John, "Shakespeare's Influence on *Moby Dick* or Where There's a Will, There's a Whale," *Cahiers Elisabethains*, 13 (April 1978), 41–48.
634

645. Magretta, Joan, "Radical Disunities: Models of Mind and Madness in *Pierre* and *The Idiot*," *Studies in the Novel*, 10 (Summer 1978), 234–50.
304

646. Bucho, Luella M., "Melville and Captain Delano's *Narrative of Voyages*: The Appeal of the Preface," *American Notes & Queries*, 16 (June 1978), 157–60.
200

646a. Beidler, Philip D., "*Billy Budd*: Melville's Valedictory to

Emerson," *ESQ*, 24 (IV Quarter 1978), 215–28.
63, Emerson, 254, 338

647. Herndon, Jerry A., "Parallels in Melville and Whitman," *Walt Whitman Review*, 24 (Sept. 1978), 95–108.
669, 756

648. Sheldon, Leslie E., "Another Layer of Miltonic Allusion in *Moby-Dick*," *Melville Society Extracts*, 35 (Sept. 1978), 15–16.
499

648a. Sattelmeyer, Robert, and James Barbour, "The Sources and Genesis of Melville's 'Norfolk Isle and the Chola Widow,'" *American Literature*, 50 (Nov. 1978), 398–417.
263a, 509, 563

649. Wenke, John, "A Note on Melville and Shakespeare: Two Moments of Truth," *Melville Society Extracts*, 36 (Nov. 1978), 7.
634

650. Moses, Carole, "A Spenserian Echo in *The Confidence-Man*," *Melville Society Extracts*, 36 (Nov. 1978), 16.
663

651. Monteiro, George, "Poetry and Madness: Melville's Rediscovery of Camoes in 1867," *New England Quarterly*, 51 (Dec. 1978), 561–65.
111, 112

1979
Books

651a. Heidmann, Mark, "Melville and the Bible: Leading Themes in the Marginalia and Major Fiction, 1850–1856" (Ph.D. dissertation, Yale University, 1979).
63, 421

651b. Kowalski, Michael Lee, "The Perils of Pierre: Melville and the Popular Culture" (Ph.D. dissertation, University of California at Berkeley, 1979).
92, 171, 225a, 225b, 338, 398a, 666

Articles

652. Rosenthal, Bernard, "Herman Melville's Wandering Jews," in *Puritan Influences in American Literature*, ed. Emory Elliott (Urbana: University of Illinois Press, 1979), pp. 167–92.
28, 63, 179, 362, 639, 679

653. Karcher, Carolyn L., "Spiritualism and Philanthropy in Brownson's *The Spirit-Rapper* and Melville's *The Confidence-Man*," *ESQ*, 25 (I Quarter 1979), 26–36.
86

654. Moses, Carole, "Melville's Dark God: Christian Echoes in 'Sketch Ninth' of *The Encantadas*," *Studies in Short Fiction*, 16 (Winter 1979), 68–70.
63

655. D'Avanzo, Mario L., "Anubis and 'The Hyena' in *Moby-Dick*," *Melville Society Extracts*, 37 (Feb. 1979), 5–7.
558

656. Pancost, David W., "Donald Grant Mitchell's *Reveries of a Bachelor* and Herman Melville's 'I and My Chimney,'" *American*

Transcendental Quarterly, 42 (Spring 1979), 129–36.
501

657. Duban, James, "Satiric Precedent for Melville's 'The Two Temples,'" *American Transcendental Quarterly*, 42 (Spring 1979), 137–45.
757, 771

657a. Leonard, David Charles, "The Cartesian Vortex in *Moby-Dick*," *American Literature*, 51 (March 1979), 105–9.
123

658. Gretchko, John M. J., "Herman Melville Discovers Elijah Burritt," *Melville Society Extracts*, 38 (May 1979), 9.
99

659. Hallab, Mary Y., "Victims of 'Malign Machinations': Irving's *Christopher Columbus* and Melville's 'Benito Cereno,'" *Journal of Narrative Technique*, 9 (Fall 1979), 199–206.
383

660. Quirk, Tom, "Two Sources in *The Confidence-Man*," *Melville Society Extracts*, 39 (Sept. 1979), 12–13.
129, 502

661. Baym, Nina, "Melville's Quarrel with Fiction," *PMLA*, 94 (Oct. 1979), 909–23.
Emerson, 251, 333, 338

662. Marshall, Margaret Wiley, "*Arichandra* and *Billy Budd*," *Melville Society Extracts*, 40 (Nov. 1979), 7–10.
21, 404, 491, 492

1980
Books

662a. Kier, Kathleen E., "An Annotated Edition of Melville's *White-Jacket*" (Ph.D. dissertation, Columbia University, 1980).
13, 54, 63, 82, 146, 359, 397, 452, 499, 544, 564a, 622, 641a, 672, 719a, 759

662b. Meacham, Gloria Horsley, "Selected Nineteenth Century Interpretations of Organized Slave Resistance: Black Character and Consciousness as Represented in the Fictional Works of Harriet Beecher Stowe, Herman Melville, and Martin Robinson Delany and Related Historical Sources" (Ph.D. dissertation, Cornell University, 1980), esp. pp. 79–128.
200, 673

Articles

663. Breinig, Helmbrecht, "The Symbol of Complexity: 'I and My Chimney' and Its Significance in the Context of Melville's Later Writings," *Anglia*, 98 (1980), 51–67.
63

664. Drinnon, Richard, "Professional Westerner: Judge Hall," in *Facing West: The Metaphysics of Indian-Hating and Empire-Building* (Minneapolis: University of Minnesota Press, 1980), pp. 191–215.
317

665. McIntosh, James, "Melville's Use and Abuse of Goethe: The Weaver-Gods in *Faust* and *Moby-*

Dick," Amerikastudien/American Studies, 25 (1980), 158–73.
119, 235, 296, 299, 300, 301, 667

666. Waggoner, Hyatt H., "Hawthorne's Presence in *Moby-Dick* and in Melville's Tales and Sketches," *Nathaniel Hawthorne Journal 1977*, ed. C. E. Frazer Clark, Jr. (Detroit: Bruccoli Clark, 1980), pp. 73–79.
Hawthorne

667. Dettlaff, Shirley M., "Ionian Form and Esau's Waste: Melville's View of Art in *Clarel*," *Melville Society Extracts*, 41 (Feb. 1980), 2.
25

668. Garner, Stanton, "Rosemarine: Melville's 'Pebbles' and Ben Jonson's *Masque of Blackness*," *Melville Society Extracts*, 41 (Feb. 1980), 13–14.
405

669. Sealts, Merton M., Jr., "Melville and Emerson's Rainbow," *ESQ*, 26 (II Quarter 1980), 53–78.
119, 249, 250, 252, 253, 254, 380

670. Leonard, David Charles, "Descartes, Melville, and the Mardian Vortex," *SAB: South Atlantic Bulletin*, 45 (May 1980), 13–25.
123

671. Mendez, Charlotte Walker, "Scriveners Forlorn: Dickens's Nemo and Melville's Bartleby," *Dickens Studies Newsletter*, 11 (June 1980), 33–38.
211

672. Coffler, Gail, "Melville, Dana, Allston: Analogues in *Lectures on*

Art," *Melville Society Extracts*, 44 (Nov. 1980), 1–6.
12

673. Quirk, Tom, "Man Traps and Melville," *Melville Society Extracts*, 44 (Nov. 1980), 11–12.
651

674. Baker, S. C., "Two Notes on Browning Echoes in *Clarel*," *Melville Society Extracts*, 44 (Nov. 1980), 14–15.
85

1981
Books

674a. Heffernan, Thomas Farel, *Stove by a Whale: Owen Chase and the Essex* (Middletown, Conn.: Wesleyan University Press, 1981), esp. pp. xi, 155, 160–71, 184–209.
130

674b. Jaffe, David, *Bartleby the Scrivener and Bleak House: Melville's Debt to Dickens* (Arlington, Va.: The Mardi Press, 1981).
211, 469b

Articles

675. Marovitz, Sanford E., "Melville's Problematic Being," *Melville Society Extracts*, 45 (Feb. 1981), 2.
50, 147, 549, 692

676. Duban, James, "Melville's Use of Irving's *Knickerbocker History* in *White-Jacket*," *Melville Society Extracts*, 46 (May 1981), 1, 4–6.
382

677. Howard, Leon, "The Composition of *Moby-Dick*: Or How Melville Gave Ahab a Pegleg for New

Year's Eve," a lecture discussed in Tom Quirk, "More on the Composition of *Moby-Dick*: Leon Howard Shows Us Ahab's Leg," *Melville Society Extracts*, 46 (May 1981), 6–7.
149

678. Robillard, Douglas, "The Metaphysics of Melville's Indian Hating," *Essays in Arts and Sciences*, 10 (May 1981), 51–58.
749

679. Stessel, Edward, "Naval Warfare and Herman Melville's War Against Failure," *Essays in Arts and Sciences*, 10 (May 1981), 59–77.
329

680. Moore, Richard S., "Piranesi, 'The Blanket,' and the 'Mathematical Sublime' in *Moby-Dick*," *Melville Society Extracts*, 47 (Sept. 1981), 1–3.
95, 203

681. Hays, Peter, "Samson in *Moby-Dick*: Particular vs. Transcendental," *Melville Society Extracts*, 47 (Sept. 1981), 8.
63

682. Madison, R. D., "Melville's Edition of Cooper's *History of the Navy*," *Melville Society Extracts*, 47 (Sept. 1981), 9–10.
163

683. Allison, June W., "The Similes in *Moby-Dick*: Homer and Melville," *Melville Society Extracts*, 47 (Sept. 1981), 12–15.
369

684. Dimock, Wai-chee S., "*White-Jacket*: Authors and Audiences," *Nineteenth-Century Fiction*, 36 (Dec. 1981), 296–317.
440, 647

1982
Books

685. Bezanson, Walter E., "Historical Note," in *Israel Potter: His Fifty Years of Exile*, ed. Harrison Hayford, Hershel Parker, and G. Thomas Tanselle (Evanston and Chicago: Northwestern University Press and The Newberry Library, 1982), pp. 173–235.
9, 163, 180, 263, 266, 280, 343, 466, 544, 561, 604, 640, 650, 721

686. Madison, R. D., "Melville's Basic Source," in *Israel Potter: His Fifty Years of Exile*, ed. Harrison Hayford, Hershel Parker, and G. Thomas Tanselle (Evanston and Chicago: Northwestern University Press and The Newberry Library, 1982), pp. 277–394.
721

686a. Quirk, Tom, *Melville's Confidence Man: From Knave to Knight* (Columbia: University of Missouri Press, 1982).
29a, 43b, 63, 69, 91b, 100, 122, 149, 373a, 499, 529, 634, 754

686b. Sealts, Merton M., Jr., *Pursuing Melville 1940–1980: Chapters and Essays by Merton M. Sealts, Jr.* (Madison: University of Wisconsin Press, 1982) [including "A Correspondence with Charles Olson"].
4, 16, 16a, 28, 29, 50, 63, 83, 83a, 107, 119, 130, 190, Emerson, 247, 254, 255, 263a, 296, 327, Hawthorne, 351, 368, 408, Keats, 497b, 499, 502, 505, Plato, 548.1, 548a,

549, 550, 551, 552, 553, 554, 555, 557, 559, 560, 568, 580a, Schopenhauer, 612, 630, 634, 638, 658a, 689, 747.1, Whitman

Articles

687. Cohen, Hennig, "The Landscape in Melville's Poetry," *Melville Society Extracts*, 49 (Feb. 1982), 3.
47, 668

688. Robillard, Douglas, "A Possible Source for Melville's Goetic and Theurgic Magic," *Melville Society Extracts*, 49 (Feb. 1982), 5–6.
91, 606

689. Evans, Lyon D., Jr., "The Source of Melville's 'The Little Good Fellows,'" *Melville Society Extracts*, 49 (Feb. 1982), 13.
750

690. Scherting, Jack, "The Chaldee Allusion in *Moby-Dick*: Its Antecedent and Its Implicit Skepticism," *Melville Society Extracts*, 49 (Feb. 1982), 14–15.
751

691. Sealts, Merton M., Jr., "Melville and Whitman," *Melville Society Extracts*, 50 (May 1982), 10–12.
88, 669

692. Hirsch, Penny L., "Melville's Spenser Edition for *The Encantadas*," *Melville Society Extracts*, 50 (May 1982), 15–16.
663

693. Moses, Carol[e], "Spenserian Allusion in 'Sketch Fourth' of *The Encantadas*," *Melville Society Extracts*, 52 (Nov. 1982), 16.
663

1983
Articles

693a. Gretchko, John M. J., "New Evidence for Melville's Use of John Harris in *Moby-Dick*," *Studies in the American Renaissance* (1983), 303–11.
187a, 323, 544, 615

693b. Chai, Leon, "Melville and Shelley: Speculations on Metaphysics, Morals, and Poetics in *Pierre* and 'Shelley's Vision,'" *ESQ*, 29 (I Quarter 1983), 31–45.
254, 295, 333, 338, 551, 637, 638, 639, 697

694. Madison, R. D., "Melville's Review of Browne's *Etchings*," *Melville Society Extracts*, 53 (Feb. 1983), 11–13.
82

695. Lackey, Kris, "Additional Biblical Allusions in *Moby-Dick*," *Melville Society Extracts*, 54 (May 1983), 12.
63

696. Gretchko, John M. J., "A Note on James Colnett," *Melville Society Extracts*, 54 (May 1983), 13–14.
154

697. Roberts, Audrey, "Another Chapter for 'Benito Cereno,'" *Melville Society Extracts*, 55 (Sept. 1983), 10–11.
200

698. McAuley, David, "A Source for Melville's 'The March into Virginia,'" *Melville Society Extracts*, 55 (Sept. 1983), 12–13.
646

699. Franchetti, Lisa M., "Exaggeration in Melville's Review of

Codman," *Melville Society Extracts*, 56 (Nov. 1983), 4–6.
146

700. Hovey, Kenneth Alan, "*White-Jacket* vs. *Mr. Midshipman Easy*," *Melville Society Extracts*, 56 (Nov. 1983), 13–15.
480

701. Hamilton, William, "On 'Live in the all' Once Again," *Melville Society Extracts*, 56 (Nov. 1983), 15–16.
607

702. Bryant, John, " 'Nowhere a Stranger': Melville and Cosmopolitanism," essay read at The Melville Society meeting (28 Dec. 1983).
496

703. Horsford, Howard C., "Melville in the Streets of London," essay read at The Melville Society meeting (28 Dec. 1983).
482

704. Robillard, Douglas, "Melville and Mme. de Stael," essay read at The Melville Society meeting (28 Dec. 1983).
666, 667

1984
Book

705. Branch, Watson, Hershel Parker, and Harrison Hayford with Alma A. MacDougall, "Historical Note," in *The Confidence-Man: His Masquerade*, ed. Harrison Hayford, Hershel Parker, and G. Thomas Tanselle (Evanston and Chicago: Northwestern University Press and The Newberry Library, 1984), pp. 255–357.
43, 63, 93, 100, 122, 183a, 210, 212, 249, 274, 276, 313a, 317, 333, 341, 373a, 485, 499, 513a, 529, 634, 643a, 644a, 650, 754

Articles

705a. McIntosh, James, "Melville's Copy of Goethe's Autobiography and Travels," *Studies in the American Renaissance* (1984), 387– 407.
25, 28, 29, 116a, 235, 247, Goethe, 296, 299, 300, 301, 304, 667

706. "Melville's Milton," *Melville Society Extracts*, 57 (Feb. 1984), 7.
499

707. Wilson, James C., "The Significance of Petra in 'Bartleby,' " *Melville Society Extracts*, 57 (Feb. 1984), 10–12.
47, 667a

708. De Puy, Harry, " 'Double Dutch' Alliteration in *Pierre*," *Melville Society Extracts*, 57 (Feb. 1984), 12–13.
22, 464a

709. Madison, R. D., "Redburn's Seamanship and Dana's Guide-Book," *Melville Society Extracts*, 57 (Feb. 1984), 13–15.
188b

710. Bagchee, Shyamal, "*Billy Budd, Walden*, and Berries," *Melville Society Extracts*, 58 (May 1984), 11.
483, 711

711. Friederich, Reinhard H., "Asleep with Kings and Counselors: A Source Note on Bartleby in

the Tombs," *Melville Society Extracts*, 58 (May 1984), 13–15.
63, 83, 130a

711a. "The Crying of Lot 45: Melville's *Milton*," *Melville Society Extracts*, 58 (May 1984), 16.
499

712. Altherr, Thomas L., "Drunk with the Chase: Francis Parkman and *Moby-Dick*," *Melville Society Extracts*, [59] (Sept. 1984), 8–11.
540

713. Young, John, " 'I and My Chimney' and *Moby-Dick*," *Melville Society Extracts*, [59] (Sept. 1984), 11–15.
409

714. Sewell, David R., "Another Source for the Barber Shop Episode in *The Confidence-Man*," *Melville Society Extracts*, 60 (Nov. 1984), 13–15.
43a

1985
Articles

715. Kier, K. E., " 'A Thing Most Momentous'? or 'Part of the General Joke'?" *Melville Society Extracts*, 61 (Feb. 1985), 11–13.
544

716. Bercaw, Mary K., "The Crux of the Ass in 'The Encantadas,' "

Melville Society Extracts, 62 (May 1985), 12.
766

717. Sappenfield, James A., "A Note on the 'Pains-taking Moralist' of Melville's *Pierre*," *Melville Society Extracts*, 62 (May 1985), 12–14.
634

718. Frank, Stuart M., " 'The King of the Southern Sea' and 'Captain Bunker': Two Songs in *Moby-Dick*," *Melville Society Extracts*, 63 (Sept. 1985), 4–7.
82, 417a

719. "Herman at Christie's: On the Block—Again," *Melville Society Extracts*, 63 (Sept. 1985), 10–12.
190, 344a

720. Craven, Robert R., "Two New Sightings of the White Whale," *Melville Society Extracts*, 63 (Sept. 1985), 12–16.
52, 156a, 156b, 158, 158a

1986
Book

721. Madison, R. D., ed., "Introduction," *Journal of a Cruise* [by Captain David Porter] (Annapolis: Naval Institute Press, 1986), pp. xi–xxiv and 632 (n. 163.5–6).
563

IV

INDEX OF
SCHOLARS

Numbers refer to the entries in the preceding numbered "List of Scholarship"

A

Abel, Darrel, 326
Adler, Joyce Sparer, 556
Alexis, Gerhard T., 542
Allen, Priscilla, 419, 437, 543
Allibone, S. Austin, 76
Allison, June W., 683
Altherr, Thomas L., 712
Anderson, Charles Roberts, 121, 133, 138
Arms, George, 171
Arvin, Newton, 174, 187a, 193, 198, 204
Ashbery, John, 291b
Aspiz, Harold, 474
Asquino, Mark L., 551
Asselineau, Roger, 420
Austin, Allen, 402
Avanzo, Mario L. D', see D'Avanzo, Mario L.

B

Bach, Bert C., 442
Bagchee, Shyamal, 710
Baird, James, 273b
Baker, S. C., 674
Banta, Martha, 507a
Barbour, James Francis, 487, 615, 629, 648a
Barrett, Laurence, 178

Battenfeld, David H., 272
Baym, Nina, 661
Beidler, Philip D., 646a
Belgion, Montgomery, 168
Bell, Michael Davitt, 551a
Bell, Millicent, 223, 235, 236a, 343
Benardete, M. J., 167
Bennett, Arnold, 115
Bercaw, Mary K., 716
Bergmann, Johannes Dietrich, 479a, 484, 599a
Beringause, A. F., 377
Berkeley, David S., 552
Bernstein, John, 377a
Berthoff, Warner, 332
Betts, William W., Jr., 253, 303
Bezanson, Walter E., 259, 260, 315, 685
Bickley, R. Bruce, Jr., 517, 576
Billy, Ted, 586
Bird, Christine Murphy, 511
Birss, John Howard, 110, 111, 119, 131
Blackmur, R. P., 266a
Blair, Walter, 480
Blansett, Barbara Ruth Nieweg, 365
Boies, J. J., 335
Bond, William H., 250
Booth, Thornton Y., 361
Boudreau, Gordon Vincent, 439a, 516